FROM UNDER THE RUBBLE

FROM UNDER THE RUBBLE

by Alexander Solzhenitsyn, Mikhail Agursky,
A.B., Evgeny Barabanov, Vadim Borisov,
F. Korsakov, and Igor Shafarevich

Translated by A. M. Brock, Milada Haigh,
Marita Sapiets, Hilary Sternberg, and
Harry Willetts under the direction of
Michael Scammell

With an introduction by
Max Hayward

LITTLE, BROWN AND COMPANY — BOSTON – TORONTO

FIRST ENGLISH LANGUAGE EDITION

T 06/75

Library of Congress Cataloging in Publication Data

Main entry under title:

From under the rubble.

    Translation of Iz pod glyb.
    Includes bibliographical references and index.
    CONTENTS: Solzhenitsyn, A. As breathing and con-
sciousness return.—Shafarevich, I. Socialism in our
past and future.—Agursky, M. Contemporary socioeconomic systems and their future prospects. [etc.]
    1. Russia—Politics and government—1953- —Ad-
dresses, essays, lectures. 2. Russia—Social conditions—1945- —Addresses, essays, lectures.
3. Civilization, Modern—1950- —Addresses, essays,
lectures. I. Solzhenitsyn, Aleksandr Isaevich,
1918- II. Title.
DK274.I9413 1975   309.1′47′085   75-8883
ISBN 0-316-80372-3

Designed by Barbara Bell Pitnof

Published simultaneously in Canada by Little, Brown & Company (Canada) Limited

PRINTED IN THE UNITED STATES OF AMERICA

Introduction

MAX HAYWARD

This collection of eleven essays edited by Solzhenitsyn (who wrote three of the essays as well) opens with a brief foreword indicating that its purpose is to stir debate, after over half a century of enforced silence, on matters of fundamental principle concerning the present state of Russia. The intention is to suggest a diagnosis of the evils and difficulties that beset the country, and to point to possible long-range solutions, if only tentative ones. Although the issues are discussed primarily in Russian terms, the authors show themselves to be not uninformed about the outside world and fully conscious that the problems of the planet now override those of any one part of it.

From Under the Rubble has a forerunner in prerevolutionary Russia, namely, a famous collection of articles by a group of prominent scholars, writers and thinkers which was published in 1909 under the title *Landmarks (Vekhi)*. The contributors included the religious philosophers Nikolai Berdyayev, Sergei Bulgakov and Semyon Frank, the legal theorist B. A. Kistyakovsky, the literary critic M. Gershenzon, and the eminent economist, publicist and liberal politician Peter Struve. All of them had grown up in the climate of populist socialism and Marxism of the last decades of the nineteenth century, and had revolted against it, rejecting the whole ethos of the Russian radical intelligentsia of the 1860s, which had prepared the ground for it. Berdyayev and Bulgakov were ex-Marxists, and Struve had indeed drafted the manifesto of the Russian Social Democratic party at its founding congress in 1898. (By a nice irony, it is his grandson, Nikita Struve, who now publishes Solzhenitsyn's work in Russian in Paris.)

The contributors to *Landmarks* took a searching look at Russian society, and in particular at the intelligentsia, which they held responsible for Russia's failure to find proper means of confronting the country's multifarious problems. The main attack was against the narrowness of outlook and sectarianism that had led the majority of Russian intellectuals to seek solutions in an uncritical adaptation of the West European enlightenment in its nineteenth-century forms of positivism, atheist materialism, "scientific socialism," and so on. The authors called for a return to traditional spiritual values — which for most of them meant those enshrined in Christian teaching — as a necessary condition for a regeneration of the country's intellectual, cultural and social life. All of them were united — as Gershenzon wrote in his preface to the volume — by their "recognition of the primacy both in theory and in practice of spiritual life over the outward forms of society, in the sense that the inner life of the individual . . . and not the self-sufficing elements of some political order is the only solid basis for every social structure." [1]

Landmarks caused a tremendous stir at the time of its publication, provoking outrage in the ranks of the intelligentsia. Lenin, for example, denounced it as "an encyclopedia of liberal apostasy." The Bolsheviks' seizure of power in October 1917 was soon to overwhelm the authors of *Landmarks* and

1. As quoted in Leonard Schapiro's article on *Landmarks:* "The Vekhi Group and the Mystique of Revolution" in the *Slavonic and East European Review*, December 1955. For an excellent introduction to the wider context of the Russian nineteenth-century intellectual tradition, in which it is important to view both *Landmarks* and *From Under the Rubble*, see the same author's *Rationalism and Nationalism in Russian Nineteenth Century Political Thought*, Yale University Press, 1967.

everything they represented, but the volume remained influential. Although it was under a strict ban in Soviet Russia, constant official attacks on it in the Stalin era — particularly during the cultural purges of 1947–1948 — served to keep its memory alive among Soviet intellectuals and even, through highly selective quotation, gave some idea of its contents.

Before they were dispersed in emigration, the *Landmarks* authors, now joined by several others, managed to have printed in the Bolshevik-controlled Moscow of 1918 a second volume of essays under the title *De Profundis*. In this they spoke of the year-old October revolution as the fulfillment of their forebodings in *Landmarks* about the inevitable consequences of the intelligentsia's thirst for revolution. As Berdyayev put it in his contribution, Russia had now been seized by evil spirits like those in Gogol's nightmarish tales, or by the "possessed" of Dostoyevsky's prophetic imagination. It was not simply a change of regime, but a spiritual disaster, a self-willed descent into the abyss. *De Profundis* was confiscated and banned almost immediately. Only two copies survived in the West and it was virtually unknown and unobtainable until it was reprinted in Paris in 1967. This sequel to *Landmarks* must clearly have made a profound impression on Solzhenitsyn: the Russian title of *From Under the Rubble* (*Iz pod glyb*) is a phonetic echo of the Russian words for *De Profundis* (*Iz glubiny*).[2]

By modeling their collection of essays on *Landmarks*, Solzhenitsyn and his associates demonstrate their conviction that in order to talk meaningfully about present-day Russia it is essential to cross back over the intellectual void of the last sixty years and resume a tradition in Russian thought which is antithetical to the predominant one of the old revolutionary intelligentsia, particularly as it developed in the second half of the nineteenth century.

The publication of this joint profession of faith by a great Russian writer now living in enforced exile, and a group of

2. It is hard to give a precise rendering of the title in English. The implication is of people speaking from beneath stone blocks or masses of earth or debris that have buried them alive — see Solzhenitsyn's foreword.

vii

intellectuals still inside the country — including one of its leading mathematicians — is an eloquent response to the recent tactics of the Soviet government in its efforts to stifle dissent. The indiscriminate use of prison and the madhouse, which is still by no means in abeyance, has been supplemented by the ostensibly more subtle policy of selective banishment abroad. The hope evidently is that if some of the more powerful voices that speak "from under the rubble" are removed from the scene, those remaining behind will be demoralized and eventually silenced.

But the authors of *From Under the Rubble* demonstrate that the voices of dissent will not so easily be stilled. The central premise of the collection is that the problems of the modern world, Soviet as well as Western, can no longer be solved on the political plane. Instead, the quest for solutions must begin on the ethical level. Since their approach is spiritual in nature, the authors reject all forms of physical violence and compulsion. Their goal is to bring about in Russia a moral revolution. As they see it, the political revolutionary has always said: "Let us go and kill our enemies and then everything will be fine." But as moral revolutionaries the authors are saying, in effect, "Let us put ourselves in danger. Perhaps we shall be killed. But as a result of our acts, there may be an improvement in the life of the nation."

The authors believe that new and better relations among people can only come about if they embrace a new life of repentance and self-restraint. This can happen among nations as well as among individuals, for the authors are convinced that the concept of the nation is not an anachronism, but that it still has a relevant intrinsic value. Their idea is perhaps best summed up by Solzhenitsyn himself. Upon the receipt of the Nobel Prize for Literature in 1970, he wrote: "Nations are the wealth of mankind, its collective personalities. The very least of them wears its own special colors and bears within itself a special facet of divine intention."

Foreword

The universal suppression of thought leads not to its extinction, but to distortion, ignorance and the mutual incomprehension of compatriots and contemporaries.

For many decades now not a single question, not a single major event in our life has been freely and comprehensively discussed, so that a true appreciation of it could be arrived at and solutions found. Everything was suppressed, everything was left to molder in unintelligible chaos, without thought for the past and consequently for the future either. Meanwhile more and more events accumulated and piled up in such crushing heaps that neither inclination nor strength was left to try and sort them out.

And now people are approaching from outside and, heedlessly and irresponsibly, without let or hindrance, are making all sorts of arbitrary judgments about our recent history and the possibilities of our people. We start to protest and at once bog down in polemics, as a result of which we are in danger of missing the wood for the trees. For the voices destined to express what was known at the appropriate time fell prematurely silent, the documents perished, and the gaze of the outside researcher cannot penetrate into those dark depths beneath the piles of unsorted rubbish.

It is from out of those dank and dark depths, from under the rubble, that we are now putting forth our first feeble shoots. If we wait for history to present us with freedom and other precious gifts, we risk waiting in vain. History is us — and there is no alternative but to shoulder the burden of what we so passionately desire and bear it out of the depths.

A.S.

Contents

CONTENTS

FROM UNDER THE RUBBLE

As Breathing and Consciousness Return

ALEXANDER SOLZHENITSYN

*(Apropos of A. D. Sakharov's treatise "Reflections on Prog-
ress, Peaceful Coexistence and Intellectual Freedom.")* [1]

*This article, written four years ago, was not issued as sa-
mizdat,* [2] *but shown only to A. D. Sakharov himself. As samizdat it was needed more at that time than now, since it
related directly to this well-known treatise. Since then Sakharov's views and practical proposals have traveled a long
way, so that today the article has very little relevance to
him, and is not a polemic with him.*

*"Therefore it's too late," I hear people objecting. If only it
were. In half a century we have not succeeded in calling
anything by its right name or thinking anything through,
and fifty years from now we shall still be catching up. Because all that has so far appeared in print is quite futile.
Here, as elsewhere, such a time lag is a normal feature of
Russian life since the revolution.*

*But it is not too late because in our country a massive sec-
tion of educated society is still stuck fast in the way of think-*

1. See Andrei Dmitrievich Sakharov, *Progress, Coexistence, and Intellectual
Freedom*, trans. the New York *Times* (New York: Norton, 1968).— TRANS.
2. *Samizdat* is a recent Russian coinage meaning literally "self-
publishing." It refers to poems, essays, stories, articles, and so on, that are
typed out and passed from hand to hand to evade the censorship.— TRANS.

3

ing which Sakharov has passed through and left behind. And it is not too late for another reason, namely, that several groups in the West apparently share the same hopes, illusions and delusions.

ONE

The transition from free speech to enforced silence is no doubt painful. What torment for a living society, used to thinking for itself, to lose from some decreed date the right to express itself in print and in public, to bite back its words year in and year out, in friendly conversation and even under the family roof.

But the way back, which our country will soon face — the return of breathing and consciousness, the transition from silence to free speech — will also prove difficult and slow, and just as painful, because of the gulf of utter incomprehension which will suddenly yawn between fellow-countrymen, even those of the same generation and same place of origin, even members of the same close circle.

For decades, while we were silent, our thoughts straggled in all possible and impossible directions, lost touch with each other, never learned to know each other, ceased to check and correct each other. While the stereotypes of required thought, or rather of dictated opinion, dinned into us daily from the electrified gullets of radio, endlessly reproduced in thousands of newspapers as like as peas, condensed into weekly surveys for political study groups, have made mental cripples of us and left very few minds undamaged.

Powerful and daring minds are now beginning to struggle upright, to fight their way out from under heaps of antiquated rubbish. But even they still bear all the cruel marks of the branding iron, they are still cramped by the shackles into which they were forced half-grown. And because we are intellectually isolated from each other, they have no one to measure themselves against.

As for the rest of us, we have so shriveled in the decades of

4

falsehood, thirsted so long in vain for the refreshing drops of truth, that as soon as they fall upon our faces we tremble with joy. "At last!" we cry, and we forgive the dust-laden whirl-wind which has blown up with them, and the radioactive fallout which they conceal. We so rejoice in every little word of truth, so utterly suppressed until recent years, that we forgive those who first voice it for us all their near misses, all their inexactitudes, even a portion of error greater than the portion of truth, simply because "something at least, some-thing at last has been said!"

All this we experienced as we read Academician Sa-kharov's article and listened to comments on it at home and from abroad. Our hearts beat faster as we realized that at last someone had broken out of the deep, untroubled, cozy torpor in which Soviet scientists get on with their scientific work, are rewarded with a life of plenty and pay for it by keeping their thoughts at the level of their test tubes. It was a liberat-ing joy to realize that Western atomic scientists are not the only ones who feel pangs of conscience — that a conscience is awakening among our own scientists too.

This in itself makes Andrei Dmitrievich Sakharov's fearless public statement an important event in modern Russian history.

The work finds its way to our hearts above all because of the honesty of its judgments. Many events and phenomena are called by the names which we all use in the secrecy of our minds but are too cowardly to speak aloud. Stalin's regime is numbered among the "demagogic, hypocritical, monstrously cruel police regimes"; we are told that in com-parison with Hitlerism, Stalinism "wore a much more cun-ning disguise of hypocrisy and demagogy" because it relied on "Socialist ideology as a convenient screen." We are re-minded of the "predatory procurements" of agricultural pro-duce and the "reduction of the peasantry to a condition almost of serfdom."

True, all this is said of the past, but the present day is not forgotten. There is "great material inequality between town and country," "40 percent of our country's population finds

5

itself in a very difficult economic situation" (the context hints at, demands the word *"poverty,"* but when one's own country is in question it sticks in the throat); whereas the 5 percent in the "boss class" are as highly privileged as "the corresponding groups in the USA." "No, more so!" we feel like retorting, but the author forestalls us with his explanations: the privileges of our country's managerial group are secret, not open and aboveboard, it is a matter of purchasing loyal service to the existing system by bribes, previously in the form of "salaries in envelopes," now by "closed distribution of everything in short supply — foodstuffs, goods, and services — and privileged access to resorts." Sakharov speaks out against the recent political trials, against the censorship, against the new unconstitutional laws. He points out that "a party using such methods of persuasion and education can hardly lay claim to the role of spiritual leader of mankind." He protests against the subordination of the intelligentsia to party officials, ostensibly in defense of "the interests of the working class." He demands that truth, not caste expediency, set the limits to the exposure of Stalinism; he rightly calls for "examination of the records of the NKVD by the whole nation," and a full amnesty for today's political prisoners. And even in the most sacrosanct sphere, foreign policy, he lays on the USSR "indirect responsibility" for the Arab-Israeli conflict.

However, this level of analysis, if not this level of boldness, is within the reach of other fellow-countrymen, though they are silent. But Sakharov, with the assurance of a great scientist, leads us upward to a loftier vantage point. With sharp taps of his lecturer's pointer he reduces to fragments those idols, the economic myths of the twenties and thirties, which, lifeless as they are, have for half a century cast a spell during our school days which few can break even in old age.

Sakharov shatters the Marxist myth that capitalism brings "the productive forces to an impasse" or "always leads to the absolute impoverishment of the working class." For the first time in our country Sakharov puts in proper perspective the competition of economic systems, unforgettably represented in a classroom poster by a socialist horse leaping over a capitalist tortoise.

Sakharov reminds us of the "burden of technical and organizational risk, and of development costs, which rests on a country pioneering in technology," and with great expertise lists important technological borrowings which have made the Soviet Union richer at the expense of the West. He reminds us that "catching up" in traditional branches of industry like iron and steel proves nothing, and that in the really decisive sectors we are consistently behind. Sakharov also destroys the myth of bloodsucking millionaires: they are "not too serious an economic burden" because there are so few of them, whereas "a revolution, which brings economic development to a standstill for more than five years, cannot be considered economically advantageous to the working classes." (Why not simply call it fatal?) As for the USSR itself, the myth that there is magic in socialist competition is laid low ("it plays no obvious economic role") and we are reminded that for all those decades "our people has worked at full stretch, which has led to a certain exhaustion of the nation's resources."

True, this demolition of sacred idols is hard going, and Sakharov is at times unnecessarily lenient: he speaks only of "a *certain* exhaustion," and says that "in the provision of high living standards . . . it is a drawn game between capitalism and socialism." (I hardly think so!) But the very act of crossing the forbidden line and daring to pronounce on matters which no one except the Founding Fathers has ventured to touch takes our author a long way forward. If what we find under the capitalist system is not unrelieved decay but "the continued development of productive forces," then "the socialist world must not destroy the soil from which it sprang," for "this would be the suicide of mankind" by atomic war. (As our propagandists choose to see it, atomic war means not the suicide of mankind but the certain triumph of socialism.) Sakharov gives sounder advice: we should renounce our "empirical opportunistic foreign policy," the "method of maximum discomfiture of opposing forces without regard to

7

the general good and common interests." The USSR and the United States should cease to be antagonists and go over to cooperation in giving the broadest disinterested aid to backward countries; and a system of international supervision to ensure respect for the Declaration of the Rights of Man should be one of their highest foreign policy aims.

The author also rehearses the main dangers to our civilization, the warning signs that man's habitat is threatened with destruction, and broadly poses the problem of saving it.

Such is the level of Sakharov's noble article.

TWO

But my purpose in writing this review is not to join in the chorus of praise: it is perhaps too loud already. I am alarmed by the likelihood that many of the fundamental ideas in Sakharov's article, which are insufficiently thought out and at times clearly unsound, will merge with the swelling current of free Russian thought only to distort or hinder its development.

Let us confess that we have set down here in exaggeratedly concentrated form all that seems best in Sakharov's article. But these statements do not form a tightly organized, vigorous whole: they are thinly spaced, toned down, above all interspersed with others which contradict them and often belong to a lower level of argument.

We see a conspicuous fault in the fact that the article lavishes attention on the internal problems of *other* countries — Greece, Indonesia, Vietnam, the United States, China — while the internal situation in the USSR is exhibited in the most benevolent light, or rather, indulgently underlit. But here he is on very treacherous ground. We have the moral right to make judgments on international problems, and still more on the internal problems of other countries, only if we take cognizance of *our own* internal problems and do penance for our faults. We have no right to pass judgment on the "tragic events in Greece" until we have looked to see whether events at home are not still more tragic. Before casting an eye on "attempts to conceal this cynicism and cruelty from the American people" we should take a good look around — is there nothing similar nearer home? Where they don't just "try to conceal," but are eminently successful? And if "the poverty of twenty-two million Negroes is tragic," are not fifty million collective farm laborers still poorer? Nor should we fail to recognize that the "tragicomic forms of the personality cult" in China are merely a repetition, with slight changes (not always for the worse), of our malodorous thirties.

This is a canker which has eaten into all of us. From the very beginning, however resoundingly the word "self-criticism" was pronounced, however boldly printed, it has always been criticism of the next man. For decades a belief in our socialist superiority was instilled into us, and we were permitted to sit in judgment only on others. So when we take it into our heads to talk about ourselves nowadays, an unconscious longing to extenuate our faults deflects our pens from the straight line of hard truth. It is no easy thing for us to accept this return of free thought, to get used to it right away and at one gulp. We timidly feel that to mention aloud the defects of our social order and our country is a sin against patriotism.

This discriminatory tolerance of "one's own" and simultaneous severity toward others shows through more than once in Sakharov's work, and to begin with on the very first page: in the crucial stipulation that although the object of his work is to facilitate the rational coexistence of "world ideologies," he does not "mean by this ideological peace with those fanatical, sectarian and extremist ideologies which admit no possibility of rapprochement, no discussion or compromise, as for instance the fascist, racist, militarist or Maoist ideologies." And that is all. End of list. Period.

What an insecure, jerry-built gateway to such an important work! This arch would collapse and crush us! True, he says "for instance," indicating that the list of ideologies with which there can be no reconciliation is not full, but what strange modesty explains the omission of precisely that ideology which at the very dawn of the twentieth century declared all compromises to be "rotten" and "treacherous," all discussions with the heterodox to be idle and dangerous twaddle, and proclaimed that in armed struggle and the division of the world into red and white, into those for us and those against us, lay the only solution of social problems. Since then that ideology has had enormous success, colored the whole twentieth century, struck a chill into three-quarters of the earth. Why then does Sakharov not mention it? Does he suppose that it can be talked round by gentle persuasion? If only it were so! But no one has yet seen anything of the sort: this ideology has not become the least bit less unyielding and intransigent. Is it implicitly included in his obscure, deprecating gesture, his impenetrable "for instance"?

A paragraph later Sakharov mentions among the "extreme expressions of dogmatism and demagogy," side by side with the same old racism and fascism — *Stalinism.* But this is a poor substitute.

In the Soviet Union since 1956 there has been nothing particularly bold, new or original in mentioning "Stalinism" as something bad. The sentiment is not officially acceptable, but it has spread far and wide among the public and is often uttered in conversation. In the thirties or forties to write down "Stalinism" in such a list would have been the act of a hero and a sage, for at the time "Stalinism" was embodied in a mighty, operative system, which had convincingly shown what it could do both at home and in Eastern Europe. But to invoke "Stalinism" in 1968 is sleight of hand, camouflage, evasion of the problem.

We may justifiably wonder whether "Stalinism" is in fact a distinctive phenomenon. *Did it ever exist?* Stalin himself never tried to establish any distinctive doctrine (and given his intellectual limitations he could never have created one), nor any distinctive political system of his own. All Stalin's present-day admirers, champions and professional mourners in our own country, as well as his followers in China, adamantly insist that he was a faithful Leninist and never in any matter of consequence diverged from Lenin. The author of these lines, who in his day landed in jail precisely because of his hatred of Stalin, whom he reproached with his departure from Lenin, must now admit that he cannot find, point to, or prove any substantial deviations.

Was not the land given to the peasants during the revolution only to be taken into state ownership soon afterward (the Land Code of 1922)? Were not the factories promised to the workers, but brought under central administration in a matter of weeks? When did the trade unions begin to serve not the masses but the state? Who used military force to crush the border nations (Transcaucasia, Central Asia, the Baltic States)? What of the concentration camps (1918–1921)? The summary executions by the Cheka? [3] The savage destruction and plundering of the Church (1922)? The bestial cruelties at Solovki [4] (1922)? None of this was Stalin — the dates, and his standing at the time, are against it. (Sakharov recommends that "Leninist principles of public supervision of places of confinement" should be reestablished. He does not tell us which year's principles, nor in which camps they were practiced. The early camps around the Solovetsky monasteries — the only ones Lenin lived to see?) We credit Stalin with the bloody enforcement of collectivization, but the reprisals after the peasant risings in Tambov (1920–1921) and Siberia (1921) were no less harsh — the difference was only that they did not affect the whole country. Some people may mark up the artificially forced pace of industrialization and the strangulation of light industry to Stalin's account, but this again was not his invention.

Stalin did perhaps manifestly depart from Lenin in one respect (though he was only following the general law of revolutions): in the ruthless treatment of his *own party*, which began in 1924 and rose to a climax in 1937. Can this be the decisive difference, the distinguishing mark which tells our

3. The Cheka was the original name of the Soviet secret police (1917–1922).— TRANS.
4. The popular name for the Solovetsky Islands in the White Sea. Their monasteries served as a place of exile during the Middle Ages and after the revolution were turned into the first systematic Soviet labor camp.— TRANS.

present-day progressive historians that "Stalinism" belongs in the exclusive list of antihuman ideologies, whereas its maternal ideology does not?

"Stalinism" is a very convenient concept for those "purified" Marxist circles of ours, who strive to differentiate themselves from the official line, though in reality the difference is negligible (Roy Medvedev may be mentioned as a typical example of this trend.) For the same purpose the concept of "Stalinism" is still more important and necessary to Western Communist parties — they shift onto it the whole bloody burden of the past to make their present position easier. (In this category belong such Communist theorists as G. Lukacs and I. Deutscher.) It is no less necessary to those broad Left-liberal circles in the West which in Stalin's lifetime applauded highly colored pictures of Soviet life, and after the Twentieth Congress found themselves looking most painfully silly.

But close study of our modern history shows that *there never was any such thing as Stalinism* (either as a doctrine, or as a path of national life, or as a state system), and official circles in our country, as well as the Chinese leaders, have every right to insist on this. Stalin was a very consistent and faithful — if also very untalented — heir to the *spirit* of Lenin's teaching.

As breathing returns after our swoon, as a glimmer of consciousness breaks through the unrelieved darkness, it is difficult for us at first to regain our clarity of vision, to pick our way among the clutter of hurdles, among the idols planted in our path.

Some of them Sakharov robs of their magic and dissolves into dust with a touch of his blackboard pointer, but others he respectfully passes by and leaves standing in all their falsity.

If we accept his reservation about all the "ideologies with which there can be no compromise" and rule them out (perhaps even extending the list), what are the ones with which Sakharov recommends coexistence? The liberal and Christian ideologies? Even as things are they hold no threat to the world, they are engaged in continual dialogue. But what are we to do with his sinister list? Rather a lot of ideologies past and *present* are represented in it.

What price then the *convergence* so eagerly awaited and invoked?

And where are the guarantees that "ideologies with which there can be no compromise" will not spring up in the future?

In the same work, after so soberly assessing the economic havoc wrought by revolutions, Sakharov envisages the "possibility of decisive action" through "the struggle of revolutionary and national-liberation movements . . . when no other means than armed struggle remains. . . . There are situations in which revolution is the only way out of an impasse." Here again, the author is not contradicting himself — he has merely contracted the squint characteristic of the age — viewing all revolutions with general approval, and unreservedly condemning all "counterrevolutions." (Who, though, can calibrate a sequence of violent events, each the cause of its successor; who can determine the incubation period, before the end of which a violent upheaval is still to be called counterrevolution, but after which it becomes revolution?)

Incomplete liberation from modish dogmas imposed by others is always punished by intermittent failures of vision and overhasty formulations. Thus the Vietnamese war, in Sakharov's account, is regarded by *world progressive opinion* as a war between the "forces of reaction" and "the will of the people." When regular divisions arrive along the Ho Chi Minh trail — is that also "the people's will"? Or when "regular" partisans set fire to villages because of their neutrality and coerce a peaceful population with tommy guns — shall we put this down to "the people's will" or "the forces of reaction"? How can we Russians, with experience of our *own* civil war, pass such superficial judgments on the war in Vietnam? No, let us not wish either "revolution" or "counterrevolution" on our worst enemies.

Once permit mass violence even in the most limited context and straightway the forces of "progress" and "reaction" will pour in to help; it will swell and sweep over a whole continent, and you will be lucky if it stops even at the brink of nuclear war. What is left then of the *peaceful coexistence* mentioned in Sakharov's heading?

The sacrosanct statues around which our author treads carefully include *socialism* — which is apparently so unreservedly accepted by all that it is not mentioned in the title as a subject for discussion. In his exaltation of socialism Sakharov indeed oversteps the mark. As if it were something generally known and in no need of proof, he writes about the "high moral ideals of socialism," "the ethical character of the socialist path," and even calls this his *main conclusion* (though it would obviously be more accurately called his main pious wish).

In no socialist doctrine, however, are moral demands seen as the essence of socialism — there is merely a promise that morality will fall like manna from heaven after the socialization of property. Accordingly, nowhere on earth have we been shown ethical socialism in being (and indeed the juxtaposition of these two words, tentatively questioned by me in one of my books, has been severely condemned by responsible orators). In any case, how can we speak of ethical socialism, when we do not know whether what we are shown under that name is in fact socialism at all? Is it something that exists in nature? Sakharov assures us that socialism, "as no other social order could," has "enhanced the moral significance of labor," and that "only socialism has raised labor to the peak of moral heroism." But in the great expanses of our collectivized countryside, where people always and only lived by labor and had no other interest in life but labor, it is only under "socialism" that labor has become an accursed burden from which men flee. Let us add to this that throughout our broad country and along its roads the heaviest manual labor is performed by women, since the men moved onto machines or into administration. Then there is the annual mobilization of townspeople for compulsory seasonal labor. We might even add that millions of white-collar workers at their office desks find their labor galling and detestable. Without prolonging the list, I can say that I have met scarcely anyone in our country who looks forward to Monday more than to Saturday. And if you compare the quality of building today with the masonry of earlier ages — particularly that of the old churches — you will feel inclined to look for "moral heroism" somewhere *in the past*.

Sakharov of course knows all this himself, and what he says is the result, not of personal errors of his, but of the general hypnosis of a whole generation, which cannot wake up abruptly, cannot at once shake off the cumulative effects of *all* those indoctrination sessions. That is why we read about the "socialist principle of remuneration according to quantity and quality of labor," although the system has existed under the name of "piecework" since the beginning of time. On the other hand, when Sakharov sees anything bad in socialist reality — "dissimulation and specious growth . . . at the cost of deterioration in quality" — he puts it down for some reason not to "socialism" but to "Stalinist pseudosocialism," whatever that may be. "Some of the absurdities in our development were not an organic consequence of the socialist path but a kind of tragic accident." Where is the proof of that? In the newspapers?

In this same hypnotic trance, Sakharov contemptuously appraises nationalism as a sort of peripheral nuisance, which hinders the glorious advance of mankind, but is doomed shortly to disappear.

Ah, but what a tough nut it has proved for the millstones of internationalism to crack. In spite of Marxism, the twentieth century has revealed to us the inexhaustible strength and vitality of national feelings and impels us to think more deeply about this riddle: why is the nation a no less sharply defined and irreducible human entity than the individual? Does not national variety enrich mankind as faceting increases the value of a jewel? Should it be destroyed? And can it be destroyed?

Underrating as he does the vitality of the national spirit, Sakharov also overlooks the possible existence of vital national forces in Russia. This shows through quite comically in the passage where he enumerates the "progressive forces in our country" — and finds what? "The Left Leninist-Communists" and the "Left Westernizers." Is that all? We should be spiritually poor indeed, we should be doomed, if Russia today consisted merely of such forces as these.

The word *progress* also appears in the title of the article — meaning technical, economic and social progress in the common traditional sense, and Sakharov leaves this too among the untouched and undethroned idols, although in an adjacent passage the drift of his own ecological arguments is that "progress" has brought mankind into dangers which to say the least are grave. In the social sphere, the author considers "the system of education under state control" a "very great achievement," and expresses his "concern that a scientific method of directing . . . the arts has not yet been realized in practice." Speaking of purely scientific progress, Sakharov with some satisfaction outlines the following prospects: "Creation of an artificial superbrain," "a resultant capacity to control and direct all vital processes at the level of the individual organism . . . and of society as a whole . . . including psychological processes and heredity."

Such prospects come close to our idea of hell on earth, and there is much here to perplex us and provoke sharp protest, were it not that at a second perusal it becomes clear that the whole treatise is obviously not intended to be read formally, literally and with captious attention to detail, and that the essence of the treatise is not what is expressed on the surface, even when this is specially emphasized, not its political terminology and intellectual arguments, but the moral disquiet which informs it and the spiritual breadth of the author's proposals, even if they are not always accurately and successfully expounded.

Similarly with the prospects for technological progress. Sakharov warns us — politicians, scientists, all of us — that "the greatest scientific foresight and caution, the greatest concern for universal human values" will be necessary.

16

Clearly such an appeal is not a practical program: pleas to politicians to show the greatest care for universal human values or to scientists to proceed cautiously with their discoveries are like barriers of flimsy board around a pit-shaft — and the bottom is littered with others like them. In all the history of science, has scientific foresight ever saved us from anything? If it has, we normally know nothing of it. What happened was that a lonely scientist burned his plans without showing them to anyone.

Sakharov himself did not burn his plans in time. Perhaps this is what now gnaws at him, perhaps it is this pain that makes him come out into the marketplace and call upon mankind at least to *begin putting an end* to evil, at least to stop short of new and worse disasters!

He knows himself that caution is not enough, that "the greatest concern is not enough," but he is not armed with his own terrible weapon, he holds out his weaponless hands to us in friendship, he is not so much our teacher as a humane spiritual adviser.

Similarly, Sakharov's hopes of convergence are not a well-grounded scientific theory, but a moral yearning to cloak man's last, nuclear, sin, to avoid nuclear catastrophe. (If we are concerned with solving mankind's moral problems, the prospect of convergence is a somewhat dismal one: if two societies, each afflicted with its own vices, gradually draw together and merge into one, what will they produce? A society immoral in the warp and the woof.)

"Do not extend spheres of influence," "do not create difficulties for other countries," let "all countries aim at mutual aid," and let the great powers voluntarily hand over 20 percent of their national income — none of this is practical politics, nor does it claim to be. These again are moral exhortations. The "prohibition of all privilege" inside our country is also a mere cry from the heart, and not a practical task for the "Left Communists" and "Left Westernizers" — for how could they build up the necessary coercive force? And can privilege in any case be eliminated by decree?

17

In Russia such prohibitions, reinforced by powder and shot, have been known in the past, but privilege popped up again as soon as there was a change of bosses. Man's whole outlook must be modified so that privilege ceases to be attractive and becomes morally repellent to its possessors — only then can it be eliminated. The elimination of privileges is a moral, not a political, task. Sakharov feels this himself, this is his real view of the matter, but the language of ethical literature is lost to our generation, and so our author is forced to make shift with the inexpressive language of politics. He says of Stalinism, for instance, that "blood and mud have sullied our banner." Now obviously our author's concern is not for banners, and what he is trying to say here is: "They have sullied our souls and depraved every one of us!"

The total inapplicability of our workaday language and concepts to the author's profound moral unease can be seen in many passages in the treatise, and also in its title; what Sakharov feels most strongly about will not fit into it, and that is why it is so long and enumerative.

Intellectual freedom also figures in the title. In it Sakharov sees the "key to the progressive reconstruction of the state system in the interests of mankind."

Certainly intellectual freedom in our country would immediately bring about a great transformation and help us to cleanse ourselves of many stains. Seen from the dark hole into which we are cast, that is so. But if we gaze into the far, far future — let us consider the West. The West has supped more than its fill of every kind of freedom, including intellectual freedom. And has this saved it? We see it today crawling on hands and knees, its will paralyzed, uneasy about the future, spiritually racked and dejected. Unlimited external freedom in itself is quite inadequate to save us. Intellectual freedom is a very desirable gift, but, like any sort of freedom, a gift of conditional, not intrinsic, worth, only a means by which we can attain another and higher goal.

In accordance with his demand for freedom, Sakharov proposes to introduce the multiparty system in "socialist" countries. Obstruction to this of course comes entirely from the regime, not from the public. But let us for our part try to rise above Western conceptions to a loftier viewpoint. Do we not discern in the multiparty parliamentary system yet another idol, but this time one to which the whole world bows down? "Partia" means a *part*. Every party known to history has always defended the interests of this one *part* against — whom? Against the rest of the people. And in the struggle with other parties it disregards justice for its own advantage: the leader of the opposition (except perhaps in England) will never praise the government for any good it does — that would undermine the interests of the opposition; and the prime minister will never publicly and honestly admit his mistakes — that would undermine the position of the ruling party. If in an electoral campaign dishonest methods can be used secretly — why should they not be? And every party, to a greater or lesser degree, levels and crushes its members. As a result of all this a society in which political parties are active never rises in the moral scale. In the world today, we doubtfully advance toward a dimly glimpsed goal: can we not, we wonder, rise above the two-party or multiparty parliamentary system? Are there no *extraparty* or strictly *nonparty* paths of national development?

It is interesting that Sakharov, while praising Western democracy and enthusing about socialism, recommends for the future world society neither the one nor the other, but inadvertently reveals that his dream is quite different: "a very intellectual . . . world leadership," "world government," which is obviously impossible either under democracy or under socialism, for given universal franchise, when and where would an intellectual elite be elected to govern? We have here quite a different principle — that of authoritarian rule. Whether such a government proved very bad or excellent, the means of creating it, the principles of its formation and operation, can have nothing in common with modern democracy.

Here again, incidentally, Sakharov thinks and writes of his

19

world rulers as an intellectual elite, but in the spirit of his work, in accordance with his general view of the world, he instinctively expects it to be a moral elite.

We may be rebuked for criticizing Academician Sakharov's useful article without apparently making any constructive suggestions of our own.

If so, we shall consider these lines not a facile conclusion, but merely a convenient starting point for discussion.

POSTSCRIPT, 1973

Having decided four years later to include this earlier article in the present collection, I must enlarge on the thought with which it abruptly ended.

Among Soviet people whose opinions do not conform to the official stereotype, there is a well-nigh general view that what our society needs, what it must aspire to and strive for, is *freedom* and the multiparty parliamentary system. The adherents of this view include all the supporters of socialism, but it is also more widely held than that. Indeed, it is so nearly unanimous that to challenge it (in unofficial circles, of course) looks downright indecent.

This almost perfect unanimity is an example of our traditional passive imitation of the West: Russia can only recapitulate, it is too great a strain to seek other paths. As Sergei Bulgakov [5] aptly remarked: "Westernism is spiritual surrender to superior cultural strength."

The tradition is an old one, the tradition of the prerevolutionary Russian intelligentsia, who believed not casually and coolly, but with the zeal of martyrs, sometimes at the cost of sacrificing their lives, that their cause and that of the nation could only be (the people's) freedom and (the people's) hap-

5. Sergei Bulgakov (1871–1944), a Marxist political economist who abandoned Marxism and wrote his seminal work, *From Marxism to Idealism*, in 1903. In 1923 he was expelled from the Soviet Union and ultimately settled in Paris, where he became one of the chief organizers of the Russian Student Christian Movement.— TRANS.

piness. History knows how this worked out in practice. But leaving that aside, let us look more deeply into the slogan itself.

What was understood by "the people's *happiness*" does not concern us here. Basically, absence of poverty, material well-being (the contemporary official concept — uninterrupted rise in the level of material existence — exactly coincides). It can, I think, nowadays be acknowledged without discussion that as the ultimate aim of several generations, to be paid for with the blood of millions, this is rather inadequate. The spiritual vector of happiness was, it is true, remembered by the Cadet [6] intelligentsia (and less often by socialist intellectuals), but very vaguely, because it was more difficult to imagine it on behalf of a people they understood so little: they meant, in the first place, needless to say, education (Western style), sometimes folk-dancing, even ritual, but never of course the reading of the Lives of the Saints or religious disputation. The general conviction was expressed by Korolenko: [7] "Man is made for happiness as a bird is made for flight." This formula has also been adopted by our contemporary propaganda: both man and society have as their aim "happiness."

Although the Cadets, to bring themselves closer to the people, called themselves the "People's Freedom party," the demand for "freedom" and the concept of "freedom" had not established themselves at all firmly among our people. The peasant masses longed for *land* and if this in a certain sense means freedom and wealth, in another (and more important) sense it means obligation, in yet another (and its highest) sense it means a mystical tie with the world and a feeling of personal worth.

Can external freedom for its own sake be the goal of conscious living beings? Or is it only a framework within which other and higher aims can be realized? We are creatures born

6. An abbreviated name for members of the prerevolutionary Constitutional Democratic party.— TRANS.
7. V. G. Korolenko (1853–1921), a talented prose writer and memoirist who initially supported the Populists; also a well-known philanthropist and champion of minorities, especially the Jews.— TRANS.

with inner freedom of will, freedom of choice — the most important part of freedom is a gift to us at birth. External, or social, freedom is very desirable for the sake of undistorted growth, but it is no more than a condition, a medium, and to regard it as the object of our existence is nonsense. We can firmly assert our inner freedom even in external conditions of unfreedom. (Remember how Dostoyevsky ridicules the complaint that "our environment has destroyed us.") In an unfree environment we do not lose the possibility of progress toward moral goals (that for instance of leaving this earth better men than our hereditary endowment has made us). The need to struggle against our surroundings rewards our efforts with greater inner success.

There is, therefore, a miscalculation in the urgent pursuit of political freedom as the first and main thing: we should first have a clear idea of what to do with it. We were given this sort of freedom in 1971 (more of it from month to month) — and what did it mean to us? That every man was free to ride off with a rifle, wherever he thought fit. And to cut down telegraph wires for his own needs.

The multiparty parliamentary system, which some among us consider the only true embodiment of freedom, has already existed for centuries in some Western European countries. But its dangerous, perhaps mortal defects have become more and more obvious in recent decades, when superpowers are rocked by party struggles with no ethical basis; when a tiny party can hold the balance between two big ones and over an extended period determine the fate of its own and even neighboring peoples; when unlimited freedom of discussion can wreck a country's resistance to some looming danger and lead to capitulation in wars not yet lost; when the historical democracies prove impotent, faced with a handful of sniveling terrorists. The Western democracies today are in a state of political crisis and spiritual confusion. Today, more than at any time in the past century, it ill becomes us to see our country's *only* way out in the Western parliamentary system. Especially since Russia's readiness for

22

such a system, which was very doubtful in 1917, can only have declined still further in the half century since.

Let us note that in the long history of mankind there have not been so very many democratic republics, yet people lived for centuries without them and were not always worse off. They even experienced that "happiness" we are forever hearing about, which was sometimes called pastoral or patriarchal (and is not a mere literary invention). They preserved the physical health of the nation (obviously they did, since the nation did not die out). They preserved its moral health, too, which has left its imprint at least on folklore and proverbs — a level of moral health incomparably higher than that expressed today in simian radio music, pop songs and insulting advertisements: could a listener from outer space imagine that our planet had already known and left behind it Bach, Rembrandt and Dante?

Many of these state systems were authoritarian, that is to say, based on subordination to forms of authority varying in origin and quality. (We understand the term in the broadest possible way, taking in everything from power based on unquestionable authority, to authority based on unquestionable power.) Russia too existed for many centuries under various forms of authoritarian rule, Russia too preserved itself and its health, did not experience episodes of self-destruction like those of the twentieth century, and for ten centuries millions of our peasant forebears died feeling that their lives had not been too unbearable. If such systems have functioned for centuries on end in many states, we are entitled to believe that, provided certain limits are not exceeded, they too can offer people a tolerable life, as much as any democratic republic can.

Together with their virtues of stability, continuity, immunity from political ague, there are, needless to say, great dangers and defects in authoritarian systems of government: the danger of dishonest authorities, upheld by violence, the danger of arbitrary decisions and the difficulty of correcting them, the danger of sliding into tyranny. But authoritarian regimes as such are not frightening — only those which are answerable to no one and nothing. The autocrats of earlier, religious ages, though their power was ostensibly unlimited, felt themselves responsible before God and their own consciences. The autocrats of our own time are dangerous precisely because it is difficult to find higher values which would bind them.

It would be more correct to say that in relation to the true ends of human beings here on earth (and these cannot be equated with the aims of the animal world, which amount to no more than unhindered existence) the state structure is of secondary significance. That this is so, Christ himself teaches us. "Render unto Caesar what is Caesar's" — not because every Caesar deserves it, but because Caesar's concern is not with the most important thing in our lives.

If Russia for centuries was used to living under autocratic systems and suffered total collapse under the democratic system which lasted eight months in 1917, perhaps — I am only asking, not making an assertion — perhaps we should recognize that the evolution of our country from one form of authoritarianism to another would be the most natural, the smoothest, the least painful path of development for it to follow? It may be objected that neither the path ahead, nor still less the new system at the end of it, can be seen. But for that matter we have never been shown any realistic path of transition from our present system to a democratic republic of the Western type. And the first-mentioned transition seems more feasible in that it requires a smaller expenditure of energy by the people.

The state system which exists in our country is terrible not because it is undemocratic, authoritarian, based on physical constraint — a man can live in such conditions without harm to his spiritual essence.

Our present system is unique in world history, because over and above its physical and economic constraints, it demands of us total surrender of our souls, continuous and active participation in the general, conscious *lie*. To this putrefaction of the soul, this spiritual enslavement, human beings who wish to be human cannot consent. When Caesar, having exacted what is Caesar's, demands still more insistently that we render unto him what is God's — that is a sacrifice we dare not make!

The most important part of our freedom, inner freedom, is always subject to our will. If we surrender it to corruption, we do not deserve to be called human.

But let us note that if the absolutely essential task is not political liberation, but the liberation of our souls from participation in the lie forced upon us, then it requires no physical, revolutionary, social, organizational measures, no meetings, strikes, trade unions — things fearful for us even to contemplate and from which we quite naturally allow circumstances to dissuade us. No! It requires from each individual a moral step within his power — *no more than that.* And no one who voluntarily runs with the hounds of falsehood, or props it up, will ever be able to justify himself to the living, or to posterity, or to his friends, or to his children.

We have no one to blame but ourselves, and therefore all our anonymous philippics and programs and explanations are not worth a farthing. If mud and dung cling to any of us it is of his *own* free will, and no man's mud is made any the less black by the mud of his neighbors.

1969–October 1973

Socialism in Our Past and Future

IGOR SHAFAREVICH

This article summarizes the author's longer work on the same topic. To that work we refer the reader who may wish to acquaint himself in greater detail with the facts and arguments which support his conclusions.[1]

SOCIALISM TODAY

Every generation is liable to make the mistake of exaggerating the significance of its own era, believing itself destined to witness a key turning point in history. In fact, radical changes involving the basic principles of human life happen once in five hundred or more years. But they do happen, as did the decline of antiquity and the break with the Middle Ages. And some generations are fated to live at those times.

It can hardly be doubted that our era is a turning point. In many of its basic activities mankind has come up against the fact that further movement along the paths followed hitherto is impossible and leads into a blind alley. This is true in the

1. The work referred to is apparently a full-length book on the same subject. It has never been published, either in the Soviet Union or abroad, and does not appear to have been circulated in *samizdat*. Therefore, only the author (and perhaps a few friends) knows of its existence.— TRANS.

26

spiritual sphere, in the organization of society, and in the sphere of industrial production (because of the inconsistency of the idea of a constantly expanding industrial society). The generations that come immediately after us must choose new paths and thus determine history for many centuries to come. For this reason, problems that appear to be insoluble stand out with painful clarity, and the dangers which threaten us yawn blackly ahead. Possible ways out can be seen only dimly, and the voices which speak about them are diffident and contradictory.

There exists, however, one voice which is untinged by doubts or obscurity; there exists a doctrine which points confidently to the future of mankind — *socialism.* At present it is divided into countless currents, each claiming to be the sole exponent of socialism and considering the others to be pseudosocialist. If we eschew such narrow partisanship and examine which countries are headed by governments that have proclaimed socialism as their aim, we shall see that the greater part of mankind in Europe, Asia, Africa and Latin America has already started to move in that direction. And in the rest of the world socialist parties are contending for power and socialist teachings prevail among young people. Socialism has become such a force that even the most prominent politicians are obliged to curry favor with it and the most weighty philosophers to make obeisances to it.

All the evidence is that man has very little time left to decide for or against a socialist future. Yet this decision can determine his fate for the rest of time. Accordingly, one of the most urgent questions of our time is *what is socialism?* What is its origin? What forces does it use? What are the causes of its success? Where is it taking us?

We can judge how far our understanding of the matter has progressed simply by the number of contradictory answers that are given to any one of these questions by representatives of the various socialist movements. To avoid a multiplicity of examples we shall adduce just a few opinions concerning the *origin of socialism.*

"When feudalism was overturned and 'free' capitalist soci-

ety appeared it was immediately discovered that this freedom denoted a new way of oppressing and exploiting the
workers. Various socialist movements at once came into
being as a reflection of this tyranny and a protest against it"
(V. I. Lenin, *The Three Sources and Three Components of
Marxism*).

". . . African societies have always lived by an empirical,
natural socialism, which can be termed instinctive" (the
ideologist of "African socialism," Dudu Tiam).

"Socialism is a part of the religion of Islam and has been
closely linked with the character of its people ever since that
people existed as nomadic pagans" (the ideologist of "Arab
socialism," al-Afghani).

What kind of peculiar phenomenon is this, that it can
evoke such different judgments? Is it a collection of unconnected movements which for some incomprehensible reason
insist on sharing one name? Or do they really have something in common beneath their external variety?

The most basic and obvious questions about socialism do
not seem to have been answered at all; other questions, as
will be seen later, have not even been asked. This ability to
repel rational consideration seems itself to be yet one more
enigmatic characteristic of this enigmatic phenomenon.

In this essay I shall try to consider these questions and
suggest some possible conclusions, using the best-known
sources — the classics of socialism and composite histories.

As a first approach let me try to describe purely phenome-
nologically the general features of present-day socialist states
and doctrines. The most emphatically proclaimed and the
most widely known principle is, of course, the economic one:
socialization of the means of production, nationalization, the
various forms of state economic control. The primacy of economic demands among the basic principles of socialism is
also emphasized in *The Communist Manifesto* of Marx and
Engels: ". . . Communists can state their theory in one proposition: the destruction of private property."

If one considers this by itself, one naturally asks whether

28

there is any difference *in principle* between socialism and capitalism. Isn't socialism just a monopolistic form of capitalism, isn't it "state capitalism"? Such a doubt can indeed arise if one concentrates on economics alone, though even in economics there are many profound differences between capitalism and socialism. But in other areas we come up against the true contradictions in principle between these systems. Thus, the basis of all modern socialist states is the party, a new formation which has nothing but the name in common with the parties of capitalist countries. It is typical of the socialist states that they try to spread their brand of socialism to other countries. This tendency has no economic basis and is harmful for the state, because it usually leads to the emergence of young and more aggressive rivals in its own camp.

At the bottom of all these differences lies the fact that socialism is not just an economic system, as is capitalism, but also — perhaps above all — an *ideology*. This is the only explanation for the hatred of religion in socialist states, a hatred which cannot be explained on economic or political grounds. This hatred appears like a birthmark in all the socialist states, but with varying degrees of prominence: from the almost symbolic conflict of the Fascist state in Italy with the Vatican to the total prohibition of religion in Albania and its proclamation as "the world's first atheist state."

Turning from the socialist states to socialist teachings, we meet with the same familiar positions: abolition of private property and hostility toward religion. We have already quoted *The Communist Manifesto* on the destruction of private property. The struggle with religion was the point of departure of Marxism and an indispensable element in the social reformation of the world. In his article *Toward a Critique of Hegel's "Philosophy of Law"* Marx said: ". . . the criticism of religion is the premise for any other form of criticism. . . . An obvious proof of the German theory's radicalism, and necessarily of its practical energy, is the fact that it starts by decisively casting religion aside. . . . The emancipation of the German is the emancipation of mankind. The brain of this emancipation is philosophy" (he has the atheistic aspects of Feuerbach's atheism in mind) "and its heart is the proletariat."

S. Bulgakov,[2] in his work *Karl Marx as a Religious Type*, has shown how militant atheism, Marx's central motivation, gave birth to his historical and social ideas: the ignoring of the individual and the human personality in the historical process, "the materialist interpretation of history," and socialism. This point of view is fully confirmed in the posthumously published drafts for Marx's book *The Holy Family*. There, Marx regards socialism as the highest level of atheism: if atheism "affirms man through the denial of God," if it is the "negative affirmation of man," then socialism is "man's positive affirmation."

But socialist doctrine includes principles which are not proclaimed by the socialist states, at least not openly. Thus, anybody reading *The Communist Manifesto* with an open mind will be surprised at the amount of space devoted to the destruction of the family, to the rearing of children away from their parents in state schools, to wife-sharing. In their arguments with their opponents the authors nowhere renounce these propositions, but try to prove that these principles are higher than those on which the bourgeois society of their time was based. There is no evidence of a subsequent renunciation of these views.[3]

In modern left-wing movements which are socialist but not, for the most part, Marxist, the slogan of "sexual revolution," that is, the destruction of traditional family relationships, also plays a basic part. A clear recent example of this tendency is the "Red Army," the Trotskyist organization in Japan, which became famous after a series of murders committed by it at the beginning of the 1970s. The victims

2. See note on page 20.— TRANS.
3. The attitude to this delicate question can be traced in the various translations of *The Communist Manifesto*. In the collected works of Marx and Engels of 1929 we read: "The only reproach which it might be possible to level at Communists is that they want official and open wife-sharing instead of hypocritical and concealed wife-sharing." In the 1955 edition the words "that they want" are replaced by "that they are alleged to want."

were mostly members of the organization itself. New members were supposed to break all family ties and the murders took place when this rule was ignored. The accusation "he behaved like a husband" was considered to justify a death sentence. The murder of one partner was often entrusted to the other. Any children born were taken from their mothers and given to another woman, who fed them on dried milk.

So, among the principles which are present in many unconnected socialist states or present-day movements and which can therefore be attributed to the *basic* premises of socialism, are: *the abolition of private property, the destruction of religion, the destruction of the family.* Socialism appears before us not as a purely economic concept, but as an incomparably wider system of views, embracing almost every aspect of human existence.

SOCIALISM IN THE PAST

We may hope to evaluate socialism correctly if we can find the right scale by which to measure it. With this in mind it is natural to step back from the perhaps too narrow frame of contemporaneity, and to consider it in its wider historical context. This we shall do in relation to socialist states and to socialist teachings.

Are socialist states specific to our era, or do they have precedents? There can be no doubt about the answer: many centuries and even millennia ago there existed societies which *embodied much more fully and consistently* the socialist tendencies which we observe in modern states. Two examples will suffice.

(1) Mesopotamia in the twenty-second and twenty-first centuries B.C. Mesopotamia was one of the cradles of civilization where the first states known to historians arose in the fourth millennium before Christ. They were formed on the basis of the economies of separate temples, which collected large masses of peasants and craftsmen around them and de-

veloped an intensive agriculture based on irrigation. Toward the middle of the third millennium, Mesopotamia broke up into small kingdoms in which the basic economic units remained the separate temples. Then, the Accadian king Sargon began the era when Mesopotamia was again united in a single state. I shall summarize some of the facts about the state which in the twenty-second and twenty-first centuries united Mesopotamia, Assyria, and Elam. Its capital was Ur, and the whole period is called the era of the Third Dynasty of Ur.

Archaeologists have found huge quantities of cuneiform tablets reflecting the economic life of the time. From these we know that the basis of the economy remained the temple units, but after the unification they lost all their independence and became cells in a unified state economy. Their heads were appointed by the king, they submitted detailed accounts to the capital, and their work was reviewed by the king's inspectors. Groups of workers were often transported from one temple to another.

Agricultural workers, men, women and children, were divided into parties headed by overseers. They worked all the year round, moving from one field to another and receiving seed grain, tools and draft animals from temple and state stores. Similarly, in groups under a commander, they used to go to the stores for their food. The family was not regarded as an economic unit: provisions were issued not to the head of a family but to each worker or more often to the commander. The documents relate separately to men, women, children and orphans. Evidently there was no question of being allowed even the use, let alone the ownership, of plots of land for this category of workers.

The other groups of inhabitants fed themselves by cultivating the plots set aside for them. Thus there were fields allocated to individuals, fields for craftsmen and fields for shepherds. But these fields were worked by the same workers as the state lands, and the work was supervised by state officials.

The towns contained state workshops, of which the biggest

were in the capital, Ur. The workers received tools, raw materials and half-finished products from the state. The products of the workshops went into the state warehouses. Craftsmen, like agricultural workers, were divided into parties under overseers. Provisions were issued to them by the state stores on the basis of lists.

Agricultural workers and craftsmen figure in the accounts as workers of full strength, two-thirds strength, or one-sixth strength. On this depended the norms for their provisions. Work norms also existed which determined the scale of the worker's rations. The temples submitted lists of the dead, the sick, and of absentees (with reasons). Workers could be transferred from one field to another, from one workshop to another, sometimes from one town to another. Agricultural workers were sent to assist in the workshops and craftsmen were sent to work in the fields or haul barges. The bondage of large classes of the population is highlighted by the numerous documents concerning fugitives. These documents name the fugitives and their relatives, and they concern not only barbers or the sons of shepherds, but also priests and their sons. This picture of the life of the workers opens with regular statements about the death rate (for the removal of the dead from food lists). One document declares a 10 percent mortality among its workers; another, 14 percent; yet another, 28 percent. Mortality was particularly high among women and children, who were employed on the heaviest work, such as hauling.

(2) The empire of the Incas. This great empire, numbering several million inhabitants and covering the territory from present-day Chile to Ecuador, was conquered by Spain in the sixteenth century. The conquerors have left detailed descriptions which give an excellent picture of the life which they could see or learn about from the natives. The descriptions depict the nature of the social system there so clearly that even in modern histories of this state, the headings very often use the term "socialist."

The Inca state did not know private ownership of the means of production. Most of its inhabitants hardly owned a thing. Money was unknown. Trade played no perceptible role in the economy.

The basis of the economy, the land, belonged theoretically to the head of the state, the Inca. That is, it was state property and the inhabitants only had the use of it. Members of the governing class, the Incas, owned some land only in the sense that they received the income from it. The cultivation of these lands was done by the peasants as a form of service to the state and was supervised by state officials.

The peasant received for his use a plot of specified size and additional strips as his family grew. When the peasant died, all the land reverted to the state. There were two other large categories of land: that owned directly by the state, and that owned by the temples. All the land was worked by detachments of peasants commanded and supervised by officials. Even the moment to begin work was indicated by a signal, which consisted of an official blowing a horn from a tower specially constructed for this purpose.

Peasants also worked as craftsmen. They received raw materials from state officials and handed their products back to them. Peasants were also builders, and for this purpose they were organized into great work brigades of up to twenty thousand men. Finally, the peasants were liable for military service.

The whole life of the population was regulated by the state. For the Inca governing class there existed only one field of activity, service in the military or civilian bureaucracy, for which they were trained in closed state schools. The details of their personal life were controlled by the state. For instance, an official of a given rank could have a prescribed number of wives and concubines, a set amount of gold and silver vessels, and so on.

But the life of the peasant was, of course, much more regimented. All his activities were prescribed for each period of his life: between the ages of nine and sixteen he was to be a shepherd, from sixteen to twenty he had to serve in an Inca's house, and so on down to old age. Peasant girls could be sent by the officials to the Incas' houses as servants or concubines, and they supplied the material for the mass human sacrifices. Peasant marriages were arranged by an official once a year according to lists prepared in advance.

The peasants' diet, the size of their huts and their utensils were all laid down. Special inspectors traveled about the country to ensure that the peasants observed all these prohibitions and kept working.

The peasant received his clothing, a cape, from state stores, and in each province the cape was of a specified color and could not be dyed or altered. These measures, and the fact that each province prescribed a distinctive hairstyle, facilitated surveillance of the population. Peasants were forbidden to leave their village without the permission of the authorities. The bridges and town boundaries were guarded by checkpoints.

This whole system was supported by a schedule of punishments elaborated with striking thoroughness. Almost always they amounted to the death penalty, which was executed in an extraordinary variety of ways. The condemned were thrown into ravines, stoned, hung by the hair or the feet, thrown into a cave with poisonous snakes. Sometimes, in addition to this, they were tortured before being killed, and afterward the body was not allowed to be buried: instead, the bones were made into flutes and skins used for drums.

These two examples cannot be ignored as isolated paradoxes. One could quote many others. A hundred and fifty years after the Spanish conquest of the Incas, for example, the Jesuits constructed in a remote part of Paraguay a society on analogous principles. Private ownership of the land did not exist, there was neither trade nor money, and the life of the Indians was just as strictly controlled by the authorities.

The Old Kingdom of Egypt was close to the Mesopotamian states both in time and because of its system. The Pharaoh was considered the owner of all the land and gave it only for temporary use. The peasants were regarded as one of the products of the land and were always transferred with it. They had obligations of state service: digging canals, building pyramids, hauling barges, quarrying and transporting stone. In the state-owned enterprises craftsmen and workers received tools and raw materials from the king's stores and gave their products back to them. The bureaucracy of scribes who managed these tasks is compared by Gordon Childe with the "commissars of Soviet Russia." He writes, "Thus about three thousand years before Christ an economic revolution not only secured for the Egyptian craftsman his means of subsistence and his raw material, but also created the conditions for literacy and learning and gave birth to the State. But the social and economic organization created in Egypt by Menes and his successors as revolutionaries was centralized and totalitarian" (*What Happened in History*).[4]

One could cite other examples of societies whose, life was to a significant degree based on socialist principles. But the ones we have already indicated show sufficiently clearly that the emergence of socialist states is not the privilege of any specific era or continent. It seems that this was the form in which the state arose: "the world's first socialist states" were the world's first states of any kind.

If we turn to socialist *doctrine*, we see a similar picture here too. These teachings did not arise either in the twentieth century or the nineteenth; they are more than two thousand years old. Their history can be divided into three periods.

(1) Socialist ideas were well known in antiquity. The first socialist system, whose influence can be seen in all its countless variations right up to the present, was created by Plato. Through Platonism socialist ideas penetrated to the Gnostic sects which surrounded early Christianity, and also to Manichaeism. In this period the ideas of socialism were propagated in schools of philosophy and in narrow mystical circles.

(2) In the Middle Ages socialist ideas found their way to the masses. In a religious guise they were propagated within various heretical movements, the Catharists, the Brethren of the Free Spirit, the Apostolic Brethren, and the Beghards.

4. See Gordon Childe, *What Happened in History* (New York: Penguin Books, 1946).— TRANS.

They inspired several powerful popular movements, for example, the Patarenes of fourteenth-century Italy, or the Czech Taborites of the fifteenth century. Their influence was particularly strong during the Reformation and their traces can still be seen in the English revolution in the seventeenth century.

(3) Beginning with the sixteenth century, socialist ideology took a new direction. It threw off its mystical and religious form and based itself on a materialistic and rationalist view of the world. Typical of this was a militantly hostile attitude to religion. The spheres in which socialist ideas were propagated changed yet again: the preachers, who had addressed themselves to craftsmen and peasants, were replaced by philosophers and writers who strove to influence the reading public and the higher strata of society. This movement came to its peak in the eighteenth century, the "Age of Enlightenment." At the end of that century a new objective made itself felt, that of bringing socialism out of the salons, out of the philosopher's study, and into the suburbs, onto the streets. There followed a renewed attempt to put socialist ideas behind a mass movement.

In this writer's opinion, neither the nineteenth nor the twentieth century introduced anything that was new in principle into the development of socialist ideology.

Let us cite a few illustrations to give an idea of the nature of socialist teachings and to draw attention to certain features which will be important in the discussion to follow.

(1) Plato's *Republic* depicts an ideal social system. In Plato's state, power belongs to the philosophers, who govern the country with the help of warriors (also called guardians). Plato's main concern was with the way of life of these guardians, since not only were the philosophers to be chosen from among them, but they were also to control the rest of the population. He wanted to subordinate their life completely to the interests of the state, and to organize it so as to exclude the possibility of a split and the emergence of conflicting interests.

The first means of achieving this was the abolition of private property. The guardians were to own nothing but their own bodies. Their dwellings could be entered by anybody who wished to. They were to live in the republic like hired laborers, serving only in return for food and no other reward.

For the same purpose the individual family was also abolished. All the men and women in the guardian class were to share their mates with all the others. Instead of marriage there was to be brief, state-controlled sexual union, for the purposes of physical satisfaction and the production of perfect progeny. To this end the philosophers were to yield to distinguished guardians the right of more frequent sexual union with the more beautiful women.

Children, from the moment of birth, would not know their own fathers or even mothers. They were to be cared for communally by all the women who happened to be lactating, and the children passed around all the time. And the state would take care of their subsequent upbringing. At the same time a special role was assigned to art, which was to be purged mercilessly in the name of the same goals. A work of art was considered all the more dangerous, the more perfect it was from the aesthetic point of view. The "fables of Hesiod and Homer" were to be destroyed, and most of classical literature with them — everything that might suggest the idea that the gods were imperfect and unjust, that might induce fear or gloom, or could inculcate disrespect for the authorities. New myths were to be invented, on the other hand, to develop in the guardians the necessary civic virtues.

Apart from this ideological supervision, the life of the guardians was to be biologically controlled as well. This control began with the careful selection of parents able to provide the best progeny, and selection was based on the achievements of agriculture. Children of unions not sanctioned by the state, like those with physical imperfections, were to be destroyed. The selection of adults was to be entrusted to medicine: doctors would treat some patients, allow others to die, and kill the remainder.

(2) The philosophy of the medieval heretics was based on the opposition between the spiritual and the material worlds

as two antagonistic and mutually exclusive categories. It begot hostility toward the whole material world and in particular to all forms of social life. All these movements rejected military service, oaths or litigation, personal submission to ecclesiastical and secular authority, and some rejected marriage and property. Some movements considered only marriage a sin, but not adultery, so that this demand did not have an ascetic character but aimed at the destruction of the family. Many sects were accused by their contemporaries of "free" or "sacred" love. One contemporary states, for instance, that the heretics considered that "marital ties contradict the laws of nature, since these laws demand that everything should be held in common." In precisely the same way, the denial of private property was linked with its renunciation in favor of the sect, and the common ownership of property was fostered as an ideal. "In order to make their teaching more attractive, they introduced common ownership," according to the record of one thirteenth-century trial of some heretics.

These more radical aspects of the doctrine were usually communicated only to the elite of the sect, the "perfected," who were sharply set apart from the basic mass of "believers." But in times of social crisis the preachers and apostles of the sect used to take their socialist ideas to the masses. As a rule these ideas were mingled with calls for the destruction of the whole existing order and above all of the Catholic Church.

Thus, at the beginning of the thirteenth century in Italy the Patarene movement, led by preachers from the sect of the Apostolic Brethren, provoked a bloody three-year war. The Apostolic Brethren taught that "in love everything must be held in common — property and wives." Those who joined the sect had to hand all their property over for common use. They thought of the Catholic Church as the whore of Babylon and the pope as Antichrist, and they called for the murder of the pope, bishops, priests, monks, and of all the godless. Any action against the enemies of the true faith was proclaimed to be permissible.

A little over a hundred years later heretical sects dominated the Taborite movement, whose raids terrorized central
Europe for a quarter of a century. Of them a contemporary
says: "In the Citadel or Tabor there is no Mine or Thine, everybody uses everything equally: all must hold everything in
common, and nobody must have anything separately, and he
who does is a sinner." Their preachers taught: "Everything,
including wives, must be held in common. The sons and
daughters of God will be free, and there will be no marriage
as a union of just two — man and wife. . . . All institutions
and human decisions must be abolished, since none of them
was created by the Heavenly Father. . . . The priests' houses
and all church property must be destroyed: churches, altars
and monasteries must be demolished. . . . All those who
have been elevated and given power must be bent like the
twigs of trees and cut down, burned in the stove like straw,
leaving not a root nor a shoot, they must be ground like
sheaves, the blood must be drained from them, they must be
killed by scorpions, snakes and wild animals, they must be
put to death."

The great specialist on the history of the heresies, I. von
Döllinger, describes their social principles as follows:
"Every heretical movement that appeared in the Middle
Ages possessed, openly or secretly, a revolutionary character;
in other words, if it had come to power it would have had to
destroy the existing social order and produce a political and
social revolution. These Gnostic sects, the Catharists and Al-
bigensians, whose activities evoked severe and implacable
legislation against heresy and were bloodily opposed, were
socialists and communists. They attacked marriage, the family, and property."

These features appeared still more clearly in the heretical
movements after the Reformation, in the sixteenth century.
We shall adduce one example, the teaching of Niklas Storch,
leader of the so-called Zwickau prophets.[5] This teaching, as

5. A particular follower of his was Thomas Müntzer, who played such an important role in the Peasants' War.

described in a contemporary book, included the following propositions:

"1) No marital connection, whether secret or open, is to be observed. 2) On the contrary, any man can take wives when the flesh demands it and his passions rise, and live with them in bodily intimacy exactly as he pleases. 3) Everything is to be held in common, since God sent all people into the world equal. Similarly He gave equally to all the possession of the earth, of fowl in the air and fish in the sea. 4) Therefore all authorities, terrestrial and spiritual, must be dismissed once and for all, or be put to the sword, for they live untrammeled, they drink the blood and sweat of their poor subjects, they guzzle and drink day and night. . . . So we must all rise, the sooner the better, arm ourselves and fall upon the priests in their cozy little nests, massacre them and wipe them out. For if you deprive the sheep of their leader, you can do what you like with them. Then we must fall upon the bloodsuckers, seize their houses, loot their property and raze their castles to the ground."

(3) In 1516 appeared the book which started a new stage in the development of socialist thought, Thomas More's *Utopia*. Being in the form of a description of an ideal state built on socialist principles, it continued, after a two-thousand-year break, the tradition of Plato, but in the completely different conditions of Western Europe of the Renaissance. The most significant works to follow in this new current were *The City of the Sun* by the Italian monk Tommaso Campanella (1602), and *The Law of Freedom in a Platform* by his contemporary in the English revolution, Gerrard Winstanley (1652).

From the end of the seventeenth century and in the eighteenth, socialist views spread more and more widely among writers and philosophers and there appeared a veritable torrent of socialist literature. The "socialist novel" came into being, in which descriptions of socialist states were intertwined with romance, travel and adventure (for example, *The History of the Savarambi* by Verras; *The Republic of*

Philosophers by Fontenelle; *The Southern Discovery* by Rétif de la Bretonne). The number of new philosophical, sociological and moral tracts preaching socialist views constantly increased (for example, Meslier's *Testament; The Law of Nature* by Morelly; *Thoughts on the Condition of Nature* by Mably; *The True System* by Deschamps; and passages in Diderot's *Supplement to the "Journey" of Bougainville*).

All these works agree in proclaiming as a basic principle the common ownership of property. Most of them supplement it with compulsory labor and bureaucratic rule (More, Campanella, Winstanley, Verras, Morelly). Others depict a country divided into small agricultural communes ruled by their most experienced members or by old men (Meslier, Deschamps). Many systems presuppose the existence of slavery (More, Winstanley, Verras, Fénelon), and More and Winstanley regard it not only as an economic category but as a means of punishment upholding the stability of society. They offer frequent elaborations of the ways in which society will subordinate the individuality of its members. Thus, More speaks of a system of passes which would be essential not only for journeys about the country but for walks outside the town, and he prescribes identical clothing and housing for everybody. Campanella has the inhabitants going about in platoons and the greatest crime for a woman is to lengthen her dress or paint her face. Morelly forbids all thought on social or moral subjects. Deschamps assumes that all culture — art, science and even literacy — will wither away spontaneously.

An important part is played in these works by consideration of the way in which the family and sexual relations are to change (Campanella, Rétif, Diderot, Deschamps). Campanella assumes absolute bureaucratic control in this domain. Bureaucrats decide which man is to couple with which woman, and when. The union itself is supervised by officials. Children are reared by the state. Deschamps thinks that the menfolk of a village will be the husbands of all the women, and that the children will never know their parents.

A new view of human history was worked out. Medieval mysticism had regarded it as a unified process of the revelation of God in three stages. Now this was transformed into the idea of a historical process subject to immanent laws and likewise consisting of three stages, the last of which leads inescapably to the triumph of the socialist ideal (e.g., Morelly, Deschamps).

Unlike the medieval heresies, which had attacked only the Catholic religion, the socialist world view now became hostile to any religion, and socialism fused with atheism. In More, freedom of conscience is linked with the recognition of pleasure as the highest objective in life. Campanella's religion resembles a pantheistic deification of the cosmos. Winstanley's attitude to religion is one of outright hostility, his "priests" are merely the agitators and propagandists of the system he describes. Deschamps considers that religion will wither away, together with the rest of culture. But Meslier's *Testament* stands out for its aggressive attitude toward religion. In religion he sees the root of mankind's misfortunes, he considers it a patent absurdity, a malignant superstition. He particularly loathes the person of Christ, whom he showers with abuse in protracted tirades, even blaming him because "he was always poor" and "he wasn't resourceful enough."

The very end of the eighteenth century saw the first attempt to put the socialist ideology which had been developed into practice. In 1786 in Paris a secret society called the "Union of the Equal" was founded with the aim of preparing a revolution. The plot was discovered and its participants arrested, but their plans have been preserved in detail, thanks to the documents published by the government and to the memoirs of the plotters who survived.

Among the aims which the plotters had set themselves, the first was the abolition of private property. The whole French economy was to be fully centralized. Trade was to be suspended and replaced by a system of state provisioning. All aspects of life were to be controlled by a bureaucracy: "The fatherland takes possession of a man from the day of his birth and does not let him go until his very death." Every man was to be regarded to some extent as an official supervising both his own behavior and that of others. Everybody was to be obliged to work for the state, while "the uncooperative, the negligent, and people who lead dissolute lives or set a bad example by their absence of public spirit" were to be condemned to forced labor. For this purpose many islands were to be turned into strictly isolated places of confinement.

Everybody was to be obliged to eat in communal refectories. Moving about the country without official permission was to be forbidden. Entertainments which were not available to everybody were categorically forbidden. Censorship was to be introduced and publications "of a falsely denunciatory character" were forbidden.

SOCIALISM IN THEORY AND PRACTICE

We can now return to the basic topic of this essay. However short and disjointed our digression into the history of socialism has been, one essential conclusion is beyond doubt: socialism cannot be linked with a specific area, geographical context, or culture. All its features, familiar to us from contemporary experience, are met in various historical, geographical and cultural conditions: in socialist states we observe the *abolition of private ownership of the means of production, state control of everyday life, and the subordination of the individual to the power of the bureaucracy;* in socialist doctrines we observe *the destruction of private property, of religion,*[6] *of the family and of marriage, and the introduction of wife-sharing.*

This cannot be considered a new conclusion: many writers

6. The ideology of Plato's *Republic* appears to me to be irreligious, since religion has no place in it. The medieval heresies had the appearance of *religious* movements, but they were the sworn enemies of that specific religion which the society around them preached. The murder of monks and priests, defilement of churches and burning of crosses are characteristic of their whole history. And this fundamental hatred that they all shared was the nucleus out of which grew the other aspects of their philosophy.

have pointed to the socialist character of such societies as the empire of the Incas, the Jesuit state, or the early states of Mesopotamia, while the history of socialist doctrine has been the subject of numerous monographs (some of them even by socialists). Thus, in his book *An Outline of the History of Socialism in Most Recent Times* R. Y. Vipper writes: "one could say of socialism that it is as old as human society."

Curiously enough *this observation has not been used to evaluate socialism as a historical phenomenon.* But its significance cannot be exaggerated. It calls for a complete review and replacement of the established principles by which we seek to understand socialism. If socialism is a feature of nearly all historical periods and civilizations, then its origins cannot be explained by any reasons connected with the specific features of a specific period or culture: neither by the contradiction between the productive forces and industrial relations under capitalism, nor by the psychological characteristics of the Africans or Arabs. To try to understand it in such a way hopelessly distorts the perspective, by squeezing this great universal historical phenomenon into the unsuitable framework of economic, historical and racial categories. I shall try below to approach the same questions from the opposite point of view: that *socialism is one of those basic and universal forces that have been in operation over the entire span of human history.*

A recognition of this, of course, in no way clarifies the historical role of socialism. We can approach an understanding of this role by trying to elucidate the aims which socialism itself avows. But here we run up against the fact that apparently there are two answers to this question, depending on whether we are talking about socialism as a state structure or as a doctrine. Whereas the socialist states (modern and ancient alike) all base themselves on the one principle of the destruction of private property, socialist doctrines advance a number of other basic propositions over and above that, such as the destruction of the family.

Here we meet two systems of views, one typical of "socialist theory," the other typical of "socialist practice." How do

45

we reconcile them and which is the true version of the aims of socialism?

The following answer suggests itself (and has in some particular cases been given): the slogans about the destruction of the family and marriage and — in their more radical form — about wife-sharing, are necessary *only* for the destruction of the existing social structures, for whipping up fanaticism and rallying the socialist movements. These slogans cannot, in themselves, be put into practice; indeed, that is not their function — they are necessary only *before* the seizure of power. The only vital proposition in all the socialist teachings is the destruction of private property. And this indeed is the true aim of the movement, and the only one which should be taken into consideration in discussing the role of socialism in history.

It seems to me that this point of view is essentially false. First, because socialism, being an ideology capable of inspiring grandiose popular movements and creating its own saints and martyrs, cannot be founded on deception. It must be infused with a deep inner unity. And on the contrary, history can show us many examples of the striking candor and, in some sense, honesty with which similar movements have proclaimed their objectives. If there is any deception here it is on the side of the opponents of these movements, who are guilty of *self-deception.* How often they strive to persuade themselves that the most extreme ideological propositions of a movement are irresponsible demagogy and fanaticism. Then they are perplexed to discover that actions which seemed improbable on account of their radical nature are the fulfillment of a program which was never concealed, but was proclaimed thunderously in public and expounded in all the known writings about it. We should note furthermore that all the basic propositions of socialist doctrine can be found in the works of such "detached" thinkers as Plato and Campanella, who were not connected with any popular movements. Evidently these principles arose in their writings as a result of some inner logic and unity in socialist ideology,

46

which consequently cannot be torn into two parts, one to be used in the seizure of power and then thrown away.

On the other hand, it is easy to see why socialist ideology goes beyond the practice of the socialist states and outstrips it. The thinker or organizer behind a popular movement on the one hand, and the socialist politician on the other, even though they base themselves on a unified ideology, have to solve different problems and work in different spheres. For the creator or propounder of socialist doctrine it is important to take the system to its uttermost logical conclusions, since it is precisely in that form that they will be most accessible and most contagious. But the head of state has to consider, above all, how to retain power. He begins to feel pressures that force him to move away from a program of rigid adherence to ideological norms, the pursuit of which would jeopardize the very existence of the socialist state. It is no coincidence that for many decades the same phenomenon has been repeating itself with such monotony, namely, that as soon as a socialist movement comes to power (or at least to a share of power) its less fortunate brothers anathematize it, accusing it of betraying the socialist ideal — only to be accused of the same should fortune smile on them.

But the dividing line that separates the slogans of the socialist movements from the practice of the socialist states does not run at all between the economic principles of socialism and its demands for the destruction of the family and marriage. Indeed, the propositions relating to economics and to changing industrial relations are also not realized with equal degrees of radicalism in the various socialist states.

A dramatic attempt to embody these principles to the full was made during the period of "war communism" in our country. The aim then was to base the entire Russian economy on the direct exchange of goods, to reduce the market and the role of money to nothing, to introduce the universal conscription of industrial labor, to introduce collective working of the land, to replace trade in agricultural products by confiscations and state distribution. The term "war communism" is itself misleading because it makes us think of wartime measures evoked by the exceptional situation during the civil war. But when this policy was being pursued that term was not used: it was introduced *after* the civil war, when "war communism" was renounced and recognized as a temporary expedient.

It was precisely when the civil war had in fact been won, and plans were being worked out for the governing of the country in peacetime conditions, that Trotsky, on behalf of the Central Committee, presented to the Ninth Congress of the Party the program for the "militarization" of the economy. Peasants and workers were to be put in the position of mobilized soldiers formed into "work units approximating to military units" and provided with commanders. Everyone was to feel that he was a "soldier of work who cannot be his own master; if the order comes to transfer him he had to comply; if he refuses he will be a deserter who is punished."

To justify these plans Trotsky developed this theory: "If we accept at face value the old bourgeois prejudice — or rather not the old bourgeois prejudice but the old bourgeois axiom which has become a prejudice — that forced labor is unproductive, then this would apply not only to the work armies but to conscripted labor as a whole, to the basis of our economic construction and to socialist organization in general." But it turns out that the "bourgeois axiom" is true only when applied to feudalism and capitalism, but is inapplicable to socialism! "We say: it is not true that forced labor is unproductive in all circumstances and in all conditions."

After a year "war communism" and "militarization" were replaced by the New Economic Policy as a result of devastation, hunger and rural uprisings. But the previous views were not deposed. On the contrary, the NEP was declared to be only a temporary retreat. And indeed, those very ideas continued to permeate Stalin's activity and the pronouncements of the opposition whom he was fighting. They were stated in Stalin's last work *The Economic Problems of Socialism,* in which he called for a curtailment of trade and the circulation of money, and their replacement by a system of barter.

48

We see a similar picture in the appearance in our country of another basic feature of socialism, hostility to religion. Nineteen thirty-two saw the inauguration of the "godless five-year plan," under which the last church was planned to be closed by 1936, while by 1937 the name of God was no longer supposed to be uttered in our country. In spite of the unprecedented scale assumed by its religious persecutions, the "godless five-year plan" was not fulfilled. The unforeseen readiness of believers to submit to any tortures, the birth of an underground Orthodox Church and the steadfastness of believers of other faiths, the war, the tumultuous rebirth of religious life in the territories occupied by the Germans — all these factors forced Stalin to give up his plan of uprooting religion and to recognize its right to exist. But the principle of hostility to religion remained and found expression again in the persecutions under Khrushchev.

Let us try to examine the socialist principles relating to the family and marriage from the same point of view. The first years after the revolution, the 1920s, again provide an example of how attempts were made to put these principles into practice.

The general Marxist views on the development of the family, on which the practice of those years was based, are expounded in detail in Engels's *The Origin of the Family, Private Property and the State.* They boil down to the assertion that the family is one of the "superstructures" erected on the economic base. In particular, "monogamy arose as a consequence of the concentration of great wealth in one person's hands — that person, moreover, being a man — and the need to bequeath this wealth to the children of that man and nobody else." In socialist society "the management of the individual household will be turned into a branch of social work. The care and upbringing of children will become a social matter." Thus the family will lose all its social functions, which from the Marxist point of view means it will die out. *The Communist Manifesto* proclaims the disappearance of the "bourgeois family." But by the twenties they were already managing without this epithet. Professor S. Y. Volfson, in his lengthy work *The Sociology of Marriage and the Family* (1929), foresaw that the family would lose the following characteristics: its productive function (which it was already losing under capitalism), its joint household (people would take their meals communally), its child-rearing function (they would be reared in state nurseries and kindergartens), its role in the care of the aged, and the cohabitation of parents with children and of married couples. "The family will be purged of its social content, it will wither away. . . ."

Practical measures were taken in accordance with these ideological propositions. Thus, in his note "Ten Theses Concerning Soviet Power," Lenin proposed taking "unflinching and systematic measures to replace individual housekeeping by separate families with the joint feeding of large groups of families." And for decades afterward many people languished in houses built in the twenties, where the communal flats had no kitchens in anticipation of the gigantic "factory-kitchens" of the future. Legislation simplified the measures for entering into and dissolving marriage as much as possible, so that registration became merely one of the ways of confirming a marriage (together with its confirmation in the courts, for example), while divorce was granted at the immediate request of one of the partners. "To divorce in our country is in some cases easier than to sign out in the house register," wrote one jurist. The family was viewed by leading personalities of the time as an institution opposed to society and the state. For instance, in her article entitled "Relations between the Sexes and Class Morality," Alexandra Kollontai wrote: "For the working class, greater 'fluidity' and less fixity in sexual relations fully corresponds to, and is even a direct consequence of, the basic tasks of that class." In her opinion woman was to be regarded as a representative of the revolutionary class, "whose first duty is to serve the interests of the class as a whole and not of a differentiated separate unit."

All these actions affected life in such a way that Lenin not only did not welcome the destruction of the "bourgeois family," predicted by *The Communist Manifesto*, but said: "You know, of course, about the famous theory that in Communist society the satisfaction of sexual desires and of the need for love is as simple and insignificant as drinking a glass of water. This 'glass of water' theory has made our young people frantic, absolutely frantic. It has become the downfall of many of our young men and girls. Its adherents proclaim that this is a Marxist theory. We don't want that kind of Marxism" (Clara Tsetkin, *On Lenin*). Indeed, in an inquiry conducted by the Communist Sverdlov Institute (the famous "Sverdlovka"), only 3.7 percent of respondents indicated love as a reason for their first intercourse. As a result, in the European part of the USSR between 1924 and 1925 the proportion of divorces to marriages increased by 130 percent. In 1924, the number of divorces per thousand that took place during the first year of marriage was 260 in Minsk, 197 in Kharkov and 159 in Leningrad. (Compare: 80 in Tokyo, 14 in New York, 11 in Berlin.) A society was founded called "Down with Shame"; and "naked marches" anticipated the modern hippies by half a century.

This historical precedent seems to us to show that in more favorable circumstances the socialist principle of the destruction of the family might be realized in full, and marriage be stripped of all its functions except intercourse (spiritual or physical) between its members. Such a result may well come about in the near future, particularly in view of the increasing likelihood of government intervention in this sphere of human relations. "We shall interfere in the private relations between men and women only insofar as they disrupt our social structure," wrote Marx. But who is to say what disrupts "our structure"? In the book by Professor Volfson which we have already quoted, he writes, ". . . we have every reason to believe that by the time socialism is established, childbirth will have been removed from the powers of nature. . . . But this, I repeat, is the only side of marriage which, in our opinion, the socialist society will be able to control." Such measures were in fact used in Nazi Germany, both to avert the appearance of progeny undesirable from the point of view of the state, and in order to obtain the desired progeny. For instance, the *Lebensborn* organization created by the SS selected Aryan mates for unmarried women, and there was propaganda in favor of a system of auxiliary wives for racially pure men. And when China proclaimed the following norm for family life: "One child is indispensable, two are desirable, three are impermissible," one is entitled to think that the term "impermissible" was in some way enforced.

It has nowadays become generally recognized that the crisis of overpopulation is one of the basic dangers (and perhaps the most frightening) that threaten mankind. Under these conditions attempts by governments to assume control of family relations may well be successful. Arnold Toynbee, for instance, considers that government intervention in these most delicate of human relations is inevitable in the very near future, and that as a result the totalitarian empires of the world will place cruel restrictions on human freedom in family life, just as in economics and politics. (See his book *An Historian's Approach to Religion*.[7]) In such a situation, and particularly with the increasing impairment of the spiritual values on which mankind could lean, the coming century is bringing with it the very real prospect of a socialist transformation of family and marriage, a transformation whose spirit has already been divined by Plato and Campanella.

These and other examples lead one to the conclusion that socialist ideology contains a *unified* complex of ideas welded together by internal logic. Of course, socialism takes on a variety of forms in differing historical conditions, for it cannot help mixing with other views. This is not surprising, and we would meet the same in an analysis of any phenomenon of a similar historical scale, for instance, religion. However, it is possible to isolate a very distinct nucleus and to formulate the "socialist ideal" that manifests itself either fully or in part, with greater or lesser impurity, in a variety of situations.

Socialist theories have proclaimed this ideal in its most logical and radical form. The history of socialist states shows a chain of attempts to approximate to an ideal which has

7. Arnold Toynbee, *An Historian's Approach to Religion* (New York: Oxford University Press, 1965).— TRANS.

never yet been fully realized, but which can be reconstructed from those approximations. This reconstructible ideal of the socialist states *coincides* with the ideal of socialist doctrine, and in it we can see the unified *"socialist ideal."*

THE SOCIALIST IDEAL

The formulation of this ideal is now no longer a problem.

The basic propositions of the socialist world view have often been proclaimed: the abolition of private property, religion and the family. One of the principles which is not so often represented as fundamental, though it is no less widespread, is the demand for *equality, the destruction of the hierarchy into which society has arranged itself.* The idea of equality in socialist ideology has a special character, which is particularly important for an understanding of socialism. In the more consistent socialist systems equality is understood in so radical a way that it leads to a negation of the existence of any genuine differences between individuals: "equality" is turned into "equivalence."

For instance, Lewis Mumford (in *The Myth of the Machine*) suggests that in their social structure the early states of Mesopotamia and Egypt expressed the concept of a machine whose components were the citizens of the state. In support of his argument he refers to contemporary drawings in which warriors or workers were depicted in a completely stereotyped manner, like the components of a machine.

The classic description of the socialist concept of equality is "Shigalyovism" — the socialist utopia quoted by Dostoyevsky in *The Possessed:*

"The thirst for education is already an aristocratic thirst. As soon as there is a family or love, there is a desire for property. We shall throttle that desire: we shall unleash drunkenness, scandal, denunciations; we shall unleash unprecedented debauchery; we shall extinguish every genius in his infancy. Everything must be reduced to the common denominator, total equality.

53

"Each belongs to all, and all to each. All are slaves and equal in slavery. In extreme cases it will mean defamation and murder, but the main thing is equality. First there will be a drop in the standard of education, in learning and talent. A high level of learning and talent is accessible only to the very brainy. We must abolish the brainy! The brainy have always seized power and been despots. The brainy couldn't be anything other than despots and have always brought more debauchery than good. We will execute or exile them. We will cut out Cicero's tongue, gouge out Copernicus's eyes, stone Shakespeare to death — that's Shigalyovism! Slaves must be equal: freedom and equality have never yet existed without despotism, but there must be equality in the herd, that's Shigalyovism!"

Supporters of socialism usually declare *The Possessed* to be a parody, a slander on socialism. However, we shall take the risk of quoting a few passages in a similar vein:

"This communism, everywhere negating the *individuality* of man, is merely the logical continuation of private property, which equally negates individuality."

". . . it so overestimates the role and dominion of *material* property that it wants to destroy *everything* that cannot become the possession and *private property* of the masses; it wants to eliminate talent *by force*. . . ."

". . . finally, this movement, which aims to oppose to private property the universal ownership of private property, expresses itself in a completely animal form when to *marriage* (which is, of course, a certain *form of exclusive* private property) it opposes the *communal ownership of women,* as a result of which woman becomes a *low form of social property.*"

"In the way that a woman abandons marriage for the realm of general prostitution, so the whole world of wealth, that is, of man's objectified essence, passes from the condition of exclusive marriage with a private owner to general prostitution with the collective."

I should very much like the reader to try to guess the author of these thoughts before looking at the answer: K. Marx, sketches for *The Holy Family* (published posthumously). To calm the reader let me hasten to qualify this: Marx sees communism in *this* way only "in its initial stages." Further on, Marx depicts *"communism* as the *positive* destruction of private property," in which he scientifically foresees quite other features. According to this book, for instance, every object will become "a humanified object or an objectified human" and "man assumes his many-sided essence in many-sided ways, that is, as an integral person."

There was also a socialist movement which endowed equality with such extraordinary significance that it derived its title, the "Union of the Equal," from it. Here is their interpretation of this concept:

"We want real equality or death, that's what we want.

"For its sake we would agree to anything, we would sweep everything away in order to retain just this. Let all the arts vanish if necessary, so long as we are left with genuine equality."

The way in which equality is understood brings us to a striking correlation between socialism and religion. They consist of identical elements which, in their different contexts, possess opposite meanings. "There is a similarity between them in their diametrical opposition," says Berdyayev [8] of Christianity and Marxism. The idea of human equality is also fundamental to religion, but it is achieved in contact with God, that is, in the highest sphere of human existence. Socialism, as is clearly evident from the examples above, aims to establish equality by the opposite means of destroying all the higher aspects of the personality. It is this concept of equality to which the socialist principles of communal property and the destruction of the family relate, and it also explains the hatred of religion which saturates socialist ideology.

The socialist ideal, that basic complex of ideas which for many thousands of years has lain at the foundation of socialist

8. Nikolai Berdyayev (1874–1948), ex-Marxist, later a religious philosopher and one of the chief contributors to *Vekhi*. Expelled from the Soviet Union in 1922.— TRANS.

ideology, can now be formulated: (1) equality and the destruction of hierarchy; (2) the destruction of private property; (3) the destruction of religion; (4) the destruction of the family.

Dostoyevsky was by no means parodying when he drew his portrait:

> *Do away at last with the nobles,*
> *Do away with the tsar as well,*
> *Take the land for common owners,*
> *Let your vengeance forever swell*
> *Against church and marriage and family,*
> *And all the old world's villainy.*[9]

WHERE IS SOCIALISM TAKING US?

We concluded above that there exists a unified ideal proclaimed by socialist doctrine and implemented — with more or less faithfulness — in the socialist states. Our task now is to try to understand what essential changes in life its full implementation would produce. In doing so we will automatically arrive at a description of the aim of socialism and its role in history.

The various types of socialist system and the life of the socialist states give us an opportunity to imagine how these general propositions would be concretely embodied. We get a picture which, although frightening and apparently strange at first sight, has an integral, inner logic and is thoroughly plausible. We must imagine a world in which every man and woman is "militarized" and turned into a soldier. They live in barracks or hostels, work under commanders, feed in communal refectories, and spend their leisure hours only with their own detachment. They need permits to go out in the

9. This poem, "A Noble Personality," is quoted in *The Possessed* as a Nihilist leaflet. The imitation turned out to be so accurate that a few years after the novel's publication these lines found their way to the Third Department in the form of a leaflet which really was being distributed by Nihilists.

street at night, to go for a walk outside the town or to travel to another town. They are all dressed identically, so that it is hard to tell the men from the women, and only the uniforms of the commanders stand out. Childbirth and relations between the sexes are under the absolute control of the authorities. The individual family, marriage and the familial rearing of children do not exist. Children do not know their parents and are brought up by the state. All that is permitted in art are works which contribute to the education of the citizens in the spirit required by the state, while all the old art that does not conform to this is destroyed. Speculation is forbidden in the realms of philosophy, morality and particularly religion, of which all that remains is compulsory confession to one's chiefs and the adoration of a deified head of state. Disobedience is punished by slavery, which plays an important role in the economy. There are many other punishments and the culprit is obliged to repent and thank his punishers. The people take part in executions (by expressing their public approval or stoning the offender.) Medicine also plays a part in the elimination of undesirables.

None of these features has been taken from the novels of Zamyatin,[10] Huxley or Orwell: they have been borrowed from familiar socialist systems or the practice of socialist states, and we have selected only the typical ones which are met with in several variants.

What will be the consequences of the establishment of such a system, in what direction will it take human history? In asking this question I am not asking to what extent a socialist society will be able to maintain the standard of living, secure the population's food, clothing and housing, or protect it from epidemics. These admittedly complex questions do not form the basic problem, which is really that the establishment of a social order fully embodying the principles of so-

10. Evgeny Zamyatin (1884–1937), outstanding modernist writer. Initially a Communist, he dissented strongly from Soviet methods of government after the revolution and left the Soviet Union in 1931 after personally appealing to Stalin. He is the author of *We*, the first (and best) anti-utopian novel of the twentieth century and the inspiration for Orwell's *1984*.— TRANS.

cialism will lead to a complete alteration in man's relation to life and to a radical break in the structure of human individuality.

One of the fundamental characteristics of human society is the existence of individual relations between people. As the excellent behaviorist researches of the last decades have shown, we are dealing here with a phenomenon of very ancient, prehuman origin. There are many kinds of social animals, and the societies they form are of two types: the anonymous and the individualized. In the first (for instance, in a shoal of herrings) the members do not know each other individually, and they are interchangeable in their relations. In the second (for example, a gaggle of wild geese) relations arise in which one member plays a special role in the life of another and cannot be replaced. The presence of such relations is, in a certain sense, the factor which determines individuality. And the destruction of these individual relations is one of the proclaimed goals of socialism — between husbands and wives and between parents and children. It is striking that among the forces which, according to the behaviorists, support these individualized societies we find those of hierarchy and of territory. Likewise in human society hierarchy and property, above all one's own house and plot of land, help to strengthen individuality: they secure the individual's indisputable place in life and create a feeling of independence and personal dignity. And their destruction figures among the basic aims advanced by socialism.

Of course, only the very foundation of human society has a biological origin of that kind. The basic forces which promote the development of individuality are specifically human. These are religion, morality, the feeling of personal participation in history, a sense of responsibility for the fate of mankind. Socialism is hostile to these too. We have already quoted many examples of the hatred of religion which characterizes socialist doctrine and socialist states. In the most vivid socialist doctrines we usually find assertions that history is directed by factors independent of the human will, while man himself is the product of his social environment — doctrines which remove the yoke of responsibility which religion and morality place on man.

And finally, socialism is directly hostile to the very phenomenon of human individuality. Thus, Fourier says that the basis of the future socialist structure will be the at present unknown feeling ("passion") of *unitéisme*. In contemporary life he could only indicate the antithesis of this feeling: "This disgusting inclination has been given various names by specialists: moralists call it egoism, ideologists call it the 'I,' a new term which, however, contributes nothing new and is only a useless paraphrase of egoism."

Marx, noticing that even after the acquisition of democratic freedom society remains Christian, concluded that it is still "flawed" in that ". . . man — not man in general but each individual man — considers himself a sovereign, higher being, and this is man in his uncultivated, nonsocial aspect in an accidental form of existence, as he is in life. . . ."

And even in Bebel, in whom participation in the parliamentary game and the enticing hopes of thus obtaining power so moderated all the radicalism of socialist ideology, we suddenly discover this picture: "The difference between the 'lazy' and the 'industrious,' between the foolish and the wise cannot exist any more in the new society, since what we mean by those concepts will not exist either."

The fact that socialism leads to the suppression of individuality has frequently been remarked on. But this feature has usually been regarded as just a means for the attainment of some end: the development of the economy, the good of the whole people, the triumph of justice or universal material well-being. Such, for instance, was the point of view of S. Bulgakov, who juxtaposed socialism with the first temptation of Christ: in "turning stones to bread" socialism tried to limit all mankind's goals to the solution of purely material problems. In my opinion the whole history of socialism contradicts this view. Socialist doctrines, for instance, show surprisingly little interest in the immediate conquest of injustice and poverty. They condemn all efforts in this area as "bourgeois philanthropy," "reformism" and "Uncle Tomism," and the solution of these problems is postponed until the triumph of the socialist ideal. As always, Nechaev [11] is more candid than anyone: "If you don't watch out the government will suddenly dream up a reduction in taxation or some similar blessing. This would be a real disaster, because even under present conditions the people are moving gradually upward, and if their penury is eased by even a fraction, if they manage to get just one cow more, they will regress by decades and all our work will be wasted. We must, on the contrary, oppress the people at every opportunity like, shall we say, sweatshop owners." And so we come to the opposite point of view, that the economic and social demands of socialism are the means for the attainment of its basic *aim*, the *destruction of individuality*. And many of the purely economic principles preached by socialists (such as planning) have been shown by experience not to be organically connected with socialism at all — which, in fact, has turned out to be badly adapted to their existence.

What will be the effect on life of a change in the spiritual atmosphere such that human individuality is destroyed in all its most essential forms?

Such a revolution would amount to the destruction of Man, at least in the sense that has hitherto been contained in this concept. And not just an abstract destruction of the concept, but a real one too. It is possible to point to a model for the situation we are considering in an analogous process which took place on a much smaller scale, namely, the clash between primitive peoples and European civilization. Most ethnographers think that the main reason for the disappearance of many indigenous peoples was not their extermination by Europeans, not the diseases or alcoholism brought by the whites, but the destruction of their religious ideas and rituals, and of the way their life was arranged to give meaning to their existence. Even when Europeans seemed to be help-

11. Sergei Nechaev (1847–1882), anarchist, Nihilist and one of Russia's first professional revolutionaries. In 1873 he was convicted for organizing the group murder of an innocent fellow-conspirator and was imprisoned in the Peter-Paul Fortress in St. Petersburg. Many of his ideas were subsequently taken over by the Bolsheviks.— TRANS.

ing by improving their living conditions, organizing medical aid, introducing new types of crops and farm animals or obstructing tribal wars, the situation did not change. The natives became generally apathetic, they aged prematurely, lost their will to live, died of diseases which previously they had survived with ease. The birthrate plummeted and the population dwindled.

It seems obvious that a way of life which fully embodies socialist ideals must have the same result, with the sole difference that the much more radical changes will bring a more universal result, the *withering away of all mankind, and its death.*

There appears to be an inner organic link here: socialism aims at the destruction of those aspects of life which form the true basis of human existence. That is why we think that the death of mankind is the inescapable logical consequence of socialist ideology and simultaneously a real possibility, hinted at in every socialist movement and state with a degree of clarity which depends on its fidelity to the socialist ideal.

THE MOTIVE FORCE OF SOCIALISM

If that is the objective conclusion toward which socialism is moving, what then is its subjective aim? What inspires all these movements and gives them their strength? The picture that emerges from our deliberations has all the appearances of a contradiction: socialist ideology, whose realization in full leads to the destruction of mankind, has for thousands of years inspired great philosophers and raised great popular movements. Why have they not been aware of the debacle that is the true end of socialism? And if aware, why have they not recoiled from it? What error of thought, what aberration of the feelings can propel people along a path whose end is *death?*

It seems to me that the contradiction here is not real, but only apparent, as often happens when someone makes a proposition in an argument which seems so obvious that nobody pays any attention to it, yet it is this unnoticed proposition that embodies the contradiction. In this particular argument the obvious element seems to be the proposition that the fatal nature of socialism has never been noticed, but the closer you become acquainted with socialist philosophy, the clearer it becomes that there is no error here, no aberration. The organic connection between socialism and death is subconsciously or half-consciously felt by its followers without in the least frightening them at all. On the contrary, this is what gives the socialist movements their attraction and their motive force. This cannot of course be proved logically, it can be verified only by checking it against socialist literature and the psychology of socialist movements. And here we are obliged to limit ourselves to a few heterogeneous examples.

If Nechaev, for instance, in calling on young people to join the revolution, also warned them that "the majority of the revolutionaries will perish without trace — that's the prospect" (one of those rare prophecies that was realized in full), what attraction did he have for them? He of all people could not appeal to God, or to the immortal soul, or to patriotism, or even to a sense of honor, since "in order to become a good socialist" he proposed the renunciation of "all feelings of kinship, friendship, love, gratitude, and even honor itself." In the proclamations issued by him and Bakunin [12] one can see quite clearly what it was that attracted them and infected the others: the urge for death and "unbridled destruction," "absolute and extraordinary." A whole generation of contemporary revolutionaries was doomed to perish in that conflagration, a generation poisoned by "the most squalid living conditions," fit only to destroy and be destroyed. That was Bakunin's *sole* aim. Not only were positive ideals absent, it was forbidden even to think about them: "We refuse point-blank to work out the future conditions of life . . . we do not

12. Mikhail Bakunin (1814–1876), leading Russian revolutionary thinker of the nineteenth century and founder of Anarchism. Was a rival of Marx for the leadership of the early Communist movement.

wish to deceive ourselves with the dream that we shall have enough strength left for creation."

In the USSR our generation well remembers how we marched in columns of young pioneers and sang with fervor (as did the young people in the civil war, and the Red Guards before us):

> *Bravely shall we enter battle*
> *On behalf of Soviet power*
> *And all together we shall die*
> *In this struggle of ours.*

And the greatest fervor, the greatest élan was evoked by that phrase *"all together we shall die."*

Or here is how three of the most famous socialist writers of the last century imagined the future of the human race: Saint-Simon foresaw that mankind would perish as a result of the planet's drying up. Fourier thought the same because the earth would "stop rotating on its axis and the poles would topple down to the equator," while Engels thought it would be because the planet would cool down.

These can hardly be regarded as the fruits of scholarly minds forced to bow to the truth, however drastic it might appear to be. Moreover, these three prophecies cannot all be true.[13]

Religion predicts the end of our world too, but only after the attainment of its ultimate aim, which also supplies the meaning of its history. But socialism (on the principle of the similarity of diametrical opposites) attributes the end of mankind to some external accident and thus deprives its whole history of any meaning.

In the near future the leaders of the socialist movements will look forward with surprising sangfroid, and occasionally

13. But in spite of his different arguments, Engels had a high opinion of Fourier's idea that "the whole of humanity is fated to disappear": "This idea of Fourier's has occupied a similar place in the science of history to that occupied in the natural sciences by Kant's idea of the eventual destruction of the globe."

63

even with open satisfaction, to the destruction, if not of all mankind, then of the greater part of it. In our time Chairman Mao has already stated his conviction that the death of half the population of the globe would not be too high a price for the victory of socialism throughout the world. Similarly, at the beginning of the fourteenth century, for example, the leader of the Patarene movement in Italy, Dolcino, predicted the imminent destruction of all mankind, relying on the authority of the prophet Isaiah: "And the remnant will be quite small and insignificant."

There are many indications that a tendency to self-destruction is not foreign to mankind: we have the pessimistic religion of Buddhism, which postulates as the ultimate aim of mankind its fusion with the Nothing, with Nirvana; the philosophy of Lao-Tse, in which the ultimate aim is dissolution in nonbeing; the philosophical system of Hartmann, who predicted the deliberate self-destruction of mankind; the appearance at various times of scientific and philosophical trends setting out to prove that man is a machine, though their proofs are in each case completely different and all they have in common is their (totally unscientific) urge to establish this fact.

Finally, the fundamental role of the urge to self-destruction has long since been indicated by biology. Thus, Freud considered it (under the title of the death instinct, or Thanatos) one of the two basic forces which determine man's psychic life.

And socialism, which captures and subordinates millions of people to its will in a movement whose ideal aim is the death of mankind, cannot of course be understood without the assumption that those same ideas are equally applicable to social phenomena, that is, *that among the basic forces influencing historical development is the urge to self-destruction, the human death instinct.*

An understanding of this urge as a force analogous to *instinct* also enables us to explain some specific features of socialism. The manifestations of an instinct are always connected with the sphere of the *emotions;* the performance of an instinctive action evokes a deep feeling of satisfaction and emotional uplift, and in man a feeling of inspiration and happiness. This can account for the attractiveness of the socialist world view, that condition of ardor and of spiritual uplift, and that inexhaustible energy which can be met in the leaders and members of the socialist movements. These movements have the quality of infectiousness which is typical of many instincts.

Conversely, understanding, the capacity for learning and for intellectual evaluation of a situation, are almost incompatible with instinctual action. In man the influence of instinct as a rule lowers the critical faculty: arguments directed against the aims which the instinct is striving to achieve are not only not examined but are seen as base and contemptible. All these features are found in the socialist world view.

At the beginning of this essay we pointed out that socialism as it were repels rational consideration. It has often been remarked that to reveal contradictions in socialist teachings in no way reduces their attractive force, and socialist ideologists are not in the least scared of contradictions.

Only in the context of socialism, for instance, could there arise in the nineteenth century — and find numerous followers — such a doctrine as Fourier's in which a basic role is played by the notion of the sexual life of the planets (the North Pole of the earth, bearer of male fluid, unites with the South Pole, bearer of the female fluid). Fourier predicted that in the future socialist system the water of the seas and oceans would acquire the taste of lemonade, and that the present creatures of the sea would be replaced by antiwhales and antisharks, which would convey cargoes from one continent to another at colossal speed.[14] This will seem less surprising, however, if we recall that it is only just over two hundred years since socialist ideology assumed a rational exterior. And it was very recently (on the macrohistorical time scale) that socialism, in the form of Marxism, exchanged this exterior for a scientific one. The brief period of "scientific social-

14. As Engels said, here "purely Gallic wit combines with great depth of analysis."

ism" is ending before our eyes, the scientific wrapping no longer increases the attraction of socialist ideas and socialism is casting it off. Thus Herbert Marcuse (in "The End of Utopia") says that for the modern "avant-garde Left" Fourier is more relevant than Marx precisely because of his greater utopianism. He calls for the replacement of the development of socialism "from utopia to science" by its development "from science to utopia."

All this shows that the force which manifests itself in socialism does not act through reason, but resembles an *instinct*. This accounts for the inability of socialist ideology to react to the results of experience, or, as behaviorists would say, its inability to learn. A spider, spinning its web, will complete all the six thousand four hundred movements necessary even if its glands have dried up in the heat and will produce no silk. How much more dramatic is the example of the socialists, with the same automatism constructing for the nth time their recipe for a society of equality and justice: it would seem that for them the numerous and varied precedents which have always led to one and the same result do not exist. The experience of many thousands of years is rejected and replaced by clichés from the realm of the irrational, such as the claim that all the different socialisms of today and yesterday or created in a different part of the globe were not the real thing, and that in the special conditions of "our" socialism everything will be different, and so on and so forth.

That is the explanation for the longevity of that mass of prejudices and catchphrases surrounding socialism, like the identification of socialism with social justice or the belief in its scientific character. They are accepted without the least verification and take root in people's minds like absolute truths.

At our present turning point the depth and complexity of the problem facing mankind is becoming increasingly apparent. Mankind is being opposed by a powerful force which threatens its very existence and at the same time paralyzes its most reliable tool — reason.

Contemporary Socioeconomic Systems
and Their Future Prospects

MIKHAIL AGURSKY

Many people believe that there are only two possible socio-economic systems — the capitalist one in Western countries and the socialist one in Communist countries, and that all today's conflicts merely reflect the contradiction between them. This view is mistaken.

In fact there are perhaps more resemblances than differences between these two systems, the reason being the very existence of large-scale industry as the economic base of both.

Once it exists, whatever system directs it, large industry becomes an active influence on society in its own right. This applies particularly to such branches of mass production as automobiles, light industry, construction and electronics.

The first duty of an industry like the automobile industry is to satisfy the primary demand for automobiles. Once this need has been met, however, the industry faces the danger of a decline. This of course is catastrophic, for if there are no orders, production must stop. The automobile industry must assure itself of a steady stream of orders to survive. A switch to some product other than automobiles is impracticable, first, because the industry's plant is purpose-built for a narrow range of products and replacing it would require vast capital investment, not to mention replanning the factory, and second, because the production workers possess particular skills and would have to be completely retrained. Switching from one product to another very different one is obviously all but impossible. The vast expenditure involved would make production uneconomic for a long time, and the enterprise would also not be able to compete with firms already manufacturing similar goods. Besides, it would be unwise to discontinue the manufacture of automobiles altogether, since some residual demand for them would remain and it would in any case recover sufficiently once the first generation of automobiles was worn out. All this points to a different solution to the question, namely, stimulating demand.

Advertising helps to do this by creating a psychological atmosphere which encourages people to change their automobiles long before they are worn out. In the United States and other countries the ownership of the latest model is a status symbol. Backed by advertising, the automobile industry has reached gigantic proportions and has stimulated the growth of related industries such as metallurgy, toolmaking, and so on. Thus the stimulation of demand becomes vital to the existence not only of the automobile industry but of the entire national economy, since its decline would lead to a general economic crisis.

In his book *Future Shock* Alvin Toffler enumerates with excessive relish other examples of the stimulation of demand in various industries by boosting the output of disposables and throw-away goods — clothing, ball-point pens, diapers, food packaging, and so on. He quotes examples of the shortening of the life-span of dwelling houses so as to increase the turnover of the building industry; the built-in obsolescence of toys; the pharmaceutical industry's deliberately reducing the useful life of its drugs so as to replace them with new ones. A whole new industry has sprung up manufacturing fun goods such as badges with pornographic jokes with an expected life of only a few days.

Precisely the same stimulation of consumption is practiced in Communist countries as in the West, though the process is slower and less efficient. Thus the USSR is being drawn particularly strongly into the orbit of consumption. Although the need for automobiles is far from being satisfied as yet, at the rate new foreign-built factories are going up it can safely be assumed that the saturation point is not far off (especially considering the inadequacy of the road and service networks). Recent years have seen a revolution in housing and furniture in the USSR and we are already replacing the third generation of television sets. *Fashion*, a powerful stimulus to the working capacity of light industry, is acquiring more and more importance in the economy of the USSR. Under Soviet conditions, however, light industry is at a disadvantage, since our tastes for a long time now have been set by the West. Inflexible Soviet industry, not being the arbiter of Western fashion, is unable to keep abreast of it. This results in vast surpluses of goods which nobody wants because they have gone out of fashion.

As in the West, various kinds of fashion and leisure products are acquiring an important role in Communist economies, since they stimulate consumption and require advanced industrial processes. As in the West, planned obsolescence is widely practiced. Here too disposables are becoming widespread.

Both systems aim for constant growth in the national product and an equal expansion of consumption. The entire economic — and therefore also social — stability of both systems becomes dependent on industry's always working to capacity, and the stimulation of demand becomes vital to their existence.

There are, however, significant differences between the two systems. First of all, Communist economies, the USSR's especially, are much less efficient than Western economies. This is because the members of the ruling state-monopoly corporation have no direct interest in the results of industrial performance, their material standard of living being assured regardless of the general state of the economy. A similar tendency is observable in John Kenneth Galbraith's technostructures (as he calls the largest monopolistic conglomerates active in the Western economic system). Indeed, some of the failings of Communist economies are already beginning to become evident in these monopolistic conglomerates. Galbraith asserts that their only aim is survival. But where competition is open, the survival of such conglomerates depends basically on economic factors, which inevitably affects the welfare of their members — as P. Sweezy rightly pointed out in his review of Galbraith (*New York Review of Books*, 1973, No. 18).[1]

Under the economic conditions of communism, however, the survival of even such a senior member of the ruling corporation as a factory manager may be determined solely by noneconomic factors, since his appointment and tenure of office depend mainly on his relations with the ruling party apparatus. Given this reciprocal bond even an unsuccessful or incompetent manager can maintain his status, if, for example, he does some favors, even personal favors, for his superiors in the corporation. This tendency is reinforced by the corporation's caste system, whereby even a failed member is not dismissed from the staff but is, as a rule, transferred to some other responsible post.

The absence of proper incentives for all the echelons of this corporation makes the technological backwardness of the Communist countries inevitable. Yet how can this be reconciled with the obvious successes of Soviet military technology? The fact is that this success is determined by political, not economic, factors, and the resultant vast expenditure on the armaments industry and the meticulous quality control of military hardware carried out by the military themselves, independently of the manufacturing process. If the armaments industry's conditions were applied to civil industry, the Soviet budget would collapse under the burden of additional expenditure. Also, military production is strictly supervised by the government itself.

The second significant difference between the two systems

1. See Paul H. Sweezy, review of *Economics and the Public Purpose* by John Kenneth Galbraith in the *New York Review of Books*, vol. 20, no. 18 (November 15, 1973), p. 3.— TRANS.

is to be found in the role of competition. Although there is no free competition between enterprises in Communist countries, since their market is guaranteed, nevertheless competition is still extremely important. There is first of all personal competition for status among the members of the ruling corporation, which can be very savage. Second, the Communist economy's pace is set not by internal but by international competition, spurred by the urge for survival and expansion, considerations of international prestige, and so on. Were it not for this competition, Communist economies would be doomed to stagnate completely.

There is one more important difference between the two systems. In the West the prices of goods fall as demand rises, but in Communist countries the prices of such goods immediately rise. This increase in prices is due to the absolute monopoly of trade which in fact is one of the laws of Communist economics and one reason why Communist countries always have a lower standard of living than Western countries (although it is not the sole factor contributing to a lowering of the standard of living).

Another characteristic of Communist economies is that they do not allow unemployment. Everybody is afforded the minimum means of survival, and in that sense they enjoy greater security, although their minimum is much lower than that prevailing in advanced Western countries.

Despite their differences, the two systems are closely interconnected within the framework of the overall world economy. Communist countries, the USSR and China most of all, find it hard to compete in world markets with manufactured goods because of the low quality of their products. Therefore they have turned into exporters of raw materials, importing machine tools, consumer goods and even foodstuffs from the West in exchange. Besides this, competition between the two systems has become one of the most important stimuli of consumption growth. The West, driven by fear of revolution, tries among other things to encourage its entire population to consume as much as possible and to raise its standard of living. At the same time the Communist countries, in search of

71

the prestige essential to their future expansion, strive to boost the consumption of their own peoples.

It is possible to conclude that the Communist economy is no more than the next stage in the development of the Western economic system, where production is concentrated solely in the hands of the state.

Both these systems are profoundly flawed and, unless some means of averting it can be found, will swiftly plunge mankind into catastrophe. First of all, both systems are rapacious plunderers of the natural resources that alone can maintain the hypertrophic growth in consumption that is observable at present. Until recently these resources seemed inexhaustible, but now, particularly in the light of the energy crisis, this naïve view has been changed. Even earlier it was becoming increasingly apparent that natural resources, especially soil, water, fuel, air, and so on, were by no means infinite, and that unfettered growth in consumption would inevitably exhaust them far sooner than the natural needs of a growing population would. After all, the disappearance of just one resource vital to human life, even if all the others were plentifully available, would be sufficient to cause a catastrophe, for resources are not interchangeable.

Western countries, the United States especially, are said to use up natural resources like a "drunken sailor," but this applies even more to the USSR, where vast resources are pointlessly expended as a result of our reigning improvidence. For example, quantities of smelted metals are either thrown out into the street to rust or used in structures that are far heavier than necessary. Large quantities of agricultural produce are left to rot every year. Vast amounts of fuel are pointlessly burned. The senseless waste of Soviet resources not only continues but is increasing all the time; it has become a national habit.

But the USSR's resources are quickly being depleted, not only for these reasons, but also because it has become the largest supplier of raw materials to other countries. It is the presence of these vast resources, which the USSR can exchange for machine tools, consumer goods and foodstuffs, that allows it to compete with the West and generally support a large but inefficient economy.

It was its timber, ores, furs, and so on, that allowed the USSR to industrialize in the 1920s and 1930s when these goods were bartered for essential equipment from the United States and Germany. The world's natural resources are perhaps adequate to feed the growing population for the foreseeable future, but they are by no means sufficient to feed an exaggerated race for consumption. Unless the growth of consumption is checked, mankind will soon be faced with a critical shortage of resources. The symptoms of such a crisis are already apparent, but it will deepen further as Asia, Africa and Latin America are drawn into the sphere of expanded consumption.

Another incorrigible defect of the existing systems is their growing political instability as a result of the West's increasing dependence on external commodities markets and sources of raw materials, and the Communist countries' drive to expand. The saturation of their own markets leads the Western countries to seek new markets indiscriminately, so as to keep their industry working. This makes them increasingly dependent on raw material supplies from other countries, for the most part those that possess no manufacturing industry of their own. Therefore, if some state poses a threat to peace and freedom, business circles, fearing the loss of markets or sources of raw material, begin to put pressure on their governments to soften their policies toward that state. This is why Western countries, despite their own enormous potential, are incapable of resisting dictatorships and totalitarian regimes.

These were the roots of the Munich Agreement of 1938, when the leaders of Britain and France, under pressure from big business, opened the way to National Socialist aggression against the entire world. Earlier the business world had been instrumental in bringing about the rebirth of German industry, which was then used by the Nazis exclusively for military purposes. Western business circles were led to pursue this suicidal policy by their constitutional inability to take a long-term view of either their national interests or their own individual interests, or to make any concessions in the short term.

They are doing exactly the same thing now. With the unexpected support of frivolous social-democratic youth groups, on whom the word "socialism" displayed by the Eastern block (and by the Berlin Wall, too) has a hypnotic effect, business circles pressured West Germany's ruling Social Democratic party into elevating the existing status quo in Germany to the rank of a juridically accepted fact, in the meantime making maximum concessions to the USSR and East Germany, which latterly has become the focus of militarism in Europe. The events leading up to Brandt's resignation showed this eloquently enough. The German nation — and mankind as a whole — will pay dearly for the actions of these business circles. The West German businessmen and industrialists, however, have been rewarded with free entry to the East European and Soviet markets.

Another instance of how the selfish interests of business circles can conflict with national and world interests is the shortsighted policy pursued by French governments under de Gaulle, who were prepared to make all kinds of concessions to any totalitarian regime so long as it was sufficiently far away and posed no immediate threat to France.

The Communist countries, meanwhile, pursue their aims of worldwide expansion. At present this manifests itself mainly in the Third World, where the USSR and China compete for the control of countries supplying raw materials. Control over those resources would enable them to exert pressure on the West. At the same time they are also pursuing strategic aims. All this displays an irrational thrust for the expansion of their influence which K. Witvogel was the first to note as characteristic of totalitarian systems. The USSR and China stop at nothing to increase their influence in the Third World, supporting even the most inhuman regimes and provoking armed conflicts, as for instance in the Middle East, the Indian subcontinent, and so on.

Existing political systems are conditioned to a significant degree by economics, but political and economic systems are by no means synonymous. Political systems can be divided into two types according to the criterion of whether civil rights are guaranteed or not — democracy and dictatorship, the extreme form of which is totalitarianism, imposing on the population not only power but also ideology. Communist countries are as a rule totalitarian — at least that is how it has been to date.

But dictatorships and totalitarian regimes can exist in the West too — for example, totalitarian Nazi Germany and the dictatorial regimes of Greece, Haiti, Chile, Uganda, Iraq and Libya, to name but a few.

Therefore the nationalization of production and the absence of guarantees for private property are not the only conditions for the absence of democracy. The real causes are the selfish interests of various groups which, given the chance, subordinate the rest of the population of the country, although in Communist countries the absence of democracy is the essential prerequisite of their existence.

Many people believe it to be self-evident that existing democratic systems represent some sort of absolute good. The intelligentsia of Communist countries, who regard contemporary parliamentary states as ideally free and democratic, are particularly prone to this view. But the stumbling block to such a view is the question of why so many people in these parliamentary states are dissatisfied with them — for dissatisfied they undoubtedly are. Powerful left-wing movements are rocking such ancient and seemingly stable parliamentary states as France and Italy. They accuse these states of lacking democracy, of corruption and so forth, while paradoxically idealizing precisely those states that defenders of parliamentarianism call totalitarian.

A man who has been accustomed to breathing fresh air all his life does not notice it, and never realizes what a blessing it is. He thinks of it only occasionally when entering a stuffy room, but knows that he need only open the window for the air to become fresh again. A man who has grown up in a democratic society and who takes the basic freedoms as much for granted as the air he breathes is in much the same position. People who have grown up under democracy do not value it highly enough. Yet there are weighty reasons for their dissatisfaction with this society.

In the first place political struggle in a democracy bears the essential stamp of totalitarianism — not, of course, of the kind prevailing in totalitarian countries, but enough to be irritating. In all conscience it is hardly credible that the entire vast range of existing philosophies and viewpoints could be contained in the political programs of two or three main parties. But political activity outside these parties, which have taken on the form of large bureaucratic organizations, is largely pointless, since it requires the spending of a great deal of money to achieve any effect.

The overwhelming majority of voters and politicians adhere to the parties out of conformism, which is reinforced by vast propaganda machines, or else for career reasons. The tyranny of the majority can be oppressive indeed, especially if the majority is very little bigger than the minority. How oppressive and pernicious such a tyranny can be has been well known since the time of the Athens Republic.

A parliamentary system guarantees dissenters many personal freedoms, but does nothing to shield society from the massive propaganda of conformism, which exerts great pressure on people and is extremely difficult to resist. Let us suppose there is a religious minority which for reasons of conscience does not wish to read pornographic literature, and even less to see it in the hands of its children. In a contemporary democracy such a minority will be unable to live according to its convictions, since the entrepreneur who profits from pornographic literature enjoys unlimited freedom to exploit any of the mass media for its popularization. This is bound to have an effect at least on the children of this minority, if not on the adults.

One of democratic society's gravest defects is its lack of control over the mass media. While this is a good guarantee of basic freedoms, the price paid for it is rather high.

The mass media in today's democracies are commercial, which accounts for their size and their truly astronomical circulation figures. The information industry plays a vital role in stimulating consumption. It tries to appeal to the widest possible range of human perceptions, exploiting the sexual urges more and more and transforming them into a force that destroys society.

Furthermore, those who control the mass media, and also journalists, can at times become more influential than politicians. Since in a democracy the mass media enjoy unlimited freedom, nobody can put pressure on a publisher or journalist and have him removed. These people, unlike politicians or judges, are elected by nobody, yet their real power is immense.

Other democratic freedoms are also being turned inside out. The freedom to acquire arms, intended to make life more secure, can now make life in countries like the USA more dangerous, since weapons can be acquired by people who will use them to the detriment of others.

The freedom to strike, so vital to workers defending their rights, can be used by thugs both criminal and political for disreputable purposes, such as blackmailing employers. It has now become one of the chief sources of inflation.

Freedom of movement within a country, freedom to enter and leave a country, can easily be abused by criminals or by hostile totalitarian states for the purposes of espionage and so forth.

In a modern democratic society life is stressful, and that is one reason for the dissatisfaction. This tension makes many people who have grown up in democracies envy totalitarian countries, where life is much calmer and slower moving, where many of the alarms that upset people in the democracies do not exist.

Oddly enough, life in totalitarian countries, indeed any life under conditions of constraint, does at first sight have some attractions. Russians before the abolition of serfdom and the Jewish ghettos of the Middle Ages were noted for the measured rhythm of their existence: every man knew his station

77

in life and his prospects, he did not rebel, he was apparently psychologically far more contented than the modern inhabitant of a democratic country.

Where there are no freedoms, there is no requirement to participate in the political struggle. A man who lives in a totalitarian society is obliged to follow a prescribed political line, and so long as he does so — as the majority generally do, at least once totalitarianism has been in control for a few years — he feels much more secure than if he had to choose between conformity and resistance.

The inhabitant of a totalitarian society is called upon to make far fewer decisions than a man living in a democratic society. For example, if there is no freedom of movement in a totalitarian country, nobody will have to think about where to live. If there is no choice of employment, that is another agonizing choice less. If free competition and free enterprise do not exist, there is no need to engage in this competition, which many in any case find unendurable. At the same time, the inhabitant of a totalitarian state may be much less well off than the inhabitant of a democracy, but since his country's overall standard of living is so different, he is perfectly content with his situation and secure in his modest future.

The inhabitant of a totalitarian society is not bothered by most of the temptations which would trouble his peace of mind in a democracy: the exploitation of sex, for example, provided this is prohibited by law. And the same applies to the preservation of the family and marriage.

The inhabitant of a totalitarian country (so long as he is loyal) feels far safer than the inhabitant of a democracy, since where he lives there is no freedom to acquire or carry weapons, police regulations are stricter, and so on.

Totalitarian regimes limit the flow of disturbing or worrying news. The media in these countries are as a rule forbidden to report crimes, accidents and natural disasters occurring at home (though not in hostile countries). At the same time they are instructed to maintain optimism by filtering out anything that might encourage fears of impending world catastrophe, and so forth.

For this reason very many people living in totalitarian countries, having survived terror and been brainwashed by propaganda, are not only genuinely content with their position, but virtually consider themselves to be the happiest people on earth. This, however, engenders an inferiority complex vis-à-vis the democracies, so that the inhabitants of totalitarian countries often turn into implacable enemies of freedom, ready and willing to destroy everything that reminds them of the free will they have lost. This also applies in many respects to the intellectuals of these countries, who often display a pathological fear of freedom.

So far I have talked about the defects of contemporary democracy. But the defects of totalitarianism are of a completely different order. Democracy's faults pale into insignificance beside the enormities of totalitarianism, such as the deaths of tens of millions of people in Soviet and German death camps and prisons. So long as totalitarianism continues to exist, it organically bears the seeds of lawlessness within itself, although the crimes of the Nazi period in Germany or 1918–1956 in the USSR cannot, in the nature of things, occur often.

But totalitarian societies are neither eternal nor unshakable. They age and disintegrate under the impact of many factors.

First of all, in striving to extend their sway over the largest possible area, they lose their capacity for effective government, especially such giants as the USSR and China.

Totalitarian countries are riven by conflicts of various kinds — national, social and political. Another important factor undermining their stability is the revival of religious consciousness, the natural enemy of totalitarianism, which lays claim to total control of the human spirit. All this goes to make totalitarian societies short-lived.

But even the democracies of today are becoming less and less stable, and there are forces growing and consolidating within them that threaten to bury them altogether. The reason is that these societies have lost the basic, valuable first principles of democracy. The democracies came into being and took shape in concrete historical conditions, when their populations exercised a high degree of self-discipline based on ethics. As the influence of religious values declined, this discipline began to diminish, posing a growing threat to democratic society.

The free sale of arms in the USA in the nineteenth century was no threat, but now that the self-discipline which once prevented their abuse has been lost, it has become a serious menace. A simple prohibition on the sale of weapons would accomplish nothing, since vast quantities are already in the hands of the public and could be withdrawn only by the application of draconian measures unthinkable in a democracy.

It goes without saying that the evaluative approach to the mass media has also disappeared. We can take as an example the extremely sympathetic and well-intentioned journal *Index*,[2] which is devoted to a worldwide struggle against censorship. In it there is a regular chronicle recording infringements of freedom of the press. Consciously rejecting the evaluative approach to censorship, its compilers place facts about the tyrannical persecution of any manifestation of independent thought in the USSR or Czechoslovakia side by side with reports of some mild administrative measure taken against a neo-Nazi journalist in West Germany.

A significant contributory factor to the destabilization of the democracies is the ability of totalitarian states to meddle unpunished in their internal affairs, while the latter permit no shadow of interference in their own.

The only reason, indeed, why democratic societies still exist is that their populations have not yet altogether lost their self-control. One may conclude that existing systems, from both the economic and the political point of view, are possessed of a large quantity of faults, and the superiority of one over the other may be regarded simply as the lesser of two evils.

2. *Index on Censorship*, a quarterly journal published in London by Writers and Scholars International Ltd.— TRANS.

Let us now attempt to paint a rough picture of the socio-economic system of the future. It will resemble the present socioeconomic system of neither West nor East. It would be incorrect to call the future society socialist, since this term has been devalued many times over by the historical practice of the last fifty years. Socialism consciously rejects spiritual and moral values, it preaches violence as the means of social struggle, thereby arriving at a negation of the concept of social justice which it advances.

Is there a real alternative to the systems of today? Is it possible to create a system free from their glaring faults? A just and rational system can be built only on a foundation of spiritual and moral values. And that means that the point of departure for the solution of social, economic and political questions should be the principle of social justice for all and the renunciation of violence as a means of solving social problems. There should also be a complete renunciation of the totally outdated (and never correct) theory of the workers' exercising some sort of hegemony over society, and of the ideology that turned out to be nothing but a convenient smoke screen for the establishment of totalitarian regimes by tiny groups of intellectuals. Workers in Communist countries have far fewer rights than in the West. Enormous numbers of workers are in any case a specific characteristic only of our present systems and in the future, the class of persons permanently engaged in servicing manufacturing equipment may well disappear altogether.

Violence, as the experience of the Russian and other revolutions has shown, can only aggravate the faults of the system that preceded the revolution. The Marxist theory of the class struggle has become not a means of defending the workers' interests but an ideology to justify terror and hegemony over them. Marxism has in general become an anachronism, an obstacle to further progress, although of course parts of it will still have relevance for the future.

It is essential to eradicate the idea that productivity is the yardstick of a society's progressiveness. The aim of the future should not be productivity growth, not the constant rise of production and consumption, but the maintenance of productivity, production and consumption at the level compatible with the restrictions dictated by the interests of society and the real level of resources.

In the economy of the future manufacture should be broken down into smaller units, but the units should have an advanced scientific and technological base. Enterprises will have to be small enough for every employee to understand the production process and be genuinely able to participate in its management. These enterprises will have to be universal, so that they are capable of manufacturing a large variety of products. Present knowledge indicates that such installations could have great potential. For this they will have to be sufficiently productive to be able to manufacture items individually or in short runs.

The problem of small enterprises is already attracting a great deal of attention, especially in the United States. Their number is increasing and their importance growing. According to a survey of metal-processing machinery in the United States (*American Machinist*, 1973, No. 22, pp. 143–149), the significance of small manufacturing plants with less than a hundred employees has grown considerably. Fifteen percent of the eleven million people employed in mechanical engineering in the United States now work in them, and over 40 percent of the metal-processing machinery is concentrated in them.

There is another problem that demands attention — the use of computers to control small enterprises. At present such enterprises are limited in what they can perform. But there is no doubt that in the near future more sophisticated enterprises will appear on the scene, capable of manufacturing complex products on a one-off or short-run basis. Technically this is perfectly feasible. With the aid of enterprises of this kind, it should be possible to supply most of the consumer goods and machinery we require.

Let us suppose that these enterprises were at the disposal of communes or municipalities. Their output would be intended not for sale or disposal, but for their own use. In that case the enterprise would be in action only when the commune or municipality really needed something from it. With a high level of amortization it would not require a great deal of the time of those who worked in it, and work there could be combined with agricultural labor or intellectual activity. Manufacturing in this form would do away with workers as a specialized group whose interests were predominantly linked with production.

The abolition of the gulf between physical and intellectual labor, as also between industrial and agricultural work, will be one of the essential features of the future. That is how the ideologist of anarchy, Prince P. Kropotkin, pictured the future. He saw future society as being composed of communes where physical labor would be combined with the intellectual. He thought people could spend part of their time in physical labor, producing essential foodstuffs and manufactured goods. The kibbutzim of Israel approach this ideal to some extent, though at present they work mainly for the outside consumer.

Communes or municipalities with these enterprises at their disposal will not, of course, be able to do everything for themselves: a certain amount of economic centralization will also be necessary. In the first place there will have to be a mining industry, unless the problem of resources is to be solved in some other way. Second, it will be essential to produce the means of production. And third, we will need specialized scientific research.

The mining industry will be much smaller than at present because of the sharp fall that will take place in the demand for resources. Nevertheless, the extraction of resources will require centralized effort. The same applies to the production of the means of production and the pursuit of scientific research. Therefore the decentralized economy will have to be combined with elements of centralization in areas where local groups cannot cope.

Naturally the total output of manufacturing will be much less than in contemporary systems and the productivity of labor will also be correspondingly lower. But that will repre-

83

sent a major step toward social progress, since both output and the productivity of labor will be at the level necessary to satisfy the optimum (but not maximum) needs of society.

This society of the future, while living within the means of its real resources, would assure man's daily needs without the monstrous excesses of the contemporary world, and it would be stable. But it should be clearly understood that a fundamentally decentralized economy of this kind would probably be incompatible with the existence of a large urban population; either the urban population must greatly decrease in numbers, or the structure of the city must be completely changed.

It would be a great blessing if we could start laying the foundations of such a system now within the framework of contemporary society. The question of small enterprises has been discussed before, and has been opposed by such advocates of large-scale industry as John Kenneth Galbraith. He asserts that: "The small firm cannot be restored by breaking the power of the larger ones. It would require, rather, the rejection of the technology which since earliest consciousness we are taught to applaud. It would require that we have simple products made with simple equipment from readily available materials by unspecialized labor" (J. K. Galbraith, *The New Industrial State*, Moscow, Progress, 1969, p. 70).[3] But this is a mistaken view, being based on an incorrect assessment of the small enterprise's potential. The very concept of the small enterprise becomes viable precisely as a result of technological progress. Therefore it is most important to overcome the prejudice which states that generalized production is always less efficient than specialized production. Technological progress and the decentralization of the economy are not incompatible. What is more, when Galbraith wrote the lines quoted above, the idea of highly automated small enterprises had still not come into being.

The political structure of future society, to an even greater degree than its economy, will have to be founded on spiritual

3. See John Kenneth Galbraith, *The New Industrial State* (Boston: Houghton Mifflin, 1967).— TRANS.

and moral values. This must make it totally unlike totalitarianism, but simultaneously unlike today's democratic societies. The society of the future must be democratic, but first, it will need a high degree of self-discipline capable of warding off many conflicts, and second, in order to avoid the mistakes of the past, some key aspects of social life will have to be controlled, though the control must not be of a totalitarian nature.

A high degree of economic decentralization will inevitably lead to political decentralization, preserving democracy at all levels of government. The central government should be limited to the fulfillment of the most basic functions, such as the initiation of legislation and the supervision of its observance, the exploitation of natural resources, the directing of large-scale scientific research, and so forth.

We should strive toward the elimination of political parties as bureaucratic organizations with their own secretariats, propaganda channels and finances. The elimination of parties is perfectly feasible, first because in a decentralized society the central authority will confer no particular privileges, and second because the psychological basis of the political parties will also disappear. The contemporary class structure of society, which fuels political antagonism, will disappear, as will the so-called intelligentsia (as a social class, not as a spiritual entity), since the polarity between physical and mental work will also have been eliminated. And this is the base on which all parties are built. There will of course always be groups of like-minded people who can combine for the pursuit of certain common aims. The point is that the creation of special bureaucratic organizations with their secretariats, finances, and so on, is dangerous to society, whatever views their adherents propound.

The center of gravity will shift to the individual small commune, and everyone will be able to defend his own point of view alone or in alliance with others. A man in whom trust is reposed at elections will have the opportunity to carry out any program without being committed to party discipline. Any man will be eligible for election as a deputy, but voting

85

must be for him personally and not for the party he represents.

It is vital that society should take control of the mass media. These are at present used for two purposes, the relative importance of which depends on the socioeconomic system. In Western countries it is commercial purposes which predominate, while in Communist countries it is propaganda. Both these uses of the mass media are extremely dangerous.

The mass media must be freed from their commercial and propagandist character. Without their commercial function their size will be greatly reduced, if only by the amount of advertising. And this will also change their content. Censorship of the mass media is absolutely indispensable, but it should be exercised not by bureaucratic organizations but by elected persons.

In fact the managers of the mass media, like the censors, will have to be freely elected in exactly the same way as the government and the judiciary and they must be independent of the organs of power. The censor is just as important to society as a judge, for example. Perhaps his responsibility is even greater than a judge's, since the moral and spiritual health of society will depend on him. Censorship must be carried out according to clear and unambiguous terms of reference laid down by constitutional statute. Naturally there must also be a right of appeal against the censor's decisions, which must in no case be absolute.

One of the censorship's particular tasks must be to ensure that information about varieties of crime does not turn into a cult that glamorizes crime, and that the public should not be artificially involved in other people's family scandals, and so on. Incidentally, this sort of information is strictly censored in the mass media of totalitarian countries, but there the restrictions are demagogic in nature and are intended to maintain illusions about the supposed perfection of totalitarianism.

But in order to avoid the restriction of intellectual freedom, everybody must be given the opportunity to express his opinions, even if only for limited circulation, so that, for instance, they could be available for consultation in libraries.

It would be presumptuous to try to fill in the contours of the future socioeconomic system in any more detail. Indeed, it would be difficult, though others could possibly discern, and may still do so, additional essential features overlooked here. The establishment of such a system will obviously take considerable time, and considerable difficulty will be experienced on the way. What seems obvious is that any future socioeconomic system must be built without violence and without the unconsidered imposition of stereotypes from above. It must be created organically out of existing systems.

But is this vision of the future only a figment of the imagination? Does the surrounding world not suggest the opposite, that the conflicts inherent in contemporary systems will only intensify in the future? And would it not be more honest to admit it? After all, pessimistic thoughts of this nature are entertained both by positivists and by religious people with their eschatological view of the world.

Perhaps it will be as the pessimists believe, but that will happen only if mankind completely loses that flame, or even that spark that has inspired its best achievements. Those who have survived so much and still preserve this spark tend to believe that it is inextinguishable. And that gives weighty reasons for historical optimism.

Separation or Reconciliation?
The Nationalities Question in the USSR

IGOR SHAFAREVICH

Of all the urgent problems that have accumulated in our life, the most painful seems to be that concerning relations between the various nationalities of the USSR.[1] No other question arouses such explosions of resentment, malice and pain — neither material inequality, nor lack of spiritual freedom, nor even the persecution of religion. Here are some examples.

In our Central Asian cities I and many others have often heard the cry: "Just wait till the Chinese come, they'll show you what's what!" This is said as a rule by moderately educated people, who cannot be unaware of what the arrival of the Chinese would entail for *them*, if only on the basis of what happened to the Kirghizians, who were lucky enough to get away after being deprived of all their possessions and driven out of China. (And the Tibetans, for example, according to the radio, were subjected to mass castrations.) They know all this, but they say it all the same. Evidently the pitch of emotion is more powerful even than the instinct of self-preservation, as in the western Ukraine in 1941, when detachments of the Ukrainian Nationalist Union harried the re-

1. There are fifteen union republics and over a hundred different nationalities in the USSR.— TRANS.

treating Soviet forces, and their officers made deals with the Germans, although they could not have failed to foresee, on the basis of the experience of the Poles, what in fact actually happened six weeks later — the arrest of the entire officer corps and the liquidation of most of the detachments.

One gets the same impression when one compares the treatment of the national question in *samizdat* with that of other seemingly no less burning problems — the fate of those imprisoned in the labor camps, for instance, or the incarceration of the sane in mental hospitals. It is noticeable that the authors of the vast majority of *samizdat* works voluntarily keep within certain limits, observe certain self-imposed restraints; they do not incite hatred or envy of the better off, or advocate violence. It seems that certain lessons of the past have been so thoroughly assimilated that they have set unshakable new standards of thought.

Yet when the nationalities question comes up these taboos evaporate. One finds indignant descriptions of one people living better than another, or, if they live worse, still receiving more than they have earned. *Samizdat*-published schemes for the resolution of the nationalities question usually include demands for the forcible resettlement of various populations and transparent hints that even harsher measures would be in order. One is left with the impression that, when writing about this area, the authors on the contrary tend to forget everything the past has taught us.

Suspicion and friction between nations is not an exclusively Soviet tendency — one sees it the world over. And we can try to understand our own problems only if we recognize them as local manifestations of natural laws common to all mankind.

The twentieth century was not expected to be the century of unprecedentedly extreme nationalism. In the last century it was generally agreed that the national problem was withering away, that the smaller nations would slowly merge into the larger, that the differences between the large nations would gradually diminish, and that in the not too distant future mankind would fuse in worldwide unity, perhaps even

89

all speaking one language. The exact opposite has turned out to be the case. Countries that have lived for centuries in national accord have been engulfed by national enmities. Unsuspected varieties of nationalism have appeared on the scene — Breton, Walloon and Welsh, for example. Enmity between peoples has reached an unprecedented peak of mutual hatred, leading to the extermination of whole peoples, as in the Nigerian civil war.

That was not the nineteenth century's only miscalculation, not the only case where the dominant ideology of the time was diametrically opposed to the future whose foundations it laid. At that time it seemed that man was faced with the clear prospect of constructing a life increasingly based on the principles of humanitarianism, respect for the rights of the individual, and democracy. Russia seemed to be blocking the road of progress precisely because she was insufficiently liberal and democratic internally. Dostoyevsky alone, apparently, felt in his bones that the world would suffer quite a different fate.

The actual historic role of the twentieth century, as it turned out, was to put large parts of mankind in thrall to an ideology that pursued the maximum suppression of the individual. Socialism, which had existed for centuries as a theory, started to materialize in the form of socialist states. This process has continued in fits and starts throughout the twentieth century, expanding with almost monotonous regularity, and there is no reason to suppose it has ended yet. We should bear this basic twentieth-century trend in mind when seeking to understand the national question, both in our own country and in the world as a whole.

At the beginning of the twentieth century the picture of the world was defined by the roles played in it by the "great powers" — the strongest states, led by peoples inspired by the belief that they were destined to play a special role in the world. In this situation socialist movements had the choice of two strategies: either to exploit these great nations' aspirations, their faith in their own mission, or else to suppress those aspirations. Both strategies were tried. Experience showed that although it could be useful to exploit national feelings to buttress the stability of an existing socialist state (especially in times of grave crisis and war), when it came to the seizure of power and drawing fresh nations into the socialist ideology, there was incomparably more to be gained from whipping up the ideology of antinationalism, especially when it was directed against the large nations and accompanied by a certain encouragement of patriotism among smaller peoples. This strategy, therefore, became the basic weapon of Marxist-oriented socialist movements, whose fundamental ideology was internationalism, the denial and destruction of patriotism, and the doctrine of the division of nations into two hostile cultures. This philosophy, so foreign to the spirit of states possessing a strong national and especially religious identity, helped to destroy them, and itself gathered strength as these states underwent periods of crisis. Whichever was cause and whichever effect, it is obvious that we have here two manifestations of a single process.

The Russian Empire, standing on a foundation of Orthodoxy, was the first to fall victim to this process; then Austria-Hungary, with its thousand-year-old roots in the Holy Roman Empire. A quarter of a century later came the end of Greater Germany as a single, united state. And even among the victors, the British Empire soon ceased to exist.

All these political catastrophes were accompanied by vicious ideological attacks on the leading peoples in those countries and on their claim to a special historic mission. For example, in postwar (that is, post–Second World War) Germany their whole literature set itself the aim of demonstrating to the German people its sinfulness and ineradicable guilt before all mankind. On both the individual and the national level, repentance is one of the most uplifting emotions of the spirit, and the Germans certainly had plenty to repent. But repentance loses its point when purification is carried out with no higher end in view: then it becomes an act of spiritual suicide. We Russians know only too well how this theme of an "accursed past" can deprive a nation of its history! And there would seem to be a certain symbolism in the

91

close personal ties that exist between the German writers of this penitent generation and the politicians who seek to persuade the Germans that the greatest service they can do the world is to reconcile themselves forever to the perpetual division of their country, in other words, accept the death of the German nation.

Finally, in the USA the savage anti–Vietnam War campaign was scarcely inspired by heightened moral sensitivity or a greater sense of responsibility. If it was, why did the genocide of the entire Ibo nation in Nigeria, which led to more deaths than the whole Vietnam War, pass almost unremarked? Even some leading antiwar figures openly admitted that the war was not the real issue. "End the Vietnam War, and we'll find something else to protest about," as one of them said. One gets the impression that what the protesters were really attacking was America's claim to a special world role, the sense of being a great nation, which has still not abandoned the Americans.

Whenever great empires have crumbled, national consciousness has always sharpened in the separate nations composing them and ethnic groups have separated out and aspired to recognition as independent states. Here again, cause and effect are inseparable. National separatism both acted as a force for the destruction of the old empire and simultaneously expanded to fill the vacuum created in people's hearts by the destruction of the sense of imperial unity and a unifying purpose. A similar dual trend is increasingly apparent in the twentieth century: both the destruction of great states ruled by a national idea, and the fission of mankind into ever smaller national units.

It seems to me that if we look at the situation in this light, we have some hope of understanding why the national question is particularly explosive in our country, for the present relationships between the nationalities are the consequence of *contradictory* historical processes. On the one hand, the separation out of the different nations and their drive for maximum possible independence have coincided with the subordination of all life to socialist ideology. These processes have been so inextricably intertwined that in many cases it has been impossible to distinguish between the manifestations of one and the manifestations of the other. For example, tendencies toward non-Russian separatism were first deliberately encouraged as a counterweight to Russian patriotism, but then were treated as the greatest menace. On the other hand, these nationalist aspirations soon came into conflict with socialist ideology's deepest-rooted tenets — hostility to the very idea of nationhood and the drive to suppress both the idea itself and the individual human personality.

In this way the national life of many peoples has fallen victim to that very force — socialist ideology — that not so long ago assisted and encouraged them to develop a system of views expressing an intolerant, radical nationalism. So deeply has this ideology penetrated the national outlook and so strong is its imprint that those who argue from national positions can hardly be persuaded that ideology, of all things, is the root cause of their misfortunes.

This has given rise to the concept — which I consider fundamentally erroneous — underlying practically every study of the national question in our country known to me (I refer, of course, only to uncensored literature). This concept is a very simple one: *All the problems of the non-Russian peoples are due in the long run to Russian oppression and the drive for Russification. The regions inhabited by these nations are Russian colonies. These peoples therefore have a clear task before them: to rid themselves of Russian colonial dominion.*

This theory has quite understandable attractions. It squeezes a complicated problem into the framework of a few simple and universally acceptable propositions. It is generally agreed that colonialism is the disgrace of the twentieth century and that colonies should become independent as soon as possible. Therefore all you need do is acquire "colonial" status in the eyes of the world and you are at once guaranteed the automatic support of colossal forces. And this means you can also offer your people an extremely clear and simple way forward. But primitively simple solutions to complex problems do not exist! We must be careful to verify the basic premise — that non-Russian peoples of the USSR are the colonial subjects of the Russian people — not only to discover the truth, but also because a conclusion based on a false premise cannot prove a reliable guide for the peoples who propose it.

The arguments generally used to demonstrate the non-Russian peoples' dependent and colonial status in the USSR do at first appear to carry conviction. The commonest are as follows:

(1) Great riches are extracted from the territory inhabited by non-Russians and go to enrich the Russian-inhabited part of the USSR.

(2) The density of the indigenous populations is declining; they are being diluted. Two reasons are given: the deportation of indigenous populations (in the past) and the immigration of large numbers of Russians (now). Russians come as workers in the new industrial enterprises, which are often created for no good economic reason and are irrelevant to the development of the particular region.

(3) National cultures are suppressed. Distinctive national tendencies in art are prohibited and their manifestations punished. History is compulsorily rewritten so as to belittle the people's national identity. Historical relics are destroyed instead of preserved, ancient cities and streets are given new names unrelated to the nation's past.

(4) National religions are suppressed.

(5) The national languages are increasingly superseded by Russian.

However, these arguments take on a different aspect if we ask: could they not be applied to the Russian people as well? Let us examine them in order.

(1) As some studies of the national question show, the Russian people enjoys a lower standard of living than many other peoples — the Georgians, Armenians, Ukrainians, Latvians or Estonians.

Sometimes this is explained away as characteristic of a peculiar kind of colonialism — Russian-type colonialism. Is this not an attempt to blind us to the basic contradiction with new terminology? It seems obvious to me that this is a general phenomenon: an enormous part of the wealth produced by *all* the nations is not returned to them. It is easy enough to guess where it goes: on the maintenance of a vast military machine and civil bureaucracy, on space exploration, on aid to revolutionary movements in Asia, Africa and Latin America, and most of all on making good the shortcomings of the economy.

(2) Few, if any, would maintain that in the past — during collectivization, for example — the Russians were less subject to deportation than other peoples. As for the present day, attention should be drawn to a universal cause — the disproportionate development of the economy based on no nation's interest. In this cause masses of Russians and non-Russians are uprooted and diverted from their national tasks. While documents written by Ukrainians complain of Russian migration into the Ukraine, Estonians and Latvians complain, not only of floods of Russians settling in their lands, but of floods of Ukrainians too.

(3) The suppression of Russian national culture began at a time when other nations were still being actively encouraged to assert their national identity. Many *samizdat* studies of the national question still accuse the Russians of "great power chauvinism." But when this term was invented, more than half a century ago, it amounted to nothing less than an invitation to stamp out any manifestation of Russian national consciousness.

In the last century, long before the state took a hand, all-powerful liberal public opinion declared Russian patriotism to be reactionary, a disgrace to Russians and a menace to everybody. And to this very day Russian national consciousness lives under unwinking, hostile surveillance, like a transported criminal under police supervision. Here is a recent dire warning. A group of anonymous authors published a sequence of interconnected articles, an anthology almost, in No. 97 of the *Vestnik Russkogo Khristianskogo Studenches-*

kogo Dvizhenia (Herald of the Russian Student Christian Movement).[2] The Latin word forming the first article's title, and that which was meant to attract the reader at first glance in all the articles, was a call to Russia to repent. And which, of all Russia's transgressions, did the authors consider the most heinous? The belief, it turns out, that Russia has a historic mission, that she too has something of her own, a new word, to offer the world; or, as the authors put it, "Russian messianism." This is the sin they call on Russians to repent; this, they say, should be Russia's main aim in the future. Their own stated aim is so to change the nation's consciousness that it dare not imagine its life *has* some aim! What other nation has ever been subjected to such sermons?

Several generations of Russians have been brought up on such a horrendous version of Russian history that all they want to do is to try and forget we ever had a past at all. Russia was the "gendarme of Europe" and the "prison of the peoples," its history consisted of "one defeat after another" and was always characterized by one and the same phrase: "the accursed past."

Even the broom of new names that has swept away everything linking us with our past has scarcely affected another people more cruelly than the Russian. Let me suggest a simple experiment for those who wish to try it: get on a bus passing through the center of Moscow and listen to the names of the stops as the driver calls them out. It will immediately strike you that streets retaining their old, original names are rare exceptions — it is as if some brush had painted out all reminders of the fact that the Russian people once had a history.

(4) Similarly with the suppression of religion. The Russian Orthodox Church was suffering its first blows while Islam, for example, was still being handled with kid gloves. In this first push, indeed, an important role was assigned to the exploitation of the religious politics of other nations: for example, an independent, autocephalous Georgian church was

2. Published in Russian by the Y.M.C.A. Press in Paris.— TRANS.

SEPARATION OR RECONCILIATION?

set up, and attempts were made to create a similar church in the Ukraine.

(5) It is only with the fifth and last of the above arguments that one cannot disagree: all this activity is indeed taking place mainly in the Russian language, as the state language of the USSR. But what do the Russians gain from that?

Other painful features of national life are also worth mentioning — above all, the catastrophic decline of the village, which has always been the mainstay of national identity. But in this respect too the Russians have suffered no less than other peoples.

I think the theory of "Russian colonialism" is not only unfair to the Russians but also erroneous in fact, and therefore damaging to the other peoples by impeding a proper understanding of their own national life. In fact, *the basic features of national life in the USSR are a direct result of the hegemony in our country of socialist ideology. This ideology is the enemy of every nation, just as it is hostile to individual human personality. It is able to exploit the aspirations of this or that people temporarily, for its own purposes, but its fundamental trend is toward the maximum destruction of all nations. The Russians no less than others are its victims; indeed, they were the first to come under fire.*

If we accept this view of how the nations came to their present pass, we must correspondingly adjust our practical attitude to present problems. Since the blame for the present situation cannot be laid at one people's door, it follows that to a certain extent *all the peoples are to blame.* This seems a more constructive view to me, since it frees our minds from bondage to external causes, over which we generally have no control, and instead concentrates them on causes hidden within ourselves, over which by definition we have much more control. A similar dilemma confronts the individual: is the fundamental course of his life determined by external factors (material circumstances, social environment, and so on), or is it inherent in himself? In the final analysis the

97

question is one of free will. The same question confronts the nation. But if one acknowledges the preeminence of inner causes, if one acknowledges that a nation's fate is determined more by its own actions and outlook on life than by external factors, then it follows that the inner causes will not be changed by simply breaking with the Russians. In other words, once the concept of "colonization" has been exploded, the concept of "decolonization" also needs rethinking. All I mean by this is that we must rid ourselves of certain habits of thought, of the unverifiable and undebatable conviction that breaking away from the Russians and creating one's own state is the automatic solution to all the problems of every nation. I think I see here a profound analogy with the position of those Russian intellectuals who gave in to the temptation to take a novel — and for us quite new and unusual — way out of their situation by emigrating. In both cases there is an underlying wish to "escape from your own shadow" — to solve by external means problems that are essentially within.

We have all had a hand in creating the problems that now confront us: the Russian Nihilists, the Ukrainian "Borotbists," [3] the Latvian riflemen [4] and many others have each done their bit. How can we hope, separately, to disentangle the knot that we all helped to tighten?

Our forefathers unanimously declared Russia to be the "prison of the peoples," adding the words of their favorite battle cry: ". . . we'll raze it to the ground, and after that . . ." The razing of the "prison of peoples" was a phenomenal success, but after that . . . After that, for example, a group of Estonian nationalists has written to the United Nations, claiming that the very existence of the Estonian nation is threatened. And they called for the final rupture of all relations with the peoples of the USSR, the expulsion of Rus-

3. "Borotbists" was the name of a Ukrainian Communist party at the time of the October revolution which was allied with the Bolsheviks. In later years it was disbanded and most of its surviving leaders executed.— TRANS.
4. A reference to the Latvian rifle regiments of the tsarist army which went over to Lenin during the October revolution and actively supported the Bolsheviks against rival factions and later the Whites.— TRANS.

sians and Ukrainians from Estonia and the stationing of UN troops there. Has history not taught us at least this, that it is hardly the height of political wisdom to throw away centuries-old alliances like useless trash, and that it is necessary to begin, not by razing to the ground, but rather by *changing* and *improving?*

A common history has welded the nations of our land together. The experience it has endowed us with is unique in the world, no other peoples possess it. Strange as it may sound, in many respects we are now immeasurably further along the historical road than many peoples we are in the habit of only "catching up with." The phase in which Western Europe and the USA now find themselves is remarkably reminiscent of the "Nihilist" era in Russia, that is, the period of a hundred years ago. Our experiences and suffering lay a moral obligation on us. We are now able to perceive and tell the world things that nobody else can tell: this is where I see the historic mission of the peoples that inhabit what was once Russia and is now the Soviet Union. They can point the way out of the labyrinth in which mankind is now lost. And this is the only way in which any of our peoples can influence the fate of mankind and hence their own fate. Each people must of course consult its own conscience and decide whether to take this mission upon itself. No nation must be judged or condemned for deciding one way or the other. But I trust it would not be regarded as tactless interference if I express my own opinion on this question, which is one that vitally affects us all.

Why is it thought that different peoples cannot live within the bounds of a single state of their own free will and to the benefit of all? If they cannot, surely one is entitled to doubt that different individuals can do so. Recent decades, it is true, have shown a tendency toward the formation of ever smaller states, but this by no means proves that this trend is correct. The small and minuscule states that have appeared in recent times are too weak: they are doomed in all possible respects to become dependents and hangers-on of larger states. They can acquire power only by acting together, sub-

99

ordinating their individuality to a common purpose, and always choosing the course of action that will offend nobody — in other words, the most trivial. That is the origin of mob rule by nations, a spectacle we are witnessing in the United Nations at the moment. But the process is still only in its infancy. At present there are about two thousand nations in the world, but only some one hundred and fifty states. If the trend toward nation-states continues, the existing states will have to be broken down by a factor of ten or more. But even the formation of pocket-handkerchief states brings no relief from familiar troubles: we see that they are plagued by the same sores of international and intertribal strife. Yet this is the ideal solution propounded in many a *samizdat* study of the national question. One of them even suggested the interesting idea that there is nothing to prevent any village declaring itself a state. It is worth thinking this idea through in earnest and trying to picture such a "state." Who will supply it with the simplest agricultural machinery and electric light, where will it find its teachers and doctors? And what if all mankind follows this happy example and splits itself up into villages? One has only to imagine it and it becomes clear how much the author of this theory is prepared to sacrifice for the sake of universal separatism.

There is nothing to indicate the necessity of dismembering states into national atoms. On the contrary, different peoples in cooperation can give birth to a culture of a higher quality than any of them in isolation. However large the nation, its culture acquires a new dimension it would not otherwise have. And the geniuses of small nations achieve worldwide significance, something that would be impossible unless they were part of a more powerful kindred culture, as the Scotsman Walter Scott was of the greater English culture. But the most vivid illustration comes from our own culture — I refer, of course, to Gogol. Great as his genius was, I do not think he could have blossomed so profoundly or attained such a pinnacle of human achievement had he not been enriched by Russian culture. And his influence on mankind would have been negligible if all Russian culture had not been illuminated with his light. Similarly with Shevchenko: [5] his prose in Russian demonstrates his desire to be a Russian as well as a Ukrainian writer.

I believe this path is not closed to the peoples of our country, but finding it will not be at all easy. It will require much effort and goodwill, and changes in our usual attitudes. It would be a great pity if readers were to think that I am advocating this effort for the non-Russian peoples only; in many respects it is precisely the Russians who ought to be breaking their old habits.

I do not think Russians suffer from the national arrogance that Western Europeans display in their relations with their Eastern neighbors and even more toward non-Europeans. Russians mix easily with other peoples and often place too low a value on their own culture.

But power-mania is the vice of every great nation and is not at all foreign to the Russians. If a large country's armies are unloosed against a small neighbor, and if they successfully carry it off, then the overwhelming majority of the populace feels pride and satisfaction — this has unfortunately been the psychology of many nations for centuries past, and the Russians are no exception. But if we want to preserve even the shadow of a hope of living side by side in one state with our present neighbors, we cannot permit ourselves this any more. And therefore when the journal *Veche* (Assembly) [6] begins its existence by describing Skobelev's [7] conquests in Central Asia, as if the most important wars in our history were those that subjugated other peoples, it looks like some sort of deliberate provocation.

But in our attitude to other nations there is another vice

5. Taras Shevchenko (1814–1861), the most famous Ukrainian poet and writer, who was exiled for his criticisms of the tsarist government's social and national policies.— TRANS.

6. A *samizdat*, or clandestine journal, that appeared in the Soviet Union from January 1971 until early 1974 and took a strongly Russian nationalist line.— TRANS.

7. Mikhail Skobelev (1843–1882), a Russian army officer, one of the conquerors of Turkistan and a prominent commander in the Russo-Turkish war.— TRANS.

that is typically Russian: the inability to see the line that divides us from other nations, the lack of inner conviction in their right to exist within their own national identity. How often have I heard Russians wondering naïvely why the Ukrainians, Byelorussians or Lithuanians won't learn proper Russian and turn into proper Russians. All the jokes, mockery and tactless puns on the Ukrainian language have their root in an unwillingness to recognize the Ukrainians as a separate nation and in a failure to understand why these "Russians" so strangely distort our language.

This may be due to a perversion or misunderstanding of our natural sense of equality, for we tend to think of all these people as our equals and immediately (without consulting them) class them as Russians. But it is easy to understand how other peoples, especially small ones, are horrified and infuriated by the sight of the immense Russian tide advancing on them, ready to swallow them up without a trace.

Most animals capable of killing their own kind are endowed by nature with inhibitions which make such killings impossible: no wolf can tear open the throat of another wolf vanquished in battle, no raven can peck out the eye of another raven. Neither men nor nations are equipped with the same inhibitions; they can instill them only by a process of *spiritual development*. This is the task facing the Russian people. We cannot count on our neighbors for sympathy, or even absence of hostility, unless we can not only see the Estonians, for example, as people equal to ourselves in every respect, but also realize how much our life has been enriched by the proximity of this small, courageous people, who are prepared to make any sacrifice other than renounce their national individuality.

Is the picture I have endeavored to paint here a feasible one? I very much want to hope it is, but to be honest I am not sure it will work out. There is too much deep-seated resentment and perhaps too little time left to neutralize it. And perhaps the national question is the most distressing one simply because it is the most difficult — it demands that such complexly organized and individual entities as nations should learn to live together without losing their individuality. And perhaps we should be looking for other, less obvious ways of solving it.

But of one thing I am convinced: this question is insoluble unless we renounce our ingrained prejudices and what Dostoyevsky called "shortcuts to thought." It is insoluble on a basis of hatred and mutual recrimination and these must be abandoned. To this end we must endeavor to change habits that have been built up over decades and centuries, transforming the forces of repulsion into forces of attraction. This is essential not at all simply in order to try to preserve the links that exist between our country's peoples; everyone with a responsible attitude toward the destiny of his own people, however he regards its future, should feel bound to exert every effort in the same direction.

Some affinity of outlook and a certain ability to understand one another are essential, not only in order to be able to live together, but also in order to be able to part company.

As V. Maklakov [8] once intriguingly put it: nationalists generally demand plebiscites, believing that so long as the majority in their region plump for secession, they should be granted independence. In other words, they believe the question can be settled by a majority vote in their region, although they are, of course, a minority in the state as a whole. Conversely, their will, which is a minority one in the state as a whole, is supposed to prevail, while the minority in their own region, who oppose secession, must bow to the majority.

Of course there can come a moment in the history of nations when all spiritual links are broken and living together in one state only exacerbates mutual animosity. But Maklakov's idea strikes me as an interesting paradox, which demonstrates, by taking a logical conclusion to absurdity, that neither plebiscites nor the introduction of United Nations forces can solve the delicate and organic problems facing the

8. V. A. Maklakov (1870–1957) was a leading member of the Constitutional Democratic party ("Cadets") before the October revolution. In 1938 he published his memoirs, *The First State Duma*.— TRANS.

nations of today. Whatever the ultimate solution may be, the only healthy path to it is through the rapprochement of peoples. The only alternative that remains is the path of force, along which each solution is doomed to be only temporary and to lead inexorably to the next, even graver crisis.

There are, at least, real grounds for hope that in many respects the lessons of the past have not been totally wasted on our peoples. Our experience has inoculated us against many temptations — but not all. *Class* hatred can probably never again light the flame that engulfs our house in time of trouble — but national hatred easily could. We can feel its warning tremors already, and they enable us to judge how destructive it could be once it erupted onto the surface. We must not be so naïve as to suppose that any man could direct this elemental force into acceptable channels — the forces of hatred and violence are subject to their own laws and always consume those who unleash them.

And who can say which nations will survive yet another cataclysm, perhaps more terrible than any they have been obliged to endure so far?

Herein lies the last reason for the extreme acuteness of the national question — it may well become a question of the continued existence of our peoples.

Repentance and Self-Limitation
in the Life of Nations

ALEXANDER SOLZHENITSYN

ONE

The Blessed Augustine once wrote: "What is the state without justice? A band of robbers." Even now, fifteen centuries later, many people will, I think, readily recognize the force and accuracy of this judgment. But let us note what he is about: an ethical judgment about a small group of people is applied by extension to the state.

It is in our human nature to make such judgments: to apply ordinary, individual, human values and standards to larger social phenomena and associations of people, up to and including the nation and the state as a whole. And many instances of this transference can be found in writers through the ages.

The social *sciences*, however, and particularly the more modern of them, strictly forbid such extensions of meaning. Only economic, statistical, demographic, ideological, to a lesser extent geographical, and — very dubiously — psychological procedures are held to guarantee the serious scientific character of research into society and the state, while the evaluation of political life by ethical yardsticks is considered totally provincial.

Yet people do not cease to be people just because they live in social agglomerations, nor do they lose the age-old human impulses and feelings — we all know the spectrum; all they do is express them more crudely, sometimes keeping them in check, sometimes giving them free rein. It is hard to understand the arrogant insensitivity of the modern trend in the social sciences: why are the standards and demands so necessarily and readily applied to individuals, families, small groups and personal relations, rejected out of hand and utterly prohibited when we go on to deal with thousands and millions of people in association? The arguments in favor of such an extension are certainly no weaker than those for deducing the complex psychological delusions of societies from crude economic processes. The barrier against transference of values is in any case lower where the principle itself undergoes no transformation, where we are not being asked to beget the living upon the dead, but only to project the self onto larger quantities of human beings.

The transference of values is entirely natural to the religious cast of mind: human society cannot be exempted from the laws and demands which constitute the aim and meaning of individual human lives. But even without a religious foundation, this sort of transference is readily and naturally made. It is very human to apply even to the biggest social events or human organizations, including whole states and the United Nations, our spiritual values: noble, base, courageous, cowardly, hypocritical, false, cruel, magnanimous, just, unjust, and so on. Indeed, everybody writes this way, even the most extreme economic materialists, since they remain after all human beings. And clearly, whatever feelings predominate in the members of a given society at a given moment in time, they will serve to color the whole of that society and determine its moral character. And if there is nothing good there to pervade that society, it will destroy itself, or be brutalized by the triumph of evil instincts, no matter where the pointer of the great economic laws may turn.

And it is open to every one of us, whether learned or not, to choose — and profitably choose — not to evade the exami-

REPENTANCE AND SELF-LIMITATION

nation of social phenomena with reference to the categories of individual spiritual life and individual ethics.

We shall try to do this here with reference to only two such categories: repentance and self-limitation.

TWO

Whether the transference of individual human qualities to society is easy or difficult in a general way, it is immensely difficult when the desired moral quality has been almost completely rejected by individual human beings themselves. This is the case with repentance. The gift of repentance, which perhaps more than anything else distinguishes man from the animal world, is particularly difficult for modern man to recover. We have, every last one of us, grown ashamed of this feeling; and its effect on *social* life anywhere on earth is less and less easy to discern. The habit of repentance is lost to our whole callous and chaotic age.

How then can we transfer to society and the nation that which does not exist on the individual level? Perhaps this article is premature or altogether pointless? We start, however, from what seems to us beyond doubt: that true repentance and self-limitation will shortly reappear in the personal and the social sphere, that a hollow place in modern man is ready to receive them. Obviously then the time has come to consider this as a path for whole nations to follow. Our understanding of it must not lag behind the inevitable development of self-generating governmental policies.

We have so bedeviled the world, brought it so close to self-destruction, that repentance is now a matter of life and death — not for the sake of a life beyond the grave (which is thought merely comic nowadays), but for the sake of our life here and now and our very survival on this earth. The *end of the world*, so often foretold by the prophets only to be postponed, has ceased to be the particular property of mystics and confronts us as sober reality, scientifically, technically and psychologically warranted. It is no longer just the danger of a nuclear world war — we have grown used to that and can take it in our stride. But the calculations of the ecologists show us that we are caught in a trap: either we change our ways and abandon our destructively greedy pursuit of progress, or else in the twenty-first century, whatever the pace of man's development, we will perish as a result of the total exhaustion, barrenness and pollution of the planet.

Add to this the white-hot tension between nations and races and we can say without suspicion of overstatement that without *repentance* it is in any case doubtful if we can survive.

It is by now only too obvious how dearly mankind has paid for the fact that we have all throughout the ages preferred to censure, denounce and hate *others,* instead of censuring, denouncing and hating ourselves. But obvious though it may be, we are even now, with the twentieth century on its way out, reluctant to recognize that the universal dividing line between good and evil runs not between countries, not between nations, not between parties, not between classes, not even between good and bad men: the dividing line cuts across nations and parties, shifting constantly, yielding now to the pressure of light, now to the pressure of darkness. It divides the heart of every man, and there too it is not a ditch dug once and for all, but fluctuates with the passage of time and according to a man's behavior.

If we accept just this one fact, which has been made plain, especially by art, a thousand times before, what way out remains to us? Not the embittered strife of parties or nations, not the struggle to win some delusive *victory* — for all the ferocious causes already in being — but simply *repentance* and the search for *our own* errors and sins. We must stop blaming everyone else — our neighbors and more distant peoples, our geographical, economic or ideological rivals, always claiming that we alone are in the right.

Repentance is the first bit of firm ground underfoot, the only one from which we can go forward not to fresh hatreds but to concord. Repentance is the only starting point for spiritual growth.

For each and every individual.

And every trend of social thought.

True, repentant political parties are about as frequently encountered in history as tiger-doves. (Politicians of course can still repent — many of them do not lose their human qualities. But *parties* are obviously utterly inhuman formations, and the very object of their existence precludes repentance.)

Nations, on the other hand, are very vital formations, susceptible to all moral feelings, including — however painful a step it may be — repentance. "An ethical idea has always preceded the birth of a nation," says Dostoyevsky (in his *Diary of a Writer*). The examples he gives are those of the Hebrew nation, founded only after Moses; and the several Moslem nations founded after the appearance of the Koran. "And when with the passage of time a nation's spiritual ideal is sapped, that nation falls, together with all its civil statutes and ideals." How then can a nation be defrauded of its right to repent?

But here certain doubts at once arise, if only the following:

(1) Is it not senseless to expect repentance from a whole nation — does this not assume that the sin, the vice, the defect is that of the whole nation? But this way of thinking — judging nations as a whole, talking about the qualities or traits of a whole nation — has been strictly forbidden to us for at least a hundred years.

(2) The mass of the nation as a whole does not perform united actions. Indeed, under many systems of government, the mass can neither obstruct nor contribute to the decisions of its leaders. *What* should it repent of?

And finally, even if we dismiss the first two points:

(3) How can the nation as a whole express its repentance? Surely only through the mouths and by the pens of individuals?

Let us try to answer these questions.

REPENTANCE AND SELF-LIMITATION

THREE

(1) Those who set the highest value on the existence of the nation, who see in it not the ephemeral fruit of social formations but a complex, vivid, unrepeatable organism not invented by man, recognize that nations have a full spiritual life, that they can soar to the heights and plunge to the depths, run the whole gamut from saintliness to utter wickedness (although only individuals ever reach the extremes). Of course, great changes occur with the passage of time and the movement of history. That shifting boundary between good and evil, of which we spoke, oscillates continuously in the consciousness of a nation, sometimes very violently, so that judgments, reproaches, self-reproaches and even repentance itself are bound up with a specific time and pass away with it, leaving only vestigial contours behind to remind history of their existence.

But then, individuals too change beyond recognition in the course of their lives, under the influence of events and of their own spiritual endeavors (and man's hope, salvation and punishment lie in this, that we are capable of change, and that we ourselves, not our birth or our environment, are responsible for our souls!). Yet we venture to label people "good" or "bad," and our right to do so is not usually questioned.

The profoundest similarity between the individual and the nation lies in the mystical nature of their "givenness." And human logic can show no cause why, if we permit value judgments on the one mutable entity, we should forbid them in the case of the other. To do so is a mere face-saving convention, or perhaps a precaution against their careless misapplication.

If we continue to base ourselves on intuitive perceptions, to consult our feelings and not the dictates of positivist knowledge, we shall find that national sympathies and antipathies *do exist* in the vast majority of people. Sometimes they are shared only by a particular circle, large or small, and can only be uttered there (not too loudly for fear of offending against the spirit of the times), but sometimes these feelings (of love, or alas more often than not of hate) are so strong that they overwhelm whole nations and are boldly, even aggressively, trumpeted abroad. Often such feelings arise from fallacious or superficial experience. They are always relatively short-lived, flaring up and dying down again from time to time, but they *do exist*, and very emphatically. Everyone knows it is so, and only hypocrisy forbids us to talk about it.

The changing conditions of its life, and changing external circumstances, determine whether a nation has anything to repent of *today*. Perhaps it has not. But because of the mutability of all existence, a nation can no more live without sin than can an individual. It is impossible to imagine a nation which throughout the course of its whole existence has no cause for repentance. *Every* nation without exception, however persecuted, however cheated, however flawlessly righteous it feels itself to be today, has certainly at one time or another contributed its share of inhumanity, injustice and arrogance.

There are only too many examples, hosts of them, and this article is not a historical inquiry. It is a matter for special consideration in each particular case how much time must elapse before a sin ceases to weigh on the national conscience. Turkey bears the still-fresh guilt of the Armenian massacres, yet for centuries before that she persecuted the Balkan Slavs — is the guilt for the latter still a living thing, or a thing of the past? (Let the impatient reader not rebuke me for not beginning immediately with Russia. Russia's turn of course will come soon enough — what else would you expect from a Russian?)

(2) No one would now dispute that the British, French and Dutch peoples as a whole bear the guilt (and marks on their souls) for the colonial policies of their governments. *Their* system of government allowed for considerable obstruction to be placed in the way of colonialism by society. But there was little obstruction of this sort, and the nation was drawn

into this seductive enterprise, with some individuals participating, others supporting and others merely accepting it.

Here is a case much nearer to hand, from the middle of the
twentieth century, when public opinion in Western countries
practically determines government behavior. After the Second World War the British and American authorities made a
deal with their Soviet counterparts and systematically
handed over in southern Europe (Austria and Italy) *hundreds
of thousands* of civilian refugees from the USSR (over and
above repatriated troops) who had no desire to return to their
native land, handed them over deceitfully, without warning,
contrary to their expectations and wishes, and in effect sent
them to their death — probably half of them were destroyed
by the camps. The relevant documents have been carefully
concealed up to now. But there were living witnesses,
knowledge of these events filtered out to the British and
Americans, and during the past quarter of a century there
have been plenty of opportunities in those countries to make
inquiries, raise an outcry, bring the guilty to judgment. But
no one has raised a finger. The reason is that the West today
sees the sufferings of Eastern Europe in a distant haze. Complacency, however, has never purged anyone of guilt. It is
just because of this complacent silence that the vile treachery
of the military authorities has seeped into and stained the national conscience of those countries. Yet the voice of repentance has still not been heard.

In Uganda today the mettlesome General Amin expels
Asians supposedly on his own personal responsibility, but
there is no doubt that he has the self-interested approval of a
population which battens on the spoils of the deported. This
is how the Ugandans have set out on the path of nationhood,
and, as in all countries which previously suffered oppression
and now frantically aspire to physical might, repentance is
the very last feeling they are about to experience.

It would be much less simple to demonstrate the responsibility of the Albanians for the behavior of their fanatical
ruler, whose own country bears the full brunt of his tyranny
only because he lacks the strength to turn upon others. But

the enthusiastic layer of the population which keeps him in orbit must surely have been recruited from ordinary Albanian families?

This is the peculiar feature of integrated organisms — that all their parts benefit and suffer alike from the activity of each organ. Even when the majority of the population is quite powerless to obstruct its political leaders, it is fated to answer for their sins and their mistakes. Even in the most totalitarian states, whose subjects have no rights at all, we all bear responsibility — not only for the quality of our government, but also for the campaigns of our military leaders, for the deeds of our soldiers in the line of duty, for the shots fired by our frontier guards, for the songs of our young people.

"For the sins of the fathers" — the saying is thousands of years old. How, you may ask, can we repent on their behalf — we weren't even alive at the time! We are even less responsible than the subjects of a totalitarian regime! But the saying is not an idle one, and we have only too often seen and still see children *paying* for the fathers.

The nation is mystically welded together in a community of guilt, and its inescapable destiny is common repentance.

(3) Individual expressions of this common repentance are dubiously representative, for we cannot know whether those who make them speak with authority. And they are extremely difficult for the people who make them. Individual repentance is one thing: the counsels of outsiders, or even of those close to you, carry no weight once you have wholeheartedly committed yourself. But the man who takes it upon himself to express the repentance of a nation, on the other hand, will always be exposed to weighty dissuasions, reproaches, and warnings not to bring shame upon his country or give comfort to its enemies. Moreover, if in your own person you pronounce words of repentance on behalf of society as a whole, you must inevitably *distribute* the blame, indicating the various degrees of culpability of various groups — and that necessarily changes the spirit and tone of repentance and casts a shadow on it. It is only at a historical distance that we can

unerringly judge to what degree one man has expressed a genuine change of heart in his nation.

But it can happen — and Russia is a striking example of this — that repentance is expressed not just once and momentarily by a single writer or orator, but becomes the normal mood of all thinking society. Thus in the nineteenth century a repentant mood spread among the Russian upper-class intelligentsia (and so overwhelmed them that the penitents ceased to acknowledge any good in themselves or any sin in the common people), then gathered force, took in the middle-class intelligentsia as well, and, translating itself into action, became a historical movement with incalculable — and even counterproductive — consequences.

The repentance of a nation expresses itself most surely and palpably in its *actions*. In its finite actions.

Even in our own calculating and impenitent age we see a powerful movement of repentance in the country which bears the guilt for two world wars. Not, alas, in the whole nation. Only in that half (or three-quarters) where the ideology of hate does not stand like an impregnable concrete wall in the way of repentance.

This repentance, not just in words, in protestations, but in real actions, in large *concessions*, was dramatically manifested to us in Chancellor Brandt's *"Canossa-Reise"* to Warsaw, to Auschwitz, and then to Israel, and found further expression in his whole *Ost-Politik*. From a practical point of view, this policy seems less carefully weighed and balanced than "policies" generally are. It was born, perhaps, of moral imperatives, in the cloudy atmosphere of penitence which hung over Germany after the Second World War. This is what makes it remarkable — that an ethical impulse, rather than political calculation, lies behind it — and it is just the sort of noble and generous impulse which one longs to see today in other nations and countries (and above all in our own!). It would have vindicated itself in practical terms too if it had met with a similar spiritual response from the East European partners, instead of grasping political greed.

It is, however, only fitting that a Russian author, writing for

Russia, should turn to the question of Russia's need to repent. This article is written with faith in the natural proclivity of Russians to repent, in our ability even as things are now to find the penitential impulse in ourselves and set the whole world an example.

Significantly, one of the fundamental proverbs expressing the Russian view of the world was (at any rate before the revolution) *"God is not in might but in right."* This belief may be partly natural to us, but was powerfully reinforced by the Orthodox faith, which was once sincerely embraced by the whole mass of the people. (It is only nowadays that we are persuaded, almost to a man, that "might is right," and act accordingly.)

We were generously endowed with the gift of repentance: at one time it irrigated a broad tract of the Russian character. Not for nothing was the "day of forgiveness" such a high point in our calendar. In the distant past (until the seventeenth century) Russia was so rich in penitential movements that repentance was among the most prominent Russian national characteristics. Upsurges of repentance, or rather of religious penitence on a mass scale, were in the spirit of pre-Petrine Russia: it would begin separately, in many hearts, and merge into a powerful current. This is probably the noblest and only true way of broad, popular repentance. Klyuchevsky,[1] studying the economic documents on ancient Russia, found many cases of Russians moved by repentance to forgive debts, to cancel debt-slavery or set their bondsmen free, and this did much to soften the force of cruel laws. Inordinate accumulations of wealth were mitigated by lavish bequests to charity. We know how very many penitents retired to religious settlements, hermits' cells and monasteries. The chronicles and ancient Russian literature alike abound in examples of repentance. And Ivan the Terrible's terror never became so all-embracing or systematic as Stalin's, largely because the tsar repented and came to his senses.

1. Vasily Klyuchevsky (1841–1911), most distinguished Russian national historian of the nineteenth century, author of *A Course of Russian History.* — TRANS.

But with the soulless reforms of Nikon [2] and Peter the Great began the extirpation and suppression of the Russian national spirit, and our capacity for repentance also began to wither and dry up. The monstrous punishment of the Old Believers — the burnings at the stake, the red-hot pincers, the impalements on meat hooks, the dungeons — followed for two and a half centuries by the senseless repression of twelve million meek and defenseless fellow-countrymen, and their dispersal to the most uninhabitable regions of the country or even expulsion from the country — all this is a sin for which the established Church has never proclaimed its repentance. This was bound to weigh heavily on the whole future of Russia. Yet all that happened was that in 1905 the persecuted were forgiven (too late, far too late, to save the persecutors).

The whole Petersburg period of our history — a period of external greatness, of imperial conceit — drew the Russian spirit even farther from repentance. So far that we managed to preserve serfdom for a century or more after it had become unthinkable, keeping the greater part of our own people in a slavery which robbed them of all human dignity. So far that even the upsurge of repentance on the part of thinking society came too late to appease angry minds, but engulfed us in the clouds of a new savagery, brought a pitiless rain of vengeful blows on our heads, an unprecedented terror, and the return, after seventy years, of serfdom in a still worse form.

In the twentieth century the blessed dews of repentance could no longer soften the parched Russian soil, baked hard by doctrines of hate. In the past sixty years we have not merely lost the gift of repentance in our public life but have ridiculed it. This feeling was precipitately abandoned and made an object of contempt, the place in the soul where

2. Patriarch Nikon was patriarch of the Russian Orthodox Church under Tsar Aleksei Mikhailovich from 1652 to 1667 (although the latter half of this period was spent in retirement). He initiated a series of sweeping reforms in ecclesiastical and secular custom designed to modernize and strengthen the Church, but resulting in serious schism. His reforms were accepted, but simultaneously led to his own downfall as patriarch. Meanwhile the schismatics, who clung to the old customs and rites, became known as the "Old Believers."— TRANS.

116

repentance once dwelt was laid waste. For half a century now we have acted on the conviction that the *guilty* ones were the tsarist establishment, the bourgeois patriots, social democrats, White Guards, priests, émigrés, subversives, kulaks, henchmen of kulaks, engineers, "wreckers," [3] oppositionists, enemies of the people, nationalists, Zionists, imperialists, militarists, even modernists — anyone and everyone except you and me! Obviously it was *they*, not we, who had to reform. But they dug their heels in and refused to. So how could they be made to reform, except by bayonets (revolvers, barbed wire, starvation)?

One of the peculiarities of Russian history is that our evil doing has always, even up to the present day, taken the same direction: we have done evil on a massive scale and mainly in our own country, not abroad, not to *others*, but at home to our own people, to ourselves. No one has borne so much of the suffering as the Russians, Ukrainians and Byelorussians. So that as we awaken to repentance we shall have to remember much that concerns only us, and for which outsiders will not reproach us.

Will it be easy for us honestly to remember it all, when we have lost all feeling for truth? We, the present older and middle generations, have spent our whole lives floundering and wallowing in the stinking swamp of a society based on force and fraud — how could we escape defilement? Are there naturally angelic characters — gliding as it were weightlessly above the slime without ever sinking into it, even when their feet touch its surface? We have all met such people — Russia is not so short of them as all that. They are the "just," we have all seen them and marveled ("such funny people"), profited from their goodness, repaid them in kind in our better moments, for we can't help liking them, and then plunged back into the depths to which we are doomed. We have floundered, some (the lucky ones) ankle-deep, some knee-deep, some waist-deep, some up to our necks, according to the changing circumstances and our peculiarities of

3. The name applied to alleged industrial saboteurs in the twenties. — TRANS.

117

character, while some were totally immersed and only occasional bubbles from a not quite dead soul reached the surface to remind us of their existence.

But who, if not we ourselves, constitutes *society?* This realm of darkness, of falsehood, of brute force, of justice denied and distrust of the good, this slimy swamp was formed by *us,* and no one else. We grew used to the idea that we must submit and lie in order to survive — and we brought up our children to do so. Each of us, if he honestly reviews the life he has led, without special pleading or concealment, will recall more than one occasion on which he pretended not to hear a cry for help, averted his indifferent eyes from an imploring gaze, burned letters and photographs which it was his duty to keep, forgot someone's name or dropped certain widows, turned his back on prisoners under escort, and — but of course — always voted, rose to his feet and applauded obscenities (even though he felt obscene while he was doing it) — how, otherwise, could we survive? How, moreover, could the great Archipelago have endured in our midst for fifty years unnoticed?

Need I mention the common or garden informers, traitors and sadists of whom there must surely have been more than one million, or how could such an Archipelago have been managed?

And if we now long — and there is a glimmer of hope that we do — to go forward at last into a just, clean, honest society — how else can we do so except by shedding the burden of our past, except by repentance, for we are all guilty, all besmirched? We cannot convert the kingdom of universal falsehood into a kingdom of universal truth by even the cleverest and most skillfully contrived economic and social reforms: these are the wrong building bricks.[4]

4. The line of repentance becomes easier and clearer to follow if it is compared with the line traced by the defense of civil rights. Here is a fresh recent example that puts the whole thing in a nutshell. Some years ago a now well-known dissident wrote a film script in the course of his normal, officially approved artistic career which was highly thought of and allowed onto the country's cinema screens — which means it is not difficult to guess at its spiritual value. On the occasion of some recent diplomatic triumph it

But if millions pour out their repentance, their confessions, their contrite sorrow — not all of them perhaps publicly, but among friends and people who know them — what could all this together be called except "the repentance of the nation"?

But here our endeavor, like any attempt to summon a nation to repentance, runs into objections from within: Russia has suffered so much that she cannot be asked to repent as well, she must be pitied, not tormented with reminders of her sins.

And it is true. No country in the twentieth century has suffered like ours, which within its own borders has destroyed as many as seventy million people over and above those lost in the world wars — no one in modern history has experienced such destruction. And it is true: it is painful to chide where one must pity. But repentance is always painful, otherwise it would have no moral value. Those people were not the victims of flood or earthquake. There were innocent victims and guilty victims, but they would never have reached such a terrifying total if they had suffered only at the hands of others: *we, all of us,* Russia herself, were the necessary accomplices.

An even harsher, colder point of view, or rather current of opinion, has become discernible of late. Stripped to essentials, but not distorted, it goes like this: the Russian people is the noblest in the world; its ancient and its modern history are alike unblemished; tsarism and Bolshevism are equally irreproachable; the nation neither erred nor sinned either before 1917 or after; we have suffered no loss of moral stature and therefore have no need of self-improvement; there are no

was thought appropriate to exhibit this film once more, but the name of the now offending scriptwriter was cut out. And what was the scriptwriter's reaction? What would have been the most natural thing to do? The line of repentance would have indicated joy and satisfaction that he had, as it were, been automatically relieved of the disgrace of this former spiritual compromise and reprieved of an ancient sin. Might he not even have made a public statement about his feelings of absolution? Well, the scriptwriter certainly made a public statement, but it was a *protest,* asserting his right to have his name on the film. The infringement of his civil rights struck him as more important than the opportunity to purge himself of a previous sin. [A.S., 1974.]

nationality problems in relations with the border republics — Lenin's and Stalin's solution was ideal; communism is in fact unthinkable without patriotism; the prospects of Russia-USSR are brilliant; blood alone determines whether one is Russian or non-Russian. As for things spiritual, all trends are admissible. Orthodoxy is not the least bit more Russian than Marxism, atheism, the scientific outlook, or, shall we say, Hinduism. God need not be written with a capital letter, but Government must be.

Their general name for all this is "the Russian idea." (A more precise name for this trend would be "National Bolshevism.")

"We are Russians, what rapture," cried Suvorov.[5] "And how fraught with danger to the soul," added F. Stepun [6] after our revolutionary experiences.

As we understand it patriotism means unqualified and unwavering love for the nation, which implies not uncritical eagerness to serve, not support for unjust claims, but frank assessment of its vices and sins, and penitence for them. We ought to get used to the idea that no people is eternally great or eternally noble (such titles are hard won and easily lost); that the greatness of a people is to be sought not in the blare of trumpets — physical might is purchased at a spiritual price beyond our means — but in the level of its *inner* development, in its breadth of soul (fortunately one of nature's gifts to us), in unarmed moral steadfastness (in which the Czechs and Slovaks recently gave Europe a lesson, without however troubling its conscience more than briefly).

In what we may call the neo-Muscovite period the conceit of the preceding Petersburg period has become grosser and blinder. And this has led us even farther from a penitential state of mind, so that it is not easy to convince our fellow-countrymen, to force on them an awareness that we Russians are not traversing the heavens in a blaze of glory but sitting forlornly on a heap of spiritual cinders. And unless we re-

5. Alexander Suvorov (1729–1800), celebrated general who led the Swiss and Italian campaigns against Napoleon.— TRANS.
6. Fyodor Stepun (1884–1965), Russian philosopher who was expelled from the Soviet Union in 1922.— TRANS.

cover the gift of repentance, our country will perish and will drag down the whole world with it.

Only through the repentance of a multitude of people can the air and the soil of Russia be cleansed so that a new, healthy national life can grow up. We cannot raise a clean crop on a false, unsound, obdurate soil.

FOUR

If we try to make an act of national repentance we must be ready for hostility and resistance on the one hand, and impassioned efforts to lead us astray on the other. S. Bulgakov [7] has written that "only suffering love gives one the right to chastise one's own nation." [8] You would think it was impossible to take it upon oneself to "repent" on behalf of a nation to which one felt alien or even hostile. Yet people eager to do just this have already come forward. Given the obscurity of our recent history, the destruction of archives, the disappearance of evidence, our defenselessness against all sorts of presumptuous and unproven judgments and all sorts of galling distortions, we can probably expect many such attempts. And we already have the first of them, a fairly resolute effort which claims to be nothing less than an act of "national repentance."

We cannot pass it by unexamined. I am speaking of articles in the *Vestnik RSKD* [9] No. 97, and particularly "Metanoia" (self-condemnation, self-examination — a term taken from the same Bulgakov writing in 1910) by the anonymous NN, and "Russian Messianism" by the pseudonymous Gorsky.

Even the boldest works of *samizdat* always have an eye to the surrounding *circumstances*. But here, writing in a foreign publication and anonymously, the authors have absolutely no apprehension either for themselves or for their readers and therefore seize the chance to pour out their hearts for just

7. See note on page 20.— TRANS.
8. In *Two Cities*, Moscow, 1910, 2nd edition, p. 289.
9. See pages 95 to 96 and note on page 96.— TRANS.

once in their lives — an urge entirely understandable to any Soviet person. Their tone could not be sharper, and the style becomes informal, even impertinent. The authors fear neither the authorities nor the critical reader: they are will-o'-the-wisps, safe from discovery; there is no arguing with them. This makes them still more uncompromising in their conduct of the case against Russia. There is not the slightest hint that the authors share any complicity with their countrymen, with the rest of us; there is nothing but denunciation of the irredeemably vicious Russian people and a tone of contempt for those who have been led astray. Nowhere do we feel that the authors think of themselves and their readers as "we." Living among us, they call on us to repent, while they themselves remain unassailable and guiltless. (The punishment for this alienness extends even to their language, which is quite un-Russian and in the tradition of those instant translations from Western philosophy which people were forever rushing out in the nineteenth century.)

These articles solemnly bury Russia, with a bayonet thrust just in case — just as prisoners in the camps are buried: it's too much trouble to make sure whether the man's dead, just bayonet him and sling him in the burial trench.

Here are a few of their statements.

"When it began its revolt against God, the Russian people *knew* that the socialist religion could be made a reality only through despotism!" (Gorsky).

When were we, in our birchbark sandals, so mature and perceptive? The revolt was started by the intelligentsia, but it too *did not know* what can be so effortlessly formulated in the seventies of the twentieth century.

"More Evil has been brought into the world by Russia than by any other country" (NN).

We shall not say that Russia has brought little evil into the world. But did the so-called Great French Revolution, did France, that is, bring less? Is there any way of calculating? What of the Third Reich? Or Marxism as such? Not to go any further. . . . And there is another side to the question: perhaps our inhuman experience, paid for mainly with our own blood and that of the peoples nearest akin to us, has even benefited some of earth's more distant inhabitants? Perhaps in some places it has taught the obtuse ruling classes to make a few concessions? Perhaps the liberation of the colonial world was not entirely uninfluenced by the October revolution — as a reaction to it, to prevent a repetition of what happened to us — God alone can know, and it is not for us to judge which country has done most evil.

"In the revolution the people proved to be an imaginary quantity. . . . Its own national culture is completely alien to the Russian people." The proof: "In the first years of the revolution icons were found useful for firewood, and churches for building material" (Gorsky).

There you have it: anybody who feels like it can come along with a snap judgment, because our chronicles have been obliterated. If the people proved to be an imaginary quantity — how can it be blamed for the revolution, whatever other charges are brought against it? If it proved to be an imaginary quantity — who was resisting the revolution in the peasant risings which inundated Tambov and Siberia? The people had to be reduced to "imaginary" status by long years of destruction, oppression and seduction — and this destruction is just what Gorsky appears not to know about. It was a complicated process — and how simple he has made it. In 1918 Russian peasants rose in defense of the Church — *several hundred* such risings were put down by Red arms. Of course, after the clergy had been destroyed, after defenders of the faith among the peasantry and in urban parishes had been massacred and all the rest terrorized — while the Komsomols [10] and Communist youth organizations grew up in the meantime — after all this they did indeed go and wreck the churches with crowbars (but even then it was mainly the work of Komsomol members who were specially hired for this purpose). Ever since, in the northern regions, icons have been, not "sold for a song" to treasure-hunters from Moscow, as our well-informed author writes (true, they

10. Komsomol: the Russian abbreviation for the League of Young Communists, the youth arm of the Communist party.— TRANS.

sometimes change hands for a bottle), but *given away:* it is considered a sin to take money for them. Whereas the progressive young intellectuals who receive such a gift quite often do a profitable trade with foreigners.

But most of the heat and space in this bulky publication are devoted to the denunciation of *Russian messianism.*

"Overcoming the national messianic delusion is Russia's most urgent task." Russian messianism is more tenacious of life than Russia itself: Russia, we are told, is dead, of "archaeological" interest, like Byzantium, but its messianism is not dead, it has simply been reborn as Soviet messianism (Gorsky).

This cunning perversion of our history comes as such a surprise that it is not immediately discernible. The author begins by tracing in exaggeratedly academic fashion the "history" of our ill-starred and deathless messianism, which however was for some reason not always discernible in Russia: for two centuries (the fifteenth to the seventeenth) it was in evidence, then missing for the next two, then it reemerged in the nineteenth century (apparently the intelligentsia was "carried away" by it — does anyone remember anything of the kind?), it disguised itself during the revolution as "proletarian messianism," and in recent decades has torn off its mask and once more revealed itself as Russian messianism. So, traveling via dotted lines, sophistries, and abrupt transitions, the idea of the Third Rome suddenly surfaces again in the guise of the Third International! [11] With the obsessive thoroughness of hate, our whole history is arbitrarily distorted for some never quite graspable purpose — and all this is speciously represented as an act of *repentance!* The blows seem to be aimed only at the Third Rome and messianism — then suddenly we discover that the breaker's hammer is not smashing dilapidated walls but pounding the last spark of life

11. "Third Rome" refers to the medieval Russian religious belief that after the fall of Constantinople (the "second Rome") in 1492, Moscow would become the center of Christendom and a "third Rome." The "Third International," or Comintern, was a world organization of Communist parties that existed from 1919 to 1943 with the aim of conquering the world for communism.— TRANS.

out of the long dormant, barely surviving Russian national consciousness. See how keen his aim is:

"The Russian idea is the main content of Bolshevism"! "The crisis of the Communist idea is the crisis of that source of faith by which Russia lived so long" ("for centuries," according to the context).

See how they turn us inside out and trample us. Russia "lived so long" by the Orthodox faith, as everybody knows. But the main content of Bolshevism is unbridled militant atheism and class hatred. Still, according to our neo-Christian authors, it all comes to the same thing. The tradition of fanatical atheism is received into the tradition of ancient Orthodoxy. Is the "Russian idea," then, the "main content" of an international doctrine which came to us from the West? When Marat called for "a million heads" and asserted that the hungry have the right to *eat* the well-fed (how well we know such situations!) — was this also the "Russian messianic consciousness" at work? Sixteenth century Germany seethed with communistic movements — so why, when this "Russian idea" was about, did nothing similar happen during the Time of Troubles in seventeenth-century Russia?

"Revolution could exercise its fatal fascination only because of Russia's ecumenical pride" (NN).

How can we tie these loose ends together? If tsarism rested on "Russia's ecumenical pride," how can revolution, which brought down the tsarist structure in ruins, also *originate* in "Russian pride"?

"Proletarian messianism is taking on a blatantly Russophile character" (Chelnov).

This is in our own day, when half the Russian people live like serfs, without internal passports. Have we memory and courage enough to recall the first fifteen years after the revolution, when "proletarian messianism took on a blatantly" *Russophobe* character? The years from 1918 to 1933, when "proletarian messianism" destroyed the flower of the Russian people, the flower of the old classes — gentry, merchants, clergy — then the flower of the intelligentsia, then the flower of the peasantry? What shall we say of the time *before* it acquired its "blatantly Russophile character," and had a blatantly Russophobe character?

"Bolshevism is an organic outgrowth of Russian life" (NN and Chelnov).

Whether this is so or not will be much debated for a long time to come. And it cannot be decided in heated polemics, but only by detailed and carefully documented research. *Quiet Flows the Don* [12] — the authentic version, undistorted by illiterate interpolations — offers more useful evidence than a dozen modern publicists. Our scholars and artists will long be debating whether the Russian revolution was the consequence of a moral upheaval that had already taken place among the people, or vice versa. And when they do, let none of the circumstances passed over here be forgotten.

Of course, once it was victorious on Russian soil the movement was bound to draw Russian forces in its wake and acquire Russian features! But let us remember the international forces of the revolution too! Did not the revolution throughout its early years have some of the characteristics of a foreign invasion? When in a foraging party, or the punitive detachment which came down to destroy a rural district, there would be Finns and there would be Austrians, but hardly anyone who spoke Russian? When the organs of the Cheka [13] teemed with Latvians, Poles, Jews, Hungarians, Chinese? When in the critical early phases of the civil war it was foreign and especially Latvian bayonets that turned the scales and kept the Bolsheviks in power? (At the time this was not a matter for shame or concealment.) Or later, throughout the twenties, when the Russian tradition and all trace of Russian history were systematically ferreted out in all fields of culture, eliminated even from place-names, in a way seen only under enemy occupation — was this self-

12. The epic novel about the Russian revolution and civil war, published by Mikhail Sholokhov in 1928. Ever since publication there have been persistent, but unproven, rumors that Sholokhov was not the true author. Early in 1974, Solzhenitsyn authorized the publication in Russian in Paris of an anonymous work ("The Rapids of *The Quiet Don*") purporting to prove that the author was not Sholokhov but a White Cossack officer and prerevolutionary writer named Fyodor Kryukov.— TRANS.
13. See note on page 11.— TRANS.

destructive urge also a manifestation of the "Russian idea"? Gorsky notes that in 1919 the borders of Soviet Russia roughly corresponded with those of the Muscovite state — ergo Bolshevism was supported mainly by Russians. But this geographical fact could equally well be interpreted to mean simply that it was mainly Russians who were forced to shoulder the burden of Bolshevism. And can we think of any people on earth in the twentieth century which when trapped by the incoming tide of communism has pulled itself together and stood firm? So far there is not a single example of this, except South Korea, where the United Nations came to the rescue. South Vietnam might have been another case, but has apparently been thrown off balance. And right now, are we to say that communism in Cuba or in Vietnam "is an organic outgrowth of Russian life"? Is "Marxism one of the forms taken by the populist-messianic mentality" in France too? Or in Latin America? Or in Tanzania? And does all this come from the unwashed monk Filofei?

What a state of disrepair twentieth-century Russian history is in, how grotesquely distorted and full of obscurities, if people so self-confidently ignorant of it can offer us their services as judges. Because of our complacency we may live to see the day when fifty or a hundred years of Russian history will have sunk into oblivion, and nobody will be able to establish any reliable record of them — it will be too late.

The publication of these articles is not fortuitous — the idea is perhaps to take advantage of our helplessness, turn recent Russian history inside out, blame *us* Russians *alone* not only for our own misfortunes but also for those of our erstwhile tormentors and nowadays pretty well the whole planet. These accusations are typical of their authors, plucked out of thin air and shamelessly fabricated, and it is easy to foresee already how they intend to go on searing our wounds with them.

This article has not been written to minimize the guilt of the Russian people. Nor, however, to scrape all the guilt from mother earth and load it onto ourselves. True, we were not vaccinated against the plague. True, we lost our heads. True, we gave way, and then caved in altogether. All true. But we have not been the first and only begetters in all this time since the fifteenth century!

We are not the only ones, there are many others. Indeed, almost everyone when the time comes gives way, gives up, sometimes under less pressure than we succumbed to, and at times even eagerly. (The brief period of our history from February to October 1917 has turned out to be a compressed résumé of the later and present history of the West.)

Thus, at the very beginning of our repentance we have been warned: the path ahead will bristle with such insults and slanders. If you are the first to repent, earlier and more fully than others, you must expect predators in the guise of penitents to flock around and peck your liver.

Nonetheless, there is no way out, except that of repentance.

FIVE

It may turn out that we are already incapable of following the path of our dreams, reaching out and acknowledging our mistakes, our sins, our crimes. In that case there is no moral escape route from the pit into which we have fallen. And every other way out is illusory, no more than a short-lived social delusion.

But if it turns out that we are still not utterly lost and can find in ourselves the strength to pass through this burning zone of general national repentance, of *internal* repentance, for the harm which we have done here in our own country, to ourselves, will it be possible for Russia to stop at that? No, we shall have to find in ourselves the resolve to take the next step: to acknowledge our *external* sins, those against other peoples.

There are plenty of them. To clear the international air and convince others of our sincere goodwill, we must not conceal these sins, not tuck them away nor slur over them in our remembrance. My view is that if we err in our repentance, it should be on the side of exaggeration, giving others the benefit of the doubt. We should accept in advance that there is no neighbor toward whom we bear no guilt. Let us behave as people do on the day of forgiveness, and ask forgiveness of all around us.

The scope of our repentance must be infinite. We cannot run away even from ancient sins; we may write off other people's sins as ancient history, but we have no right to do it for ourselves. A few pages further on I shall be talking about the future of Siberia — and whenever I do so my heart sinks at the thought of our age-old sin in oppressing and destroying the indigenous peoples. And is this really ancient history? If Siberia today were densely populated by the original national groups the only step we could ethically take would be to cede their land to them and not stand in the way of their freedom. But since there is only a faint sprinkling of them on the Siberian continent, it is permissible for us to seek our future there, so long as we show a tender fraternal concern for the natives, help them in their daily lives, educate them, and do not forcibly impose our ways on them.

A historical survey would be out of place in this article — and besides, space does not permit it. It would contain crimes enough — as for instance those we committed against the mountain peoples of the Caucasus: the Russian military encroachment in the nineteenth century (condemned at the proper time by the great Russian writers) and the deportations of the twentieth century (which Caucasian writers themselves dare not deal with).

Repentance is always difficult. And not only because we must cross the threshold of self-love, but also because our own sins are not so easily visible to us.

If we take the Russo-Polish theme — here too there is an endless tangle of crimes. To unravel it would teach us much about human relations in the broadest sense. (Today, when both the Poles and we ourselves are crushed by brute force, such a historical inquiry may seem inappropriate. But I write for posterity. Someday it may seem appropriate.)

So much has been said about our guilt toward Poland that

it has left a deposit on our memory, and we need no more persuasion. The three Partitions. The suppression of the 1830 and 1863 risings. After that, Russification: Polish-speaking elementary schools were completely forbidden, in high schools even the Polish language was taught in Russian (as an obligatory subject) and pupils were forbidden to speak Polish among themselves in their living quarters! In the twentieth century there was the stubborn struggle to deny Poland its independence, and the crafty ambiguities of Russia's leaders in 1914–1916.

At the same time, how frequent were the expressions of penitence from the Russian side, from Herzen [14] onward, how unanimous was the sympathy of all educated Russian society for the Poles, so much so that in the councils of the Progressive Bloc, Polish independence was regarded as a war aim no less important than Russian victory.

If the most recent happenings have inspired no such cry of repentance in Russia, it is only because we are so crushed, but we all remember, and there will yet be occasion to say it out loud: the noble stab in the back for dying Poland on 17 September 1939; the destruction of the flower of the Polish people in our camps, Katyn in particular; and our gloating, heartless immobility on the bank of the Vistula in August 1944, whence we gazed through our binoculars at Hitler crushing the rising of the nationalist forces in Warsaw — no need for them to get big ideas, we will find the right people to put in the government. (I was nearby, and I speak with certainty: the impetus of our advance was such that the forcing of the Vistula would have been no problem, and it would have changed the fate of Warsaw.)

But just as some individuals more readily open their hearts to repentance, and others are more resistant and offer not a single chink, so, I think, with nations — some are more and some less inclined to repent.

14. Alexander Herzen (1812–1870), famous Russian political figure and thinker and editor of the émigré journal the *Bell*, which he published from London after his forced emigration from Russia in 1847.— TRANS.

In previous centuries Poland in its prime, strong and self-confident, was busy just as long and just as energetically annexing our territory and oppressing us. (Galician Ruthenia and Podolia in the fourteenth to sixteenth centuries; then Polesia, Volynia and the Ukraine were incorporated under the Union of Lublin in 1569. In the sixteenth century came Stefan Batory's campaign against Russia, and the siege of Pskov. At the end of the sixteenth century the Poles put down the Cossack rising under Nalivaiko. At the beginning of the seventeenth century — the wars of Zygmunt III, the two false claimants to the Russian throne, the occupation of Smolensk, the temporary occupation of Moscow, the campaign of Wladyslaw IV. At that point the Poles almost deprived us of our national independence, and the danger for us was no less serious than that of the Tartar invasion, since the Poles were out to destroy the Orthodox faith. In their own country they systematically oppressed the Orthodox, and forced them into the Uniate church. In the mid-seventeenth century came the repression of Bogdan Khmelnitsky, and even in the middle of the eighteenth the crushing of the peasant rising at Uman.) Well then, has any wave of regret rolled over educated Polish society, any wave of repentance surged through Polish literature? Never. Even the Arians, who were opposed to war in general, had nothing special to say about the subjugation of the Ukraine and Byelorussia. During our Time of Troubles, the eastward expansion of Poland was accepted by Polish society as a normal and even praiseworthy policy. The Poles thought of themselves as God's chosen people, the bastion of Christianity, whose mission was to carry true Christianity to the "semipagan" Orthodox of savage Muscovy, and to be the propagators of Renaissance university culture. And when some people openly voiced their second thoughts and regrets about this when Poland went into decline in the second half of the eighteenth century, they were of a political and never of an ethical nature.

True, one cannot always draw the line between a general

national characteristic and the imprint of a particular social order. The Polish social order, with its weak elected kings, its all-powerful magnates and the utterly undisciplined selfishness of the gentry, led to the noisy self-assertion of nationhood, which ruled out self-limitation and made repentance seem inappropriate. In such a society educated Poles felt themselves to be participants and authors of all that was done, and not detached observers, whereas repentance was made easier for Russians in the nineteenth and early twentieth century by the fact that those who condemned official policy could consider themselves uninvolved: it was all *their* doing, the tsar did not consult society.

But perhaps Polish penitence expressed itself in deeds? For more than a century Poland experienced the misery of dismemberment, but then under the Versailles treaty gained independence and a great deal of territory (once more at the expense of the Ukraine and Byelorussia). Poland's first action in its relations with the outside world was to attack Soviet Russia in 1920 — it attacked energetically, and took Kiev with the object of breaking through to the Black Sea. We are taught at school — to make it seem more awful — that this was the "Third Campaign of the Entente" and that Poland concerted its actions with the White generals in order to restore tsarism. This is rubbish. It was an *independent* act on the part of Poland, which waited for the rout of all the main White forces so as *not* to be their involuntary ally and so that it could plunder and carve up Russia for itself while the latter was most helplessly fragmented. This did not quite come off (though Poland did extract an indemnity from the Soviets). Then in 1921 came its second foreign-policy initiative: the illegal detachment of Vilnius and the surrounding area from a weak Lithuania. And neither the League of Nations, nor all the admonitions and appeals to the Polish conscience, had any effect: Poland still clung to the piece it had grabbed to the very day of its collapse. Can anyone remember the nation repenting in this connection? (Poland's aggressive acts, incidentally, were carried out by the socialist Pilsudski, one of

Alexander Ulyanov's [15] codefendants.) In the Ukrainian and Byelorussian lands annexed under the treaty of 1921, a policy of relentless Polonization was carried out, even Orthodox sermons and Scripture lessons had a Polish accent. And in the infamous year of 1937, Orthodox churches were demolished (more than a hundred of them, including Warsaw Cathedral) on the Polish side of the frontier too, and priests and parishioners were arrested.

How can we possibly rise above all this, except by mutual repentance?

And is it not true that the degree of our repentance, individual or national, is very much influenced by an awareness of guilt on the other side? If those whom we hurt have previously hurt us, our guilt feelings are not so hysterical, their guilt modifies and mutes our own. The memory of the Tartar yoke in Russia must always dull our possible sense of guilt toward the remnants of the Golden Horde. Our guilt feelings toward the Estonians and Lithuanians are always more painful and shameful than any we have toward the Latvians or Hungarians, whose rifles barked often enough in the cellars of the Cheka and the backyards of Russian villages. (I ignore the inevitable noisy protests that these were "not the same people," that one cannot transfer the blame from one set of people to another. We are not the same people either. But we must all answer for everything.)

This is yet another argument in favor of general repentance. What relief, what rapturous relief it gives us when our enemies acknowledge their guilt toward us! How gratefully eager we are to outstrip them in repentance, to surpass them in magnanimity!

But repentance loses all sense if it goes no farther: if we have a good cry and then go on as before. Repentance opens up the path to a new relationship. Between nations as between individuals.

15. Alexander Ulyanov (1866–1887), Lenin's elder brother, was executed with four others in 1887 after an unsuccessful attempt to assassinate Tsar Alexander III. Pilsudski and one other defendant were pardoned.— TRANS.

The repentance of a nation, like any other kind, assumes the possibility of *forgiveness* on the part of the injured. But it is impossible to expect forgiveness before you yourself have made up your mind to forgive. The path of mutual repentance and mutual forgiveness is one and the same.

Who has no guilt? We are all guilty. But at some point the endless account must be closed, we must stop discussing whose crimes are more recent, more serious and affect most victims. It is useless for even the closest neighbors to compare the duration and gravity of their grievances against each other. But feelings of penitence can be compared.

This picture does not seem to me an idyll, unreal and irrelevant to our modern situation. On the contrary. Just as it is impossible to build a good society when relations between people are bad, there will never be a good world while nations are on bad terms and secretly cherish the desire for revenge. Neither a "positive" foreign policy nor yet the most skillful efforts on the part of diplomats to draw up tactfully incomplete treaties so that each side can find some balm for its national pride — none of this can smother the seeds of discord and prevent even more conflicts from arising.

At present the whole atmosphere of the United Nations is saturated with hatred and spite — remember how the Assembly went wild with joy (some uninhibited members are said to have jumped up on the benches) when ten million Chinese on Taiwan were thrown out of the human family for refusing to submit to totalitarian aggression.

Without the establishment of radically *new*, really good relations between nations the entire quest for "world peace" is either utopian or a precarious balancing act.

The stock of mutual guilt mounts especially high in multinational states and federations, like Austria-Hungary in the past, or the USSR, Yugoslavia, Nigeria and other African states with a multiplicity of tribes and races today. If such states are to achieve internal stability and be held together by something other than coercion, the peoples who live in them cannot possibly manage without a highly developed capacity for repentance. Otherwise the fires will smolder forever beneath the ashes and flare up again and again, and these countries will never know stability. The West Pakistanis were ruthless toward those of the East — and the country collapsed, but still the hatred did not die down. On the contrary, northern Nigeria, with the help of British and Soviet arms and with the whole world indifferently looking on, took a cruel revenge on the eastern regions and preserved the unity of the country, but unless this wrong is righted by repentance and kindness on the part of the victors, that country will not enjoy stability and health.

Repentance is only a clearing of the ground, the establishment of a clean basis in preparation for further moral actions — what in the life of the individual is called "reform." And if in private life what has been done must be put right by deeds, not words, this is all the more true in the life of a nation. Its repentance must be expressed not so much in articles, books and broadcasts as in national *actions*.

With regard to all the peoples in and beyond our borders forcibly drawn into our orbit, we can fully purge our guilt by giving them genuine freedom to decide their future for themselves.

After repentance, and once we renounce the use of force, *self-limitation* comes into its own as the most natural principle to live by. Repentance creates the atmosphere for self-limitation.

Self-limitation on the part of individuals has often been observed and described, and is well known to us all. (Quite apart from the pleasure it gives to those around us in our everyday lives, it can be universally helpful to men in *all* areas of their activity.) But so far as I know, no state has ever carried through a deliberate policy of self-limitation or set itself such a task in a general form — though when it has done so at difficult moments in some particular sector (food rationing, fuel rationing, and so on) self-limitation has paid off handsomely.

Every trade union and every corporation strives by all possible means to win the most advantageous position in the economy, every firm aims at uninterrupted expansion, every party wants to run its country, medium-sized states want to become great ones, and great ones to rule the world.

We are always very ready to limit *others* — this is what all politicians are engaged in — but nowadays the man who suggests that a state or party, without coercion and simply in answer to a moral call, should limit *itself*, invites ridicule. We are always anxiously on the lookout for ways of curbing the inordinate greed of the *other man*, but no one is heard renouncing his *own* inordinate greed. History knows of several occasions on which the greed of a minority was curbed, with much bloodshed, but who is to curb the inflamed greed of the *majority*, and how? That is something it can only do for itself.

The idea of self-limitation in society is not a new one. We find it a century ago in such thoroughgoing Christians as the Russian Old Believers. In the journal *Istina* (No. 1,1807), in an article by K. Golubov, who corresponded with Ogarev [16] and Herzen, we read:

"A people subjects itself to great suffering by its immoral acquisitiveness. That which is obtained by revolt and sequestration can have no true value. These are rather the fruits of the overweening behavior of a corrupt conscience: the true and lasting good is that which is attained by *farsighted self-limitation*" (emphasis added).

And elsewhere: "Save through self-restriction, there is no other true freedom for mankind."

After the Western ideal of unlimited freedom, after the Marxist concept of freedom as acceptance of the yoke of necessity — here is the true Christian definition of freedom. Freedom is *self-restriction!* Restriction of the self for the sake of others!

Once understood and adopted, this principle diverts us — as individuals, in all forms of human association, socie-

16. Nikolai Ogarev (1813–1877), poet and friend of Herzen, who lived abroad for much of his life. He attempted to form a nationwide revolutionary organization out of a series of populist groups calling themselves "Land and Liberty."— TRANS.

ties and nations — from *outward* to *inward* development, thereby giving us greater spiritual depth.

The turn toward *inward* development, the triumph of inwardness over outwardness, if it ever happens, will be a great turning point in the history of mankind, comparable to the transition from the Middle Ages to the Renaissance. There will be a complete change not only in the direction of our interests and activities but in the very nature of human beings (a change from spiritual dispersal to spiritual concentration), and a greater change still in the character of human societies. If in some places this is destined to be a revolutionary process, these revolutions will not be like earlier ones — physical, bloody and never beneficial — but will be *moral revolutions,* requiring both courage and sacrifice, though not cruelty — a new phenomenon in human history, of which little is yet known and which as yet no one has prophetically described in clear and precise forms. The examination of all this does not lie within the scope of our present article.

But in the material sphere too this change will have conspicuous results. The individual will not flog himself to death in his greed for bigger and bigger earnings, but will spend what he has economically, rationally and calmly. The state will not, as it does now, use its strength — sometimes even with no particular end in view — simply on the principle that where something will give, one must exert pressure, if a barrier can be moved, move it — no, among states too the moral rule for individuals will be adopted — do not unto others as you would not have done unto you: instead, learn to use to the full what you have. Only thus can a well-ordered life be created on our planet.

The concept of unlimited freedom is closely connected in its origin with the concept of *infinite progress,* which we now recognize as false. Progress in this sense is impossible on our earth with its limited surface area and resources. We shall in any case inevitably have to stop jostling each other and show self-restraint: with the population rapidly soaring, mother earth herself will shortly force us to do so. It would be spiritually so much more valuable, and psychologically so much easier, to adopt the principle of self-limitation — and to achieve it through *prudent self-restriction.*

Such a change will not be easy for the free economy of the West. It is a revolutionary demolition and total reconstruction of all our ideas and aims. We must go over from uninterrupted progress to a *stable economy,* with *nil growth* in territory, parameters and tempo, developing only through improved technology (and even technical successes must be critically screened). This means that we must abjure the plague of expansion beyond our borders, the continual scramble after new markets and sources of raw material, increases in our industrial territory or the volume of production, the whole insane pursuit of wealth, fame and change. No incentive to self-limitation has ever existed in bourgeois economics, yet the formula would so easily and so long ago have been derived from moral considerations. The fundamental concepts of private property and private economic initiative are part of man's nature, and necessary for his personal freedom and his sense of normal well-being. They would be beneficial to society *if only* . . . if only the carriers of these ideas on the very threshold of development had *limited themselves,* and not allowed the size of their property and thrust of their avarice to become a social evil, which provoked so much justifiable anger, not tried to purchase power and subjugate the press. It was as a reply to the shamelessness of unlimited money-grubbing that socialism in all its forms developed.

But a Russian author today need not rack his brains for an answer to these worries. Self-limitation has countless aspects — international, political, cultural, national, social, party-political. We Russians should sort out those which concern us.

And show an example of spiritual breadth. Show that repentance is not fruitless.

It is in this hope and faith that I am writing this article.

Our native land, after centuries of misapplying its might (both in the Petersburg and the neo-Muscovite periods), after making so many useless acquisitions abroad and causing so much destruction at home, now, before the chance is lost forever, is perhaps more than any other country in need of comprehensive *inward* development — both spiritual, and the ensuing geographical, economic and social development that will occur as a consequence.

Our foreign policy in recent decades might have been deliberately devised in defiance of the true interests of our people. We have taken on ourselves a responsibility for the fate of Eastern Europe incommensurable with our present level of spiritual development and our ability to understand European needs and ways. We are ready in our conceit to extend our responsibility to any other country, however distant, even on the other side of the globe, provided it declares its intent to nationalize the means of production and centralize power. (These, according to our Theory, are the primary features, and all the rest — national peculiarities, way of life, thousand-year-old cultural traditions — are secondary. We meddle indefatigably in conflicts on every continent, lay down the law, shove people into quarrels, shamelessly push arms till they have become our most important item of export. We are what Soviet newspapers until the forties called "traders in blood.") [17] In pursuit of all these artificial aims, which are of no use to our nation, we have exhausted our strength and wrecked several of our generations — mainly physically in the past, but now mainly spiritually.

All these world tasks, which have been of no use at all to us, have left us *tired*. We need to get away from the hurly-burly of world rivalries. And from the exhibitionistic space race, which is useless to us: what is the point of our painful efforts to erect villages on the moon when our Russian villages have become dilapidated and unfit for habitation? In our insane industrial drive we have drawn inordinate masses of people into unnatural towns and absurd, hastily erected buildings, where they are poisoned, collapse under nervous

17. According to Western specialists our arms sales between 1955 and 1970 came to the value of twenty-eight billion dollars. In the seventies our share of the world arms trade has been 37.5 percent.

strain, and start degenerating in early youth. Sweated female labor instead of sex equality, the neglect of parental duty, drunkenness, loss of appetite for work, the decline of the school, the decadence of our native language — whole spiritual deserts are eating into our life and laying waste to great patches of it, and it is only in overcoming *these* that we can win for ourselves true and not bogus prestige. Should we be struggling for warm seas far away, or ensuring that warmth rather than enmity flows between our own citizens?

And as if this were not enough, we who boast so much about our lead over others have slavishly copied Western technical progress and unthinkingly become jammed in a blind alley, finding ourselves together with the West in a crisis which threatens the existence of all mankind.

A family which has suffered a great misfortune or disgrace tries to withdraw into itself for a time to get over its grief by itself. This is what the Russian people must do: spend most of its time alone with itself, without neighbors and guests. It must concentrate on its *inner* tasks: on healing its soul, educating its children, putting its own house in order.

The healing of our souls! Nothing now is more important to us after all that we have lived through, after our long complicity in lies and even crimes. It may be too late for the older generations, but this only means that we must work with even greater zeal and selflessness to bring up our children, so that when they grow up they will be incomparably purer than our fallen society. The *school* — that is the key to the future of Russia! But it is a complicated and contradictory problem: bad parents and teachers must rear better people to follow them. It cannot be solved in one generation. It will require immense efforts. The whole public educational system must be created anew, and not with rejects but with the people's best forces. It will cost billions — and we should take them from our vainglorious and unnecessary foreign expenditure. We must stop running out into the street to join every brawl and instead retire virtuously into our own home so long as we are in such a state of disorder and confusion.

Fortunately we have such a home, a spacious and unsullied home preserved for us by history — the Russian Northeast. Let us give up trying to restore order overseas, keep our grabbing imperial hands off neighbors who want to live their own lives in freedom — and turn our national and political zeal toward the untamed expanses of the Northeast, whose emptiness is becoming intolerable to our neighbors now that life on earth is so tight packed.

The *Northeast* means the north of European Russia — Pinega, Mezen, Pechora — it means too the Lena and the whole central zone of Siberia north of the railway line, which is to this day deserted, in places virgin territory and unknown — there are hardly any open spaces like it left on the civilized earth. And then too the tundra and permafrost of the Lower Ob, Yamal, Taimyr, Khatango, Indigirka, Kolyma, Chukotka and Kamchatka cannot be abandoned in despair, given the technological skills — and the population problems — of the twenty-first century.

The Northeast is the wind in our faces described by Voloshin: [18] "In that wind is the whole destiny of Russia." The Northeast is the outward vector, which has long indicated the direction of Russia's natural movement and development. It was appreciated by Novgorod, but neglected by Muscovite Russia, partly opened up by a spontaneous movement that took place without state encouragement, then by the forced flight of the Old Believers. Peter the Great failed to see its significance, and in the last half century it has in effect been overlooked, despite all the sensational plans.

The Northeast is a reminder that Russia is the northeast of the planet, that our ocean is the Arctic, not the Indian Ocean, that we are not the Mediterranean nor Africa and that we have no business there! These boundless expanses, senselessly left stagnant and icily barren for four centuries, await our hands, our sacrifices, our zeal and our love. But it may be that we have only two or three decades left for this work: otherwise the imminent world population explosion will take these expanses away from us.

18. Maximilian Voloshin (1878–1932), post-Symbolist poet and artist noted for his nightmarish visions of the revolution and the civil war.— TRANS.

The Northeast is also the key to many apparently intricate Russian problems. Instead of casting greedy eyes on lands which do not really belong to us, or in which we are not in the majority, we should be directing our forces and urging our young people toward the Northeast — that is the far-sighted solution. Its great expanses offer us a way out of the worldwide technological crisis. They offer us plenty of room in which to correct all our idiocies in building towns, industrial enterprises, power stations and roads. Its cold and in places permanently frozen soil is still not ready for cultivation, it will require enormous inputs of energy — but the energy lies hidden in the depths of the Northeast itself, since we have not yet had time to squander it.

The Northeast could not be brought to life by camp watchtowers, the yells of armed guards and the barking of man-eating dogs. Only free people with a free understanding of our national mission can resurrect these great spaces, awaken them, heal them, beautify them with feats of engineering.

The Northeast — more than just a musical sound and more than just a geographical concept — will signify that Russia has resolutely opted for *self-limitation,* for turning inward rather than outward. In its whole future life — national, social, personal, in the schools and in the family — it will concentrate its efforts on *inward,* not outward, growth.

This does not mean that we shall shut ourselves up within ourselves forever. This would not be in accordance with the outgoing Russian character. When we have recovered our health and put our house in order we shall undoubtedly want to help poor and backward peoples, and succeed in doing so. But not out of political self-interest, not to make them live as we do or serve us.

Some may wonder how far a nation, society or state can go in self-limitation. Unlike the individual, a whole people cannot afford the luxury of impulsive and totally self-sacrificing decisions. If a people has gone over to self-limitation, but its neighbors have not, must it be ready to resist aggression?

Yes, of course. Defense forces must be retained, but only for genuinely *defensive* purposes, only on a scale adequate to real and not imaginary threats, not as an end in themselves, not as a self-perpetuating tradition, not to maintain the size and glamour of the high command. They will be retained in the hope that the whole atmosphere of mankind will soon begin to change.

And if it does not change, the Club of Rome has done the arithmetic: we have less than a hundred years to live.

November 1973

The Direction of Change

A.B.

At the beginning of this century, to the bewilderment (and annoyance) of many who thought themselves sufficiently in tune with the "spirit of the age," there appeared in Russian society a broad movement toward philosophic idealism. A certain Kiev professor observed at the time that this interest in idealism and the amount of attention devoted to it demonstrated individual faith in the writers who preached it, rather than any genuine readiness on the part of society as a whole to abandon philosophic positivism and the various forms of philosophic materialism that had taken root in our country. One gets the impression, he said, that society is now faced with an urgent question — where does truth lie, in idealism or positivism? But society is not yet ready to provide an answer: "The ground on which the seed of idealism might bring forth abundantly has yet to be plowed. Positivism exploits this situation so as to maintain its dominance."

These words, spoken seventy years ago, have turned out to be prophetic. Positivism, unscrupulous as to means, has held on to power for nearly a century. But today Russian society faces the same question once more. Once more an answer is urgently demanded, while society seems all the less prepared for it, all the more caught unawares. "Truly one has to admit that our society is in a lamentable state. This absence of public opinion, this indifference to duty, justice and truth, this cynical contempt for human thought and dignity can lead only to despair." Pushkin's words, but they could have been uttered today. And on the face of it one is left repeating those words about "unplowed ground."

But history moves in a mysterious way and lends itself little to logical analysis. The path of reason and cognition, based on the gradual exercise of thought and the accumulation of judgments logically arrived at, is not the only one possible either for society or for the individual, and it is not the most important. There is also the path of lived spiritual experience, the path of integral intuitive perception.

Has our own history of the past seventy years not taught us something? It has been a harsh and terrible period. Many times it has seemed that "Russia was dead," that "the old Russia no longer existed," that the preference of facelessness to individuality had caused the whole nation to lose itself. But was this really so? Did not a handful of Russian poets and writers survive those years? And surely the killings and tortures we experienced did not shape only nonentities? We had our martyrs and heroes. And even when they went unheard and unrecognized they were preparing the way for the rebirth of society to some sort of a new life.

Early as it is to draw definite conclusions, I believe an answer of sorts to the question "Where is the truth?" is already emerging. Just as the body rejects a foreign implant, there is now in progress a rejection of "positive philosophy" and all its accompanying official ideology: our society is covering it with a scab of skepticism, so that this graft is no longer attached to the living soul, as it was seventy or a hundred years ago, but is rejected by it.

But that is not enough. We need new spiritual energies, a source of positive influence. Let us dare to express the cautious hope that such an influence for good already exists in our society. Mysteriously and unsuspected by the busy multitude, Christian consciousness, once almost defunct, is stealing back. In the last few years Christianity's word has suddenly and miraculously evoked a response in the hearts of many whose whole education, way of life and fashionable ideas about "alienation" and the historical pessimism of contemporary art would seem to have cut them off from it irrevocably. It is as if a door had opened while nobody was looking.

Why is this rebirth taking place in our country, where Christianity is attacked particularly systematically and with great brutality, while the rest of the world suffers a general decline in faith and religious feeling? Once again our history over the last fifty years provides a clue to one of the reasons. We have passed through such bottomless pits, we have been so exposed to all the winds of Kolyma,[1] we have experienced such utter exhaustion of human resources that we have learned to see the "one essential" that cannot be taken away from man, and we have learned not to look to human resources for succor. In glorious destitution, in utter defenselessness in the face of suffering, our hearts have been kindled by an inner spiritual warmth and have opened to new, unexpected impulses.

Now, when the walls of our houses have become a little warmer and less collapsible, we are haunted by an obscure but insistent foreboding of impending historical change. It manifests itself in the general feeling that "things cannot go on like this" and as yet has assumed no fixed shape. But the shape of our future development is, of course, the more important question of our time. It will form itself somehow, but everything depends on how precisely.

Two factors I have mentioned — the return of Christian consciousness and the presentiment of change — mark the special responsibilities of our time.

It is hard not to link the two. In fact, backsliding and denials notwithstanding, we live in a Christian culture in a Christian age, and it is Christianity that is the fermenting agent, the "yeast of the world," causing history to rise like dough in a trough, not only in the past but in the future as

1. Kolyma: a river and a region in northeast Siberia noted for its harsh climate. Some of the worst labor camps were situated in this region.— TRANS.

well. We are profoundly convinced that Christianity alone possesses enough motive force gradually to inspire and transform our world. Therefore the only question that remains is how profoundly we succeed in understanding this fact and embodying it in our lives in our time.

Acknowledging this, we must consider what we should do and what we should strive for. Christianity is more than a system of views, it is a way of life. Much has been well written about this and well lived, beginning with the apostles and ending with our own contemporaries. It would be wrong now to snatch something hastily from this vast and priceless living experience just to drape over the feebleness of our deeds and thoughts.

The briefest inspection of our pitiful arsenal will be sufficient to convince us that it is quite unequal to the tasks before us.

When we think of the necessity for change, our thoughts follow the beaten path to "decentralization of the system" or "the struggle for social reconstruction." The most dynamic and resolute forces in our society are already hankering for such a struggle, not to mention those who are always glad to escape inner emptiness through outward activity. But as we already know, the fallacy of all revolutions is that they are strong and concrete on the negative and destructive side, and limp and abstract on the positive and creative side. This is how Dostoyevsky defined the underlying cause: "The bee knows the formula of its hive and the ant the formula of its anthills, but man does not know his formula." The reason why man does not know his formula is that, unlike the bee and the ant, which are not free, man is free. Freedom is man's formula, but he will never find it so long as he seeks it in parties and ideologies, however good they may be in themselves.

This freedom is not man's "natural" inheritance, but rather the aim of his life and a "supernatural" gift. "Servitude to sin" is how Christianity defines the normal condition of man's soul and it summons man to free himself from this servitude.

147

The path of heroic spiritual striving is the only path that can lead man — and the whole of society — to freedom. The authors of the *Vekhi* (*Landmarks*) [2] anthology wrote of these things seventy years ago (S. Bulgakov and S. Frank in particular), but few understood them at the time.

So is it not time, after almost two hundred years of obsession with the "social idea," to turn to this path, clearing our minds of the ideal of the fighter and replacing it with the ideal of the visionary. What a word — the modern tongue can scarcely pronounce it, so accustomed are we in our arrogance to reject this ideal from the lofty heights of our struggle for the "common cause"! The nearest words our vocabulary can find for this goal are now "self-improvement" and the theory of "small causes." What a blunder! What a stubborn refusal to come to our senses!

The point is not that we should cease to strive for a better social order, but that the truth about this order is one of those truths that cannot be grasped by reason, but can only be learned by living and acting, and are accessible only to a consciousness that is already enlightened. And until we bring about a change in ourselves, even the best-intentioned attempts to restructure anything "from outside" by decree or by force are doomed at best to come to naught, as in Repetilov's [3] "We are making a commotion, my friend," and at worst to end in Dostoyevsky's *Possessed*, with all the logical consequences that we know so well.

The age we are now living in is a vital one for our nation. Historical action has time limits, and if the chance is missed it will be a very long time before it presents itself again. One may well ask: "How is it that ye do not discern this time?" (Luke 12:56). Will we have the perception and determination to reform our nature from inside and through this our common life?

Suffering and sorrow ennoble the individual and society alike, so long as they are correctly understood and accepted.

2. See Introduction, pages v–vi.— TRANS.
3. Repetilov: A garrulous would-be revolutionary in *Woe from Wit*, a play in verse written by Alexander Griboyedov (1795–1829).— TRANS.

But if (like many others, for any number of reasons) we are unwilling to recognize the responsibility we bear for this present page of our history, if we attempt simply to forget these sufferings and to live as if nothing had happened, erasing them from our history, as it were, then we are doomed. Then we shall again be obliged to continue between two parallel processes: the eradication of the smallest stirrings of the living soul and thought from above, and the swelling of impotent hatred and rage from below. In this way good will be repelled on both fronts, until "history repeats itself" and punishes us for our obduracy.

We must conserve and assimilate the vast spiritual strength for which we in our country have paid so dearly. We must transform it into an inward fortress of resistance to lies and violence, to the point of laying down our lives if necessary. And this transformation must take place within our souls.

It will be very difficult. Now especially, when the path of spiritual striving is in direct conflict with every contemporary aspiration of mankind; when "rising material demands" (egged on by every kind of advertising) and the capacity to fulfill those demands are regarded to all intents and purposes as the main criterion of the level of a society's development; when incessant interference — by television, cinema, sport and newspapers — drowns the inner voice. Now the accessibility of travel and entertainment acts as a constant distraction from our inner affairs. The world has never seemed so noisy. Never has the entertainment industry, the industry of the spiritual pabulum of "mass information," so completely dominated mankind. This is why men feel such terrible spiritual chaos inside them, this is why they have lost touch with reality, this is why truth has become so dangerously relative. Genuine reality and genuine activity have been hunted down and cast out. Waves of aimless external irritation toss us hither and thither on the surface of the sea of life.

Christianity teaches the concept of "abstinence" — the cleansing of the soul, spiritual repose, the aspiration toward inner simplicity and harmony. We should begin with this, for only to the abstinent spirit is truth revealed, and only truth liberates. There is no need to begin with external solutions. We must achieve the sort of spiritual condition that enables solutions to be dictated from within by the immutable laws of compassion and love. Mysterious inner freedom, once achieved, will give us a sense of community with everybody and responsibility for all. So long as we achieve it in fact, not merely in wishful thinking, everything else will come of its own accord.

Without it, on the other hand, any social order will be no more than "iron and clay mixed by human hands."

But we are confused. In the search for a solution our eyes habitually turn toward the West. There they have "progress" and "democracy." But in the West the most sensitive people are trying, with similar alarm and hope, to learn something from us. They assume, probably not unreasonably, that our harsh and oppressed life has taught us something that might be able to counteract the artificiality and soullessness of their own world — something that they have lost in all their worldly bustle.

So perhaps if we can assimilate our experience and somehow put it to use, it may serve to complement Europe's experience. Then Russia will escape Chaadayev's [4] bitter prophecy of being nothing but a yawning void, an object lesson to other nations.

Nestor the chronicler [5] compared our people to the "eleventh hour laborers." If instead of standing around in the marketplace we answer the call of the Vineyard Owner, we shall not be too late at the end of the day to receive the same wage as the rest.

4. P. Y. Chaadayev (1793–1856), a pro-Catholic political thinker whose *Philosophical Letters* circulated clandestinely in early-nineteenth-century Russia. After one of them was published in 1836, Tsar Nicholas I placed Chaadayev under permanent house arrest and ordered medical supervision of his mental health.
5. Nestor was a Kievan monk who compiled the best known of all the Russian medieval chronicles, "The Primary Chronicle," in the eleventh century.

Russian Destinies

F. KORSAKOV

To the memory of Father Pavel Florensky

Father Pavel Florensky, who was murdered in one of the labor camps of northern Russia, so that to this day the whereabouts of his grave is unknown to the world, wrote these words sixty years ago, in his book The Pillar and Ground of the Truth: "As the end of History draws nearer, the domes of the Holy Church begin to reflect the new, almost imperceptible, rosy light of the approaching Undying Day." Father Pavel is obviously not speaking here merely in metaphors and images; his words are the testimony of a Russian genius to the reality and truth perceived by him and embodied in his published works, and show an intensity of thought in the search for Christ which is amazing even for the Russian cultural tradition.

But then, does the passing of sixty years mean anything at all in the context of such meditations on the nature of time? And are we able to say that the Undying Day has come nearer to us, in that what Russia has experienced in this century has given us a truer ability than before to sense the approach of that day, and to see more clearly the full extent of our sin in its impending fire? What significance can sixty years have, when to God a thousand years are as one day? Or have the hardships endured by the Russian people altered the true value of time, since the people's soul cries out for an end to its sufferings?

We should, of course, recognize the temptation inherent in such thoughts — the temptation to exaggerate our own troubles, to ignore the last two thousand years of human history, to forget that "the Lord chastises those whom he loves" (Heb. 12:6). But if you have not yet realized this, what are you to do when it is considered normal to pour abuse on all that is holy, and the savagery and corruption permeating our society are thought merely matters for political and philosophical speculation? What are you to do when you and your people seem to have come to the limit of human endurance, when you find yourself facing a blank wall that looms in front of you and stops all light from reaching you, when your knocking cannot be heard, when your cries are stifled as if by cotton wool, when you are already prepared to end it all, to die, even though you realize quite clearly the senselessness of self-immolation?

But one day, in the midst of your utter confusion and despair, you are suddenly brought up short by the light of an inner peace seen on the face of a chance acquaintance. A long time passes before you understand the providential meaning of this encounter, when you see passing before your mind's eye the same kind of faces one by one — faces which have accompanied every step of your life from its very beginning, and you relive each one of those encounters. You remember the girl soldier who shared a small piece of bread and a mug of soup with you when you were a hungry little boy, you remember the old man in a railway carriage, crossing himself as a church flashed by outside the icy carriage window, the old woman in black who held out her chapped, grimy palm to you. You remember also the books you always loved, not knowing why you loved them — books that breathed eternal peace, rending your soul with the sufferings of those who sought God, wrestled with God and lived in His presence. Then you visualize scenes from the history of the land where you were born and bred, and where you will be buried. And everything that formerly seemed nothing but a senseless accumulation of facts and events, the manifestation of an evil power, a fatal combination of circumstances or merely proof of the ambition, cruelty and pettiness of those in power, the stupidity and savagery of the men who for some incomprehensible reason existed around you — all this is unexpectedly illumined by the lofty concept of Destiny. You now understand His purpose in all things — in the flying snow that for half a year covers woods and pastures, cities and rivers, in the golden magnificence of autumn, in the wonderful skies of Russia — pale, cold, appeased. You re-create all this later, much later, bit by bit, drawing it from the innermost recesses of your soul, but this "new life," this unending work, begins at that moment when you submit, for the first time, to the involuntary promptings of your troubled soul and step across the threshold of a church, still glancing timidly at the others kneeling there, who have not entered merely on a passing impulse.

What have you brought with you into this church? What have you left outside its portals? Can you, having confessed and partaken of the Holy Sacraments, renounce everything that formerly filled your life — its problems, its pleasures and disappointments, its varied experiences, your own already formed and cherished ideas of good and evil, the weariness of spirit born of the world's cares? These are some of the most complex questions of our time. Today, when the ice covering the entire length and breadth of the huge landmass called Russia is in the process of breaking up, a process that has been going on underground, unnoticed for many long years, at a time when mere fashionable interest and curiosity about religion have been swept away by a genuine and avid demand for the Word of God, when priests are run off their feet trying to satisfy the spiritual needs of their flock and still fall short of the demand — today all the complicated and difficult, traditional and at the same time sharply topical, accursed Russian questions mingle and fester in this larger question.

The efficacy of the sacrament of confession necessarily requires the destruction of the strong attraction which the sin you have overcome still has for you, the effacement and scouring out of that sin from the penitent soul. Everything that is of the self, that "is not of my Heavenly Father's planting" (Matt. 15:13) must be rooted out, torn up and abandoned forever, for it is in any case subject to the threat of eternal annihilation and the agony of a second death.

Can we really imagine that this process of the soul cleansing itself of festering sin by purging itself with fire while still here in this life occurs as a single, rounded-off act of baptism or return to the Church? Does the egoistic self, having lodged securely in your soul, really depart so easily?

The genuflecting Church floats in flickering candlelight, which lights up the meek faces of those "fools in Christ" with whom you have lived side by side your whole life but whom you have never noticed; the words of the prayers, which you do not know, slip past you without entering your heart, and in your soul, still so full of impurity and self-love, a suppressed rebellion begins to stir.

But why, when you have resolved on such an incredible act of heroism, destroying your whole former life, surmounting the disgusted incredulity of your former friends and workmates, when you have renounced (as you imagine) the world and its temptations and entered the Church with (as you think) your soul bared — why are you not received with joy and gratitude, like the prodigal son, why is there no fatted calf, why is there no welcome for such courage on your part, why does no one talk to you in a language you can understand, why do they take no notice of your readiness to sacrifice yourself, nor have any respect for your learned theories combining the latest achievements of the natural sciences with modern philosophical ideas, nor your irony or artistic taste? Why does the Church seem to see no difference between you who have come so tragically to help and "save" the Church, and some old woman merely "seeking salvation" for herself through the Church in her dull, traditional way? Perhaps it is true, after all, that the Church fears those in power, that she bows to the earthly authorities and shows her gratitude to the atheist Moloch for not interfering with her and sparing her for the time being by pretending not to see that, in essence, she has nothing to offer twentieth-century man, that she is indifferent to the real suffering of our time, that she loves abstractions and provides little more than consolation and escape from the world, that all she insists on is the formal loyalty of her parishioners. Anyway, who are all these priests, archpriests and metropolitans — what are their real relations with the regime? Surely the government, which persecutes liberal thought, has some reason for closing its eyes to the existence of this undoubtedly archaic and alien institution?

The last thing I want to do is analyze the phenomenon of the "consciousness of the intelligentsia" — even in its novel situation as today's novitiate. The journal *Vekhi* [1] exhausted the subject of the decay of the intelligentsia; and the subsequent fate of the intelligentsia, unwilling to heed the warnings and prophecies of *Vekhi*, evolved exactly as the latter had predicted. The disease had already been diagnosed and the antidote indicated. So let the dead bury their dead. . . .

Nevertheless, this problem has not been solved, it still exists and you can't get away from it. Our vast country lies silent, but voices speak in its name. Some are purified and matured by sorrow and suffering, but other voices can be heard in whose modern, humanistic phraseology the inexperienced may not immediately recognize the same old devil with his horns and hooves, the same old Peter Verkhovensky,[2] with his old collection of nostrums, insolence and thoughtless ignorance.

Our land longs for the Word; its churches have been destroyed and desecrated, but Bibles and Gospels are still as much in demand on the black market as the works of modern poets. However, this happens only in Moscow and in the large towns; in the provinces, believers are reduced to blotting out the antireligious patter in atheist pamphlets, leaving only the quotations from the Scriptures intact. I cannot forget

1. See Introduction, pages v–vi.— TRANS.
2. One of the principal characters in Dostoyevsky's novel *The Possessed*. —TRANS.

the old man I saw on the steps of a Moscow church. "Christian people," he was saying, "I'm from Kursk — everything we had there has been burned. Couldn't anyone give me just one small book about God — please, in the name of Christ!"

But we have no interest in such places as Kursk and Mtsensk. After half a century of punishment for being carried away by our own personal experiences, we still continue to suffer only on our own behalf, imagining our problems to be the only ones worthy of attention and sympathy. All that stirs us is our unquenchable thirst for instant justice, we continue to nurse our own heroism, knowing nothing of true suffering — the source of that peace and light endlessly irradiating the Russian Orthodox Church. We are always beginning from a tabula rasa, always inventing new toys, but our indifference and lack of respect for the riches we already possess is not a sign of our broad-mindedness, but of unforgivable ignorance and insensitivity, which can no longer be borne and should no longer be admired. We have no sooner stepped over the threshold of the Church than, even before falling on our knees before its holiness, we venture to begin "feeding" the Church with the intelligentsia's nonsensical moralism, handing out the same old anti-Christian structure and forgetting the long road already traveled by the Russian intelligentsia, from the "childlike prattle" of Belinsky [3] to the insolence of Pisarev,[4] and from the armed bullying of the Bolsheviks to the empty "liberal thought" of today. Knowing nothing of true culture ourselves, we cut up its living body with the frivolity of a Khlestakov: [5] we swear by the names of Rublev,[6] Pushkin, Dostoyevsky and Blok,[7] while at the same time rejecting

3. V. G. Belinsky (1811–1848), the leading critic of the early nineteenth century and a champion of liberalism and socially committed literature.— TRANS.
4. D. I. Pisarev (1841–1868), a radical literary critic who considered himself one of Belinsky's heirs and became the apostle of Nihilistic materialism.— TRANS.
5. The hero of Gogol's *The Inspector-General*.— TRANS.
6. Andrei Rublev (1370–1430), a monk and Russia's greatest icon painter.— TRANS.
7. Alexander Blok (1880–1921), celebrated Symbolist poet and prominent Russian literary figure in the period leading up to the prominent revolution.— TRANS.

St. Sergius of Radonezh,[8] St. Serafim of Sarov,[9] the Fathers of Optyna [10] and Father Pavel Florensky, without whom a full understanding of the nature of their contemporaries' genius is hardly possible. Insisting that the Revelation, the Word, all that the Divine Liturgy and the writings of the Holy Fathers contain, are not enough to satisfy contemporary philosophers and contemporary man in general, we appeal to "contemporary thought" — to Western philosophy, the Enlightenment and humanism, forgetting that all the wise words of the Enlightenment led only to the Paris Convention and the guillotine, even as the selfless purity of the Russian Nihilists and the People's Will [11] group led to the Lubyanka [12] and to Kolyma.[13]

It is quite possible to imagine a model of this kind of probably quite unsanctified "return" to religion, to faith and the Orthodox Church. Such a "conversion" would not involve any doubt as to the truth of the intelligentsia's secular faith, but would be rather a renunciation of the intelligentsia environment with its self-satisfied confidence in itself. This is the same path of pride, but one which reflects a despair of really changing anything in our monstrous reality. It is the path of compromise and coming to terms with oneself — the exchange of one set of concepts for another, the interpolation of

8. A fourteenth-century monk who founded the famous Monastery of the Holy Trinity northeast of Moscow in 1337 and spearheaded a monastic revival through his example of asceticism and toil.— TRANS.
9. A nineteenth-century monk who revived the tradition of asceticism and self-renunciation in the Russian monasteries and emphasized personal humility and service to the people.— TRANS.
10. The name given to the monks of Optyna Monastery south of Moscow in the nineteenth century. The most famous of them was Father Ambrose, portrayed as Father Zossima in *The Brothers Karamazov*. The monastery was regularly visited by prominent intellectuals of the time, including Dostoyevsky, Tolstoy, and Vladimir Solovyov.— TRANS.
11. The name of a militant revolutionary organization established in 1879 with the object of overthrowing tsarism. It was responsible for the assassination of Tsar Alexander II in 1881.— TRANS.
12. The most notorious of the Soviet secret police prisons and the one to which most of the prominent victims of Stalin's purges were sent. It houses the headquarters of the secret police and is situated on Dzerzhinsky Square in the center of Moscow.— TRANS.
13. See note on page 146.— TRANS.

a certain attractive symbolism and of a beautiful metaphorical language into the commonly accepted, boringly familiar way of looking at the world. At the same time, nothing much seems to change, least of all "I Myself," with my freedom-loving, struggling soul's vast experience of life, my set code of morals, standards and truth, my great wealth of knowledge of the latest twentieth-century achievements, which surpass all previous achievements of human culture and have managed to throw off the dross of two thousand years of superstition. Besides, when I come to the Church I come into contact with the mysterious life of the people who, strangely enough (probably because of the humility and slavish obedience they have been endlessly praised for), have preserved this decaying institution in all its poetic charm. I am no longer alone, no longer one of a group of "heroes" (for whom, as the terrible past and recent experiences have shown, the road to betrayal and treachery is so simple and easy). How tempting it is now to use this beautiful ancient institution as a vehicle for one's own beneficial aims, to enrich it with modern intellectual insight, to shake up its hoary ideas and from here, from the eminence of the pulpit, to address — not the same old crowd of like-minded associates, with their sordid affairs and intrigues, but the people themselves, the whole wide country, those whom their entire history has taught to listen and to preserve the Word spoken here. After all, like Tolstoy, I have not "gone out of my mind" so that, like some old woman, I seriously believe that one and three are the same, that the world was created in six days, that angels and devils actually exist — but I "accept" the rules of the game, sanctified by centuries, I am ready even to gulp down wine diluted with water and chew dry bread "cut in the proper way," for I am convinced that all those around me "know the truth" as well as I do. Nor am I being sacrilegious when I do this — I observe the ritual in order to be not alone but with all the others: faith demands such garments, so I squeeze myself into them, for I have no other choice.

However, if in spite of my squeamishness I am willing to climb into a garment so worn-out and smelling of a thousand

years of ignorance, and, like everyone else, to wear it pretending that I find it light and comfortable, then I am in no
condition to undergo an inner transformation. I cannot "understand" — and so accept — that, for instance, the Orthodox
Church is the only true Church, that all other Christians —
and also unbelievers (about whose personal merits I may be
quite convinced) — are living in a state of untruth, enticed
and deluded by the devil, that their beliefs are definitely
heretical or misguided and have no place either in the
Church or in my consciousness; and that, for some reason, I
must unfailingly deny the relevance of their "truth" and their
"faith." Why? We cross ourselves in one way — they cross
themselves in another; they walk around the altar in a different direction, or sing "alleluia" differently; they have a
pope — we have a patriarch; for us the Spirit proceeds from
the Father, not from the Father and the Son. But is there not
something more important which reconciles all these differences? Have I really come here to exchange external injustice for an even more repugnant injustice within the
Church? Because I cannot live freely, am I to renounce the
right to think freely? Surely this leads straight to the burnings at the stake with which they used to regulate the truth in
the reign of good Tsar Aleksei Mikhailovich and which have
now, in our more humane age, been so easily replaced by
labor camps and long term prisons. And that is why I insist
on the necessity of ecumenism as a first principle — before I
have yet had a chance to become either Orthodox, or Catholic, or Protestant, with no understanding of the nature of our
tragic schisms, for I see no sane explanation for them that
would correspond to the spirit of the present age, except for
Tolstoy's formulation: "The Summ hussars consider the best
regiment in the world to be the Summ hussars, while the
yellow Uhlans consider the best regiment to be the yellow
Uhlans."

This model only superficially resembles L. Tolstoy's *Confession*. Tolstoy wrote that the family, science, business and
the salvation of mankind are "all illusion and stupid illusion," that "there is nothing humorous or witty, everything is

just cruel and stupid." All religions and philosophies — from Solomon, Buddhism and the Greek sages to Kant and Schopenhauer — were subjected by him to a frantic rational analysis and only confirmed the monstrous absurdity of life, reviewed as they were by a man who could not renounce his own rationalism. The way of faith, of attempting to understand a characteristic of consciousness shared by millions and millions of ordinary people — not "philosophers and learned men" who found a meaning in some incomprehensible "despicable false learning" — this was in fact the only way for Tolstoy, the only possibility of escape from the rope, the knife, or the railway track. The tragic events of his life — his denial of the Church and its Truth, his inability to understand the Incarnation and the Resurrection, original sin and the Atonement, his confusion when faced by the sacraments — reveal that same old tendency to deify Man, with his inability to resist temptation, that same alluring path of unswerving cast-iron logic, leading ultimately to the Antichrist and the Grand Inquisitor. In spite of this, Tolstoy's fearless integrity held no trace of self-interest, or, rather, of calculation; his soul passionately longed to find some kind of meaning in life that would not be destroyed by the inevitability of death.

In the modern model I have given there is, in spite of the similarity of the conclusions drawn, no trace of Tolstoy's tragic ability to grasp the essence of a question. Nowadays there is no attempt to understand another's experience, not even that of a close friend; everything takes the form of a fashionable world-weariness and the moralizing sophistries of Ivan Karamazov returning his "ticket." Before I have even crossed the threshold of the Church, I hold her responsible for a child's tears, not taking the trouble to consider that, outside the Church, I will never find a meaning for those tortured tears, and so will not even be able to wipe them away. I refuse to believe that my moralism, my thirst for "justice," my dream of founding a heaven on earth, has already resulted in our present-day ocean of tears, and that — as stated in the sequel to *Vekhi, De Profundis* [14] — there are grounds for regarding even Tolstoy's worldly moralism, so pure and unselfish compared with my own, as one of the sources of Russian revolutionary philosophy, with its demand for the immediate establishment of goodness on earth, and of the actual results of that demand.

One can also imagine a slight variation of the same model. I come to the Church, fully armed with faith and learning, having despaired of my former life and broken away from it. I know how much I shall benefit from my return to the Church, I have thrown all my energy and maturity of spirit into it, and the words of revelation, the ways and traditions of Orthodoxy, have become for me as unquestionably true as the laws of arithmetic. I understand the importance of the outward forms, but I still think it unreasonable that I, with all I have to offer, should be standing here in the crowd with those who are truly unenlightened, who understand nothing but the service; surely it is absurd to consider me no different from them? Besides, do I really need an intermediary in a priest's vestment, of whose human weaknesses I am in no doubt, and whose learning and spiritual gifts I have every reason to suspect? I am not, of course, a Protestant, I am aware of the undying eminence of the Mystical Church, but in this situation, considering this Church's actual empirical insignificance and slavish dependence on an atheist power, what spiritual food can it give me? And already, at this point, despite knowing about it, I have forgotten that pride of spirit is one of the worst sins, "the first and last of all evils" (St. Gregory Sinaiticus), that a little humility and meekness are worth more than all my learning, and already I want to retreat, to stay in myself! So the world of my soul becomes for me the only Church, and this shrine has nothing to do with the insignificance of historical Russian Orthodoxy. I intend to sacrifice myself for the Orthodox, to pray for their sins: they would not understand freedom, even if it were given to them, and in fact they don't need it — for how many centuries has

14. See Introduction, page vii.— TRANS.

the obedient flock consigned its would-be saviors to the flames! And so on. From here the path leads straight to the feverish fantasies of Ivan Karamazov.

However, Tolstoy and the heroes of Dostoyevsky were not the first to put their morality before humble submission to Providence. Over two thousand years ago there lived in the land of Uz a man whose sufferings and the injustice he clearly perceived caused him openly to challenge the Lord.

"Perish the day when I was born, and the night on which it was said 'A man is conceived' ": so began the revolt of Job. "Why do the wicked enjoy long life, hale in old age . . . they live to see their children settled, their kinsfolk and descendants flourishing; their houses are secure and safe. . . . They drive off the orphan's ass and lead away the widow's ox. . . . They jostle the poor out of the way. . . . The destitute huddle together . . . naked and bare they pass the night, in the cold they have nothing to cover them. . . . Far from the city they groan like dying men, and like wounded men they cry out, but God pays no heed to their prayer. . . ."

This is the tragic fate of Job, deprived of everything he possessed, covered in boils and sores, sitting in the dust, crying out for death and shaking his fists at the Lord, with his horrified friends trying to stop him. Surely Job's fate can be seen as a prophetic analogy to the fate of Russia throughout her history, to the fate of her great men and of her prophets and of thousands of simple people, who summoned God and reproached Him, who threatened Him, collected "evidence" against Him and drew up a "bill" for Him to settle — for a child's tears and for Kolyma, for the murder of the emperor and of his mother, for the destruction of sacred treasures, the corruption of the entire nation, and their own hopeless state?

It would seem that Chaadayev [15] was right when, a hundred and fifty years ago, he proclaimed that our nation does not constitute a "uniquely necessary portion of mankind," but that it exists merely in order to "provide, at some time, some great object lesson for the world." How incongruous, though significant, that these words did not so much

15. See note 4 on page 150.— TRANS.

strike holy terror into his contemporaries and following generations of Russians, as provoke in them a kind of morbid
thrill.[16] And in general, pouring abuse on your own country,
despising its history and the character of its people, excitedly
reviling all that any other country would traditionally have
been proud of — all this has been considered fashionable in
our country for many decades now. However, this perhaps
shows the greatness of our people, the kind of character they
have: a great people does not fear abuse and they will readily
laugh at themselves, even in the most distorted of mirrors, for
they know even worse things about themselves — and in this
simplicity lies the strength of a nation, the knowledge of
something else within itself, which cannot be seen except
through the eyes of love. "Don't be downcast," says one of
Leskov's [17] heroines, "other lands survive through being
praised, but ours is strengthened even by abuse."

What happens, however, when such abuse is not the result
of indifference and superficiality but is uttered by a genius,
and is echoed by people whose integrity and nobility of mind
cannot be doubted? "Love of one's country is a beautiful
thing," wrote Chaadayev, "but love of truth is even more
beautiful." So what is this truth, what does it consist of and
why should the Russian oppose it so heatedly to his country?

A few months before his death, while in the most difficult
circumstances in both his public and private life, Pushkin
wrote to Chaadayev after reading his pamphlet: "Although
personally I have a sincere affection for the Emperor, I am
far from enthused by all that I see around me. As a writer, I
am irritated, as a man with prejudices I am offended, but I
swear on my honor that I would not change my country for
anything on earth, nor wish for a different history than the
history of our ancestors, the history God gave us."

What are we to call this — ignorance, indifference, self-

16. "How sweet it is to hate your motherland and long for its destruction" — these are the words of Pecherin, one of the first Russian emigrants,
who later became a Catholic monk in the West.
17. Nikolai Leskov (1831–1895), novelist and short-story writer, noted for
the richness of his colloquial style and extensive knowledge of middle- and
lower-class life.— TRANS.

defense or perhaps even self-interest? Today we would call it ignorance, for a man's relations with the emperor, however involved, and the writer's troubles, however weighty the troubles of a genius might be, and some personal "prejudices" — what are these compared with our present *knowledge,* when we have been given *The Gulag Archipelago* and when, tomorrow perhaps, the Lubyanka archives will be thrown open so that the earth itself will shudder. Perhaps, perhaps, but can evil really be measured by quantity alone? And will the unloosed secrets of those bloodstained cellars really weigh more heavily than the tears of one tortured child? Can we find anything new to say to the Lord today which the man from the land of Uz, trembling in his frenzy, did not throw at Him, despite the piety he had shown before his tribulations came upon him? Or have we no longer any strength left, have we come to the limit of our endurance? "Who is this, whose ignorant words cloud my Design in darkness?"

The Lord knew and loved His servant Job, and marked him out by testing him. The Lord appeared to him out of the whirlwind, so that Job not only heard Him with his own ears but was also enabled to see Him. And Job repudiated what he had said and repented in dust and ashes. Can we still not see the finger of God pointing at us? Were the monsters Behemoth and Leviathan not enough of a revelation for us? And do we not recognize in today's events the whirlwind, in which the sound of a Voice (and not only a Voice) should be clearly audible to us? Do we still refuse to hear with our ears and see with our eyes, our hearts trembling at last in our unfathomable guilt for the blood that continues to gush and gush from the wounds of our Savior — can we still not see the path that is so clearly mapped out for us?

That path is straight and stony, it shines through fog, smoke and blood, so ineffably leading to the land which can only be reached through love that it would take a truly clouded mind to mistake it, walk past it or stray from it. Clearly visible under the stars, it is precisely etched across the centuries, leading from one great trial to the next and even harsher tribulation, and on the bends, like landmarks or signposts pointing the right way, stand churches, saints, wandering pilgrims and prophets. This path is like a flowing river, sweeping some things into its stream, casting others aside, but never drying up, even when the going gets so hard that it seems to have completely disappeared in blood-colored mist, and the Lord seems to have forgotten and abandoned this world. But the river keeps on flowing, its course has been set for eternity. And this miracle is no mere metaphor: the Russian Orthodox Church was made manifest to the world a thousand years ago — she survived the Tartar invasion and Peter the Great, and still exists today. And let every unbeliever place his hands in the gaping wounds of that Church's body. She stands immutably in the place where she arose, God's witness and God's Design — for nothing can distort her sacraments or corrupt her teachings.

This is indeed an enigma and a mystery, a miracle, which has borne witness so many times already that "my Father has never yet ceased His work and I am working too" (John 5:17). Although we touch upon the miraculous here, we are unable to understand its mystery, which for so many centuries has disturbed the rest of the world existing within an entirely different and more open framework. However, it is precisely the impossibility of finding a logical explanation for this reality that constitutes the Church's mysterious secret and explains the Russian's inability to tear either himself out of the Church or the Church out of himself. All the obvious advantages of that apparently open system are constantly being nullified and exhausted, and we seem to see those wonderful well-meaning impulses going up in smoke before our very eyes, so that man is brought back again and again to compromising with the age-old temptations. Whereas here everything remains for us as it has always been — each movement of the spirit, our weaknesses and our achievements, the fields around us, our mystical ties with the whole of this suffering world and with everyday life, which we can hardly escape. It all remains and, like a grain of corn, dies in the earth in order to bear much fruit; it remains and escapes into the atmosphere, together with the soul that is so hated in this world, and is "kept safe for eternal life" (John 12:25). And this is the reason why you cannot leave the Church, because your suffering, which in a moment of weakness makes you abandon her, remains within her and cannot go with you. You yourself become enmeshed in rusty barbed wire and what the outside world perhaps sees as a mere change of place, of climate or of material circumstances, a journey, here in fact becomes flight. And it is perfectly true that you cannot get away from that fact. This is indeed the Truth, that country "more beautiful" than ours, and if we listen to the rumble of the earth muttering beneath our feet and in a moment of revelation glimpse the last thousand years flashing past, we understand that there is no fatal contradiction in all this, only the dawning antinomy of love, for as someone quite truthfully said: "To live in this country is impossible; here you can only seek salvation."

As we have already said, this path has its beginnings in the extremes of despair, when you have not yet found the Truth but you know you cannot live without it. You give up all else for her, your future, your old ties and relationships, your heartfelt desire for great deeds, and you ask nothing in return — no promises, no proofs, no earthly treasures. You forget your own self, you cease to complain and grieve over your own burdens and failures; instead, you spend all your time cleansing yourself of the filth of subjectivity and pride, of pseudofreedom with all its enslaving temptations, the temptations of the age. Already, without your knowledge, while you are scrabbling on the brink of the abyss and stumbling in the dark, a light, twinkling like a precious stone, has been growing within you. You step across the threshold of the Church as her humble son.

"Day by day through the centuries, the Church has been gathering in its treasures. . . . The tears of the pure in heart have fallen on it like precious pearls. Both heaven and earth have made their contributions of joy in the communion with God, of sacred agonies of keen repentance, fragrant prayer and quiet yearning for heaven, eternal seeking and eternal finding, gazing into the unfathomable depths of eternity, and childlike peace of mind. . . . The centuries passed and all this increased and accumulated. . . ."

You fall on your knees, and are not alone . . . you are already in the Truth, and every spiritual effort you make, every sigh falling from your lips, brings to your aid the entire reserve of beneficial strength stored here.

It sounds lovely, they will say, but is quite absurd, for if the eighteenth century only contrived to ridicule it, the twentieth century has spread bloodstained filth all over it. Yet the Truth lives on, the same today as two thousand years ago, in a church full of kneeling worshipers, and though the priest may be unworthy to celebrate the Mass, angels celebrate it for him. The gates of Hell cannot prevail against the Church. You have no way back now, for if the Truth does not exist, your existence has no meaning. So you go on repeating and whispering the words your countryman left for you and paid for with his life in one of the unknown camps of the north. You are no longer concerned with your adversaries — you have parted company with them forever: "Steer clear of foolish speculations, genealogies, quarrels and controversies over the law; they are pointless and unprofitable" (Titus 3:9).

You are not alone, because beside you, cursed by men but not forgotten by God, Who has manifested His Will through it, stands your whole country, which throughout the ages has always stored all its spiritual treasures — its culture, its great achievements and its holy relics — here in the Church. You are needed by your nation — not by those who live only in fear of her, who know nothing of her past and care nothing for her future, for whom the present consists only of themselves. You are needed by the Church, and thus by its every member, for "all of us, united with Christ, form one body" (Rom. 12:5). You are needed by your country — by Russia.

Meanwhile, outside the Church walls a kind of unceasing witches' Sabbath seems to be going on: aging executioners are pensioned off and replaced by hypocrites who are ready — in the right circumstances and at the first sign — to take up their predecessors' old habits. The tide of accusations, yielding to force, subsides, only to rise again at the first smell of weakness. Purity and simplicity yield to cynicism and calculation, but later return armed with new tactical weapons. Heroism appears in so many disguises — from the most noble to the most openly selfish — that its true nature can scarcely be distinguished: wounded pride, conceit, hysteria, defiance that is frightened of its own shadow, the desire to settle accounts, inflamed ambition, undisguised opportunism, the fear of being passed by, left out or behind, curiosity, pillage, speculation — what a variety of apparel, adornments and roles, what tender solicitude it displays for the welfare of the despised people and their culture! What thunderbolts are loosed against the indifference and cowardly habits concealed beneath the traditional, centuries-old, tried and tested slave armor that openly calls itself the salvation of the individual soul, or else masquerades in the long-since-compromised religious robes of collaborationism or pitiful otherworldly loyalties. The blustering self goes on the rampage; intoxicated with its own freedom, it has no need of the Sole Way or of God's Law. The Absolute yields place to relativity, in which even conscience sinks; individuality disappears and man no longer makes a free choice, but has it made for him: profit, safety, the opinion of others, good relations with someone, praise or blame — like fairground demons they mechanically seize the next victim in line and the machinery goes into action: promises, threats, sops to hidden passions or ambitious designs. As if we had absolutely no Law at all, as if the Way had not been shown to us and no Commandments given us, obedience to which requires true courage and heroic zeal of man, qualities which do not and cannot exist in the brassy fairground obsessed by its own passions.

The praying Church floats in candlelight, the visages of the saints painted on the dark icons in the gilded frames come to life and intone, together with the rest of the Church, the ringing proclamation from the choir of the Beatitudes, announcing their recognition of the Truth in this world and of eternal life in the next: the poor in spirit, the sorrowing, the meek, those who hunger and thirst after righteousness, the merciful, the pure in heart, the peacemakers, those who are persecuted for the sake of righteousness, the slandered and abused, those who rejoice because they suffer for the sake of Christ. They have already renounced their own selves and so have found inner courage and strength — we need so many more of them! In thinking of them, the true heirs and participants in the Heavenly Kingdom, we already see the "azure of eternity" which Father P. Florensky wrote about.

Is there anything in the world nobler or more difficult than this ineffable toil?

You walk out into the church porch, with the snow trickling slowly down from a gray sky, and then into the town that has expelled you from it, you go out to meet the people you have taken your leave of. You know that, as in the "last days" in the Apostle's words, "hard times" are approaching (but when have times ever been easy in Russia?). You go out into the town, where you still live; you walk through the crowd, through the whirling fairground, and how can you help but see it, hear it and be drawn into it? But even here, "do not be afraid of the sufferings to come," for God knows "your works" and "where you live; it is the place where Satan has his throne; and yet you are holding fast to my cause and do not deny your faith in me" (Rev. 2:10–13).

You will never be alone from now on, no matter what may happen to you. What does the fairground of this world and your whole former life mean to you, when you know that everything has been arranged in accordance with God's Word? Even the Apostle Paul had insufficient time to tell of all those who "were stoned, were sawed in two, were put to the sword, went about dressed in skins of sheep and goats, in poverty, distress and misery. They were too good for a world like ours. They were refugees in deserts and on hills, hiding in caves and holes in the ground. These also, one and all, are commemorated for their faith; and yet they did not enter upon the promised inheritance because, with us in mind,

God had made a better plan, that only in company with us should they reach their perfection" (Heb. 11:37–40).

They did not enter upon the promised inheritance because, with us in mind, God made a better plan. . . . And the town weeps, curses and raves. You have just emerged from the church, having stood through the Liturgy, prayed for all those whose good works you have remembered, and asked the Savior to forgive their sins and evil actions. You plow your own furrow, carry your cross, and no one can know the end of his journey. The deeds of every man will be revealed in the end, and then it will be too late to think again, for "what appears to some men as light, to others will be a burning fire, depending upon what material and qualities it finds in each" (the Blessed Gregory the Theologian). The Truth has been set down for eternity, and nothing can prevent its being loudly proclaimed on the appointed day. It exists even now and one day it will emerge into God's light, a terrible warning of the inescapability of judgment, both earthly and divine.

What then can you do, I ask once more, for if the divine judgment (which nothing can escape) is coming and if the Day, of which we can know nothing (even though the rosy glow of the domes of our churches is getting brighter and brighter), is nigh, then surely it is only through our own courage and endeavor that the earthly judgment can be made? Can we afford to put it off, shifting the responsibility onto other shoulders, knowing in the depths of our trembling souls that this Day must come (and what if it doesn't?). This is one of our most tragic problems. I cannot take it upon myself to resolve it, but I know for sure that it cannot be resolved by hatred, without an understanding love of the country in which we live, nor by separating our country and the Truth, with which it is inextricably linked (despite our terrible history and our fear-ridden present) by the very inexorability of its destiny. In the final analysis, your personal choice and path are nothing more nor less than your choice and path. But you are not alone — never forget that! Nor should you forget that "the Truth itself," as the Blessed Makary the Great has said, "impels man to seek the Truth." And please believe that "the God of Abraham, Isaac and Jacob," as Pascal put it, "and not the God of the philosophers and learned men" will come to you one day, will take you by the hand and guide you, if you truly wish it.

The Schism Between the Church
and the World

EVGENY BARABANOV

In every Mass we profess our faith in the one, holy, Catholic and apostolic Church. We believe in its holiness, for we see in it the image of Christ's presence. And here on earth we already touch the fullness of the life to come. But we are not alone. Among unbelievers too there are many who perceive in the word "Church" the reality of a certain unknown and higher life. A desire to approach this reality and somehow to come into contact with it draws them to the churches on Easter Eve. They wait patiently for midnight, when they will hear the distant singing from inside the church, when the worshipers will come out in procession, and the cry "Christ is risen!" will resound over the crowd. They wait for the accomplishment of the shining mystery which — who knows? — might draw them as well into this profound reality called the Church, admit them to it, unfold its secret and unite it with their own spiritual life. And those who take part in the mystery itself — those in communion with the glory of Christ — feel themselves victors. "Let God arise and may his enemies be dispersed," the believers sing with fervor. And in these paschal cries the Church seems to rise to its full height. The evil of the world, its darkness and mendacity, its sinfulness and violence, are vanquished by the Resurrection.

And the waves of universal renewal and joy emanating from the celebrants seem to take a hold on the unbelievers as well. The victory seems to become real and actual, not somewhere beyond the frontiers of time and space, but here, today, now.

But the everyday, earthly, human reality of the Church presents an agonizing contrast. And this contrast also starts with the building itself. In our country a church is a "place for the performance of the rite of a religious community." This community is registered by the organs of the state. And state functionaries are appointed to supervise its life. This supervision consists in making the "liturgical department" as spiritually isolated as possible, harmless and even comic, from the point of view of the ideology of the state. And all the participants in the "rite," the hierarchs, the priests dependent on them, and laymen — in other words all the other elements that constitute the Church — meekly accept this situation and seem fully reconciled to their dependence.

Let us not hasten to accuse the Church. The fact that it has been forced to go "whither it will not" might still not have done great spiritual harm. The problem lies in *how* we define our attitude to this bondage, *how* we manage to accommodate both it and the triumphant paschal strength and joy. Currently some Christians bear this enforced bondage like a heavy obligation "for the sake of the preservation of the Church," while others have got used to it, acquired a taste for it, and have perhaps even come to like the contrast.

But despite this manifest and indubitable submissiveness of the Church to the state, even people who are far from being Christians are expecting some general renewal in it. They want to see in the Russian Church an effective force that is capable of opposing mendacious ideological bureaucratism with genuine spiritual values, of affirming moral principles and slaking the people's thirst with the "water of life."

People who know ecclesiastical life well are usually less optimistic. Having experienced within themselves all the terrible ailments and dilemmas of contemporary ecclesiastical reality, they are inclined to think that the Church will only be able to have an impact on society when society itself grows sufficiently free and democratic to liberate the Church from the political fetters imposed by the state.

For the time being I shall not discuss which of these points of view corresponds more faithfully to reality. Those who see in Christianity the affirmation of an absolute truth about man and human society are undoubtedly right. And it is only on the basis of this higher truth that it is possible to warrant the exceptional value of man, the value of his life and what he creates. Christianity alone holds the key to the deepest meaning of social life, culture and husbandry. The history of the Christian nations has evolved in the search for this meaning, notwithstanding all their frustrations and failures. Such has been Russia's path as well, after adopting the Orthodox faith from Byzantium in the tenth century and through Christianity becoming a part of European culture. Learning, art, law, and the concept of the state were all given to us by Christianity. And throughout the years of tribal feuds, foreign invasions, domestic upheavals and crises it was the Russian Church that always preserved and maintained the living cultural tradition and was the foundation of the nation's and the state's integrity. In the feats of its saints and pious men the Russian people has never ceased to behold the unfading light of a higher moral truth, which became the object of a quest that permeates the whole of great Russian literature. And looking back we realize that Christian ideas and ideals lay beneath even those aspects of life and culture which, it would seem, were not related to them on the surface. We need not mention the heritage which has become an inalienable part of the spiritual life of all mankind: the cathedrals and icons, Sergius of Radonezh and Andrei Rublev,[1] the archpriest Avvakum [2] and Serafim Sarovsky,[3] Gogol and Dostoyevsky, Tolstoy and Solovyov,[4] the pleiade of twentieth-

1. See note 6 on page 156.— TRANS.
2. Archpriest Avvakum (1620–1681), leader of the "Old Believers," a group of schismatics who refused to accept the ecclesiastical reforms of Patriarch Nikon. His *Life* is a remarkable autobiographical account of his wanderings in exile in Siberia.— TRANS.
3. See note 9 on page 157.— TRANS.
4. Vladimir Solovyov (1853–1900), philosopher, mystic and poet who was

century thinkers and, finally, those recent innumerable martyrs whose hagiographies have not yet been written and who are remembered by only a few surviving eyewitnesses.

All this is so. And many who are troubled by the fate of the Russian Church and genuinely participate in contemporary Church life do not, of course, deny it. Without belittling the highest achievements of Christian culture, without doubting the transforming power of the "good news" of Christianity, they remind us of something else as well — of the profound and agonizing *crisis* which is gnawing away at the Russian Church from within.

After the dozens of years when martyrdom was passed over in silence, when hypocrisy and servility reigned, it was two valiant priests, Nikolai Eshilman and Gleb Yakunin, who first referred publicly to this crisis. In their "Open Letter" to Patriarch Alexius, sent in November 1965, they protested not only against the illegal actions of the leaders and officials of the Council for Religious Affairs — actions which grossly violated their own legislation — but also against the craven, hypocritical position adopted by the higher ecclesiastical administration. They showed convincingly how a significant part of the governing episcopate, with voluntary silence or cunning connivance, had assisted the atheists to close churches, monasteries and religious schools, to liquidate religious communities, to establish the illegal practice of registering christenings, and had yielded to them control over the appointment and transfer of priests.

That was roughly the time of the statements by Archbishop Ermogen, imprisoned in a monastery for his protests, Boris Talantov, who died in prison, the historian and publicist Anatoly Krasnov-Levitin, who was recently released from a labor camp, and many others.

Their voices sounded again in the Lenten letter from Alexander Solzhenitsyn to Patriarch Pimen.

The patriarch did not reply to Solzhenitsyn, but his si-

one of the founders of the Symbolist movement in Russia. His ideas have recently made a comeback with many dissidents in the Soviet Union. — TRANS.

lence, and the fact that he forbade the two priests to officiate in church any more, provide eloquent proof of the justice of these reproaches.

Both Solzhenitsyn and the authors of the "Open Letter" to Patriarch Alexius (this is where they part company from the all-understanding and passive "ecclesiastical realists"), not only bear witness to the truth, but also call for the vicious circle to be broken — for people to overcome the fetters of lies, fear, lack of faith, and connivance through personal sacrifice. It was a remarkable, deeply moral and indispensable summons. But why did these calls not find any response among the Christians of the Church? What stops us, evidently, is not just the sacrifice (Christianity is sacrificial through and through, the "idea" of sacrifice is accepted by all), but something else, something profounder that firmly, though perhaps not very obviously, holds us back. What is it?

Father Sergei Zheludkov, in his open letter to Solzhenitsyn, endeavored to indicate that the main reason we were deprived of the possibility of initiative and choice was the totalitarian system of our state ("a strictly uniformly organized System, administered from a unified Center"), in which the legal Church could not be an island of freedom.

"What remains for us to do in such a situation?" he wrote. "Should we say 'All or nothing?' Should we try to go underground, which in the present System is unthinkable? Or should we somehow go along with the System and use, as long as we can, those possibilities which are open to us? The Russian hierarchy took the second choice, and the result is the evil that is happening today. *But there was no other choice.*"

Father Zheludkov examines the crisis of our ecclesiastical life in the traditional framework of the opposition of Church and state. But to what extent can such an approach to the problem give an exhaustive answer?

I will not argue as to whether or not the possibility of another choice existed in the past. But why is it that today, as in the past, the possibilities of choice are limited to two alternatives: an underground Church or joining the system? Why exclude so completely what would seem to be a fully lawful and natural path — a legal and open demand for the rights which are indispensable for the normal existence of the Church? It is evident that this question, which is implied unequivocally in Solzhenitsyn's letter and which Father Zheludkov refrained from discussing, presupposes some clear and definite answer. And we all know what it is: neither the patriarch, nor the synod, nor the Congregation of Bishops has any intention whatever of trying to obtain from the government any rights for the Church. Most likely they will not even defend them, but will surrender them wordlessly, with all the rights they already have, at the first demand of some bureaucrat. That at least is what was happening until just recently. And it is clear that we are dealing not simply with "administration from a unified Center," but with something else, which we are unwilling to give serious thought to and which we do not consider needs discussion.

But let us be candid: our spiritual life is not totally subordinated to orders from the "Center," and in any case not directly. It was not, after all, orders from above but conformist inertia that led the ecclesiastical intelligentsia to react to the letters of the two Muscovite priests and of Solzhenitsyn as to a new sort of "spiritual pride" and "temptation of the devil." Many ecclesiastical Christians seriously and repeatedly reproached them for not believing in the power of prayer, for failing to understand the essence of the Christian life and interfering in other people's business, for proudly and arrogantly breaking the peace of the Church instead of meekly knowing their place "like everyone else." These words were uttered with *total sincerity*, with a feeling of profound grief and even of compassion for the "troublemakers." But surely there is something enigmatic about this sincere grief?

The position of the Church in a totalitarian world is indeed tragic, but this tragedy inclines us to forget that our present position is inseparably bound up with the tragedies of the past — which now seem to us to have been almost idyllic. And in attempting to comprehend the profound sources of the current tragedy of ecclesiastical Christianity, shall we not

177

be forced to recognize that the fateful malaise arose long before our "strictly uniformly administered social System"? If we trace the mainstream of our history back up toward its source, will we not find, under the glitter of gilded pomp, all those so familiar features? And preserving our academic impartiality, despite the seductiveness of past eras with their majestic attempts at theocratic kingdoms and church-state "symphonies," surely we shall be obliged to acknowledge that in Byzantium and Russia ideas about the Kingdom of God and the kingdom of Caesar too often merged and became interchangeable. The subjection of the Church by the state is an old eastern tradition. The Emperors Constantine, Constantius, Theodosius and Justinian (not to mention the later period) openly interfered with the internal life of the Church, suppressing, dictating and avenging. We venerate the holiness of the Nicene Creed, but our Christian conscience will never be reconciled to the conclusion of the Council of Nicaea, when the emperor exiled all the dissenters. That was not an isolated case — practically the whole historical path of Orthodoxy is peppered with them. For the state, as history has shown from the Edict of Milan to the present, it has always been desirable to have a "tame Orthodoxy" which would serve the ends of autocratic power.

Of course the "union" of the Church and the state under Constantine, and the Church-state "symphony," whose ideologist and legislator was Justinian, differ sharply from the contemporary state of affairs. The Byzantine state considered itself a Christian state and the emperors, when they subordinated the Church to their needs, nevertheless regarded themselves as the instruments of God's will. The organism of the Church did not so much suffer from the external force of the state as secretly go along with it, from inside, in a process of identifying the Church with the empire, of erasing the borders between Church and state, of affirming their close (too close!) unity. It was in this false perspective of an ostensibly self-evident "symphony" that the historical fate of the Russian Orthodox Church developed until the 1917 revolution. And when tsarism fell, the Church suddenly found itself face to face with a hostile, atheistic state which applied rather different methods from those of the Christian Emperors.

However, we are not saying this in order to attribute all the ills of the Church solely to the negative influence of the state on the Church. This has become the usual subterfuge and resort to which people have recourse in order to avoid having to resolve all the agonizing problems of contemporary Christianity. We are talking about something else — about our ecclesiastical consciousness as such, the essence of our religious attitude to the life of the world and of our attitude to the System. There is nothing surprising in the fact that an atheistic state tries to reduce the life of the Church to the rite alone, or, in the words of believers, to turn it into a "fulfiller of needs." From the point of view of the ideology ruling in our country, religion is the "opium of the people" and as such, as a result of the destruction of its "social roots" and the building of a new society, must sooner or later become superfluous and die off. But insofar as vestiges of religion continue to exist, believers are afforded the possibility of "performing the rite," a possibility guaranteed by the Constitution.[5] At the same time it is intended that, under the influence of new forms of social life and the propaganda of a materialistic philosophy, the "vestiges of religion" among our population will finally vanish. One must admit that such a point of view is certainly clear and logical. What is surprising, however, is that this particular ideological position should begin to sap our own ecclesiastical consciousness. It goes without saying that we do not profess the necessity for us ourselves to die off, but more often than not we do regard the present state of affairs as something natural and normal.

Here we enter a world of depressing paradoxes. The first of them says that the external limitations on the life of the Church correspond to the secret desires of many ecclesiastics. These desires stem from the assumption that the Mass in

5. Nevertheless, this possibility is strictly limited by the closure of churches, by the refusal to open new ones and the imposition of constraints on seminaries and monasteries.

itself *is* Christianity, and that the Christian needs nothing besides. All the rest merely distracts and disperses. "It is not our business to interfere where we are not asked. Not all the churches have been closed, thank God, the Mass is celebrated according to the book, lots of people attend on feast days, what else do we need?" And many people coming to Christianity today try to adopt this ideology as the genuine position of the Church, and, having adopted it, make a fetish of it and a compulsory standard.

But this is exactly what the state has been dinning into the Church for half a century: "You say you are not of this world, well then, there is nothing for you to do in this world. That is why I forbid you to 'set up benefit societies, cooperatives of industrial societies; to offer material aid to your members; to organize children's and young persons' groups for prayer and other purposes, or general biblical, literary or handicraft groups for the purpose of work or religious instruction and the like, or to organize groups, circles or sections; to arrange excursions and kindergartens, open libraries and reading rooms, organize sanatoria or medical aid' " ("Concerning religious societies," Resolution of the Central Committee, 8 April 1929, para. 17).

And as if in response to these *prohibitions* there arises from the very depths of the Church's consciousness, latently and sometimes unconsciously, a certain strange understanding of Christianity, a certain weird and wonderful ecclesiology. "You are right to prohibit these things. We only multiply our sins by occupying ourselves with good works. We have not yet learned how to pray — how could we get involved in kindergartens. The Church is for prayer, and not for worldly cares."

In an ecclesiology such as this there is of course no room for the problems of the Christianization of Russia. Moreover, there comes into being a peculiar kind of Christianity which many people try to identify with the essence of Orthodoxy, or to vindicate by reference to the exceptional nature of our socio-ideological system. We have already grown accustomed to apologetics of that sort. But are they needed today? And if so, by whom? The crisis in our ecclesiastical life has gone too far, but we are not alone in experiencing it. The Russian Church is displaying with particular vividness just a few of the symptoms of that universal malady which has today affected Christianity, with varying degrees of severity, all over the world. Therefore many of our problems need to be examined in a wider perspective, namely, that of the general crisis of the consciousness of the Church in the secular world.

There exists not only an opposition between the Church and the state, the Church and a totalitarian system, but also a more fundamental opposition, that between the Church and the world. It is precisely here that we find the origins of the radical division of Christian life into two independent spheres, the ecclesiastical and the sociohistorical. This division has never been confirmed by dogma, and the Church has more than once pronounced against the theoretical justification of this kind of dualism. All the same, the Christian world has lived in this duality not so much in terms of its dogma as psychologically. Even before the division became overt, this schism between the two spheres of life had an impact on the hearts and minds of Christians. It turned out to be too hard to accept all the complexities and antinomies of the Gospel. And that greatest of all temptations began to rear its head — that of "simplifying" Christianity, of reducing it from being a teaching about the new *life* to a mere caring for the salvation of one's own soul. As a result of this, the earthly aspect of life and the whole structure of social relations turned out to be empty and immune to the influence of the truth.

But the genuine hope of religion, the "good news" of Christianity about the Kingdom of God, which constitutes the basic content of the Gospel, is not limited to the world beyond the grave. The Kingdom of God which Christ taught us about "is not of this world" and will be realized in full only beyond the bounds of earthly history. But through Christ it entered this world and became its leaven. And it did not just "draw near," it "resides within us." And the beginning of this new all-embracing life is the Body of Christ, the Church. Through it God summons mankind and the world to perfection, to the fullness of absolute being. If the creative transformation of the world by man is seen as the realization of the Kingdom of God with Christ and in Christ, then the world is not only pardoned and justified, but is also being realized in the highest of its possible forms.

Entry into the Kingdom of God, however, and its actual realization are impossible without renunciation and the struggle with evil. Evil and sin are triumphant in this world; "the world resides in evil," and "the people have preferred darkness to light." And it is not only from the Gospel, but from all human history and from our own experience that we know of the "power of darkness" in the world and in ourselves. Evil hinders us from going toward the light, drags us away from it with thousands of enticements, temptations and illusions. That is precisely why the Gospel teaches us not to love this world or that which is in it.

These two aspects of the Christian attitude to the world, active participation in its transformation and renunciation of its temptations, turned out to be extremely difficult to reconcile. Heavenward aspirations often went hand in hand with execration of the earth. Too often the ideal of salvation was built on a foundation of inflexible renunciation of this world. Thus salvation itself was understood as an escape from the material world into a world of pure spirituality. This gave rise to contempt for the flesh, the belittling of man's creative nature and, as a necessary consequence, a special religious individualism. For some people these tendencies have to this day remained the sole signs of a Christian life.

But the history of Christianity has another side which can with justice be called its "spiritual success," although it was often accompanied by "historical failure." I refer to the experience of Orthodoxy, its spiritual breakthrough to the eternal Divine Light, the contemplation of that Light and the union with it of the whole human being. This experience is revealed to us not only in the "mental" prayer of the ascetics, not only in theological speculation and mystical illumination, but in the very structure of the liturgical mystery, which brings us to the mystery of mysteries, the Eucharist.

This is the peak of tension: God and man meet in the most intimate and unsunderable way. And in the incomparable joy of man's union with the absolute Reality, the God-man Jesus Christ, everything is filled with unutterable light and exultation. And one involuntarily feels an urge to remain stock-still, motionless, so as to retain in oneself this joyous light. This is the origin of the experience and excitement of eastern monastic asceticism, whose aim is "to commune with the Divine Light." In his profound silence and prayer the ascetic opens himself to the action of divine grace which, as St. Symeon the New Theologian writes, "appears with all quietness and joy, and this light is the harbinger of the eternal Light, the radiance on the face of eternal bliss. . . . The mind sinks into it, becomes suffused with brightness, turns into light and unites indivisibly with the very Source of Light. . . . In this state of illumination the ascetic flickers like a flame, and he is lit internally by the Holy Ghost, and looking outward from his own life he divines the mystery of his deification. . . ."

How similar that is to the ecstasy which, according to the Gospel, was experienced by Christ's disciples on Mount Tabor.

But when the Divine Light vanished, Christ together with his disciples came down into the world. He came to earth not only for the transfiguration on Tabor. Before Him still lay the Sermon on the Mount, the cure of the sick, the entry into Jerusalem, the Last Supper, the Agony in the Garden, Golgotha and, together with death, victory over its permanence: the Resurrection.

It is impossible not to see in this the image of the historical destinies of the Church. And the Apocalypse confirms it: the Christian Church is faced with struggle; the temptation of many and their desertion; constancy and labor; and the sum of its earthly history will be victory for Him Who conquered the world, and the eternal Light of Divine Glory. We have heard of this many times, but there is always the temptation to stop, to "wait until history ends," to put up a tent here and now and contemplate — if not in the desert, or on Mount Athos, then in church, during the Mass. In the contemplation of the Light it is easy to forget the world and its eternal movement. Hence that paradox, when a great spiritual accomplishment, the revelation to man of his high and holy task, involves a major historical failure. But is it only a historical failure? Christian kingdoms crumble and perish, local churches sicken and die under the yoke of dictators, the world is convulsed by bloody revolutions and inhuman regimes, and Christians seem to hear nothing of this.

We have a certain fatal insensitivity that is indestructible and amounts to almost a contempt for history. We often talk of the "radiant universality" of Orthodoxy, but we stare with bewilderment at those who ask us to embody its light in terrestrial historical reality. Hence the tradition in which Orthodox man found it easier and more preferable to discover himself in the world of nature than to strive for the construction of the City of God on earth. He made a distinction, which was not only religious but psychological, between nature and "this world," the cosmos and history. Contemplating the divine energies which permeate the created world, he lived in tune with the one and indivisible all-embracing cosmic mystery, in which there was no room for transformations and personal initiative. Everything there is sacred, unshakable and incontrovertible till the end of time. Hence the stability of the mystique of the kingdom and the sacralization of everyday life, clothed more often than not in the heavy robes of ritualized symbolism. The kingdom and everyday life are not historical categories, but religio-cosmic ones, and in Orthodoxy they have to this day remained external to the idea of the creative personality, its spiritual impulses and moral imperatives.

All this does not mean of course that in the Christian East the personality is dissolved in a cosmic-ancestral principle or is totally absent. On the contrary, both in Byzantium and in Russia an intense ascetic struggle took place for the formation of the Christian personality. The best evidence for this are the numerous "Paterikons" and "Lives of the Saints." But those were the peaks, surrounded on all sides by steep slopes. The challenging import of these feats of asceticism is usually objectivized further down, their explosive energy is dispersed and converted into an impersonal ideology of humdrum asceticism, and becomes a double external measure for the Christian life. The Christian saints who renounced the world and history were in fact laying down new paths for the life of the world and in so doing were actually making history. Their feat of self-renunciation and their victories over the power of this world were a daring challenge to the natural order of nature, a creative vanquishment of human limitations and an active struggle with evil. But all this has nothing to do with that pseudoascetic indifference to history and contempt for the world which form the basis for the ascetic ideology which has been adapted to the human sphere. In Russia this ideology has long since become the ruling one. Particularly popular have been the ideas of obedience and humble submission to the external authorities. They opened the door to a conservative conformism not only in personal ethics, but also in the life of the Church itself. The Church and the Eucharist have lost their meaning of an integrated and creative communal life; from being a "common cause" they have become a means of individual salvation. The Christian's own religiousness has become his chief preoccupation. And in this context the concept of the Christian's responsibility for the fate of the world has irrevocably lost all meaning.

It seems at times that we Christians deliberately do not wish to understand our historical failure or to admit our historical sins. We shift the blame onto anyone we can find — the state, atheism, secularization — but ourselves always remain only innocent victims. Our consciousness is still in thrall to old patterns and principles, we seem powerless to burst the bonds of these false traditions. We have still not thrown off the medieval yoke, in which relations between the Church and the world were conceived in terms of sovereignty and submission. Christianity, however, is not about power and coercive authoritarianism, but spiritual initiative and daring. Is not the failure of attempts to establish theocracies due to the fact that they were based on contempt for and renunciation of that world which they simultaneously wanted to subjugate and harness? It was there that the ideology and practice of theocratic sovereignty and spiritual despotism originated, the desire to fix life in lasting forms. The attributes of the Church — eternity and holiness — were transferred to the theocratic kingdom. This idea of the forcible salvation of the world also meant that the world, including man and culture, had no independent value, that they could be approached in a purely utilitarian way, as a means for the realization of the Church's aims.

The world, of course, has abandoned the Church, since the traditional groove reserved for creativity turned out to be too restricted for man. The energy which had accumulated over the centuries finally burst through the dam of established authorities and forms. Today it is not the Church but the world which is creating a new civilization, and it is solving the problems with which it is faced on the basis of its own understanding of existence. The area in which the Church can directly influence the world has been sharply reduced. Among the turbulent forces creating culture and transforming society, and sometimes threatening the very stones of the Church itself, the Christian faith continues to bear witness to its existence in the mystery of the Mass and in feats of personal sanctity and prayer. But the creative spirit which transforms life and the world appears to have abandoned it. Dragging along behind the world, the Church has been left to adopt principles which at first were alien to it, but which by now have become firmly established in spite of it. Even such Western "innovations" as social Christianity, Christian economics and sociology, new church architecture and painting, new rhythms and images in the music and poetry of the liturgy — all this is, as it were, some sort of compulsory tribute to the times, an obligatory new form having no relevance to the heart of the matter. Hence the inner contradiction of modern Church life, with its precarious wobbling between the extremes of senile protectionism, modernism, and feeble imitation. However, neither the curses nor the blessings with which people try to blur the sharp dividing line between the Church and the headlong momentum of the world are able to extinguish a feeling of tragic schism.

The sense of tragedy experienced today by every sensitive Christian consciousness is not merely the tragedy of the Church and Christianity in a secular world, but the tragedy of the world itself. It is impossible for man to "settle" in the world completely without God. Although proud of its successes and attainments, the world sees every day more clearly the provisional and insufficient nature of its civilization. On the verge of having its foundations shaken to the core, it thirsts as never before for the true light.

But the most surprising fact in modern spiritual life must be considered our indifference toward this thirst, our own too easy consent to the division existing between the Church and the world. We refuse to recognize that this external division is supported not only by the "willfulness of the world," but also by our own stagnant Christianity. Is not our own double life an expression of our dual consciousness? Is it not we ourselves who have helped to reduce the meaning of the life of the Church to an "intimate little corner" of piety locked away with seven locks from the life of the world, and hostile to it? Our religious fervor is opposed not to the sinfulness of the world, but to the world itself, its life, its history, its quests and questionings. We have thoroughly assimilated and like to repeat the proposition that Christ is the "judgment of this world," this world which has not recognized and accepted Him, that He is the salvation and the life for all those who recognize and accept and perform the will of the Father revealing itself in Christ. But for some reason we forget that the Father enjoined us above all *not to judge, but to save the world.* Salvation is the eternal meaning of the Incarnation of the Word, Christ's death on the Cross, His Resurrection and the entrance of the Holy Ghost into the apostles. We forget it because our personal spiritual makeup has become more valuable to us than its objective: the transformation of the world and of life for the glory of the approaching fullness of the Kingdom of God.

"We have got used to "owning" our Christianity and keeping it to ourselves, to not sharing it, as if it were an accidental inheritance. The external division thus becomes fixed in our Christian consciousness. Both in life and in the consciousness of the self there are, as it were, two persons: one is the keeper of a spiritual heritage, the other participates in the affairs of the world, which, as a rule, have no relevance to that heritage. For a long time it was thought that the Church was victorious in the world. But when that illusion crumbled, the vanquished Christians continued to harbor feelings of resentment and of a certain humble superiority, and these feelings imperceptibly commingled with the heritage they were preserving. Sometimes it seems that proud Orthodoxy and an unshakable feeling of righteousness have become entangled with this feeling of long-standing, unextinguished and still-persisting umbrage: "Since the world once disobeyed the Church, it can go to the devil now, along with its civilization and culture. . . . We'll see then. . . ." There is a peculiar, vengeful delight about the way in which not only the smaller sects but also Christians of the Church discuss the end of the world. In this sense Berdyayev [6] was undoubtedly correct in writing that the traditional concept of hell and its eternal tortures is an ontologization of Christian vengefulness. But hell is not a transcendent absolute, it is already present here, in time, in the postlapsarian world which is "rotting" and suffering for its sinfulness. The world might rather take offense at the Church for keeping the secret of salvation to itself and being either unable or unwilling to speak about it in accessible language.

Our civilization is dual in its foundation and history. And now, in spite of a secularization that aspires to universal dominion, Christian principles continue to influence its life. The energies of Christian culture, not directly through the

6. See note on page 55.— TRANS.

Church perhaps, but obliquely and through mysterious channels, continue to penetrate through to our world. They reveal themselves to us in the experience of making a moral choice, in the quest for genuine humanity, in the aspiration for higher things, in the impossibility of making do with compromises. And here we discover that our culture itself reacts sharply and painfully to human efforts at self-deification and self-sufficiency. In the Renaissance this reaction became the dominant theme in the later works of Botticelli, Michelangelo and Titian. And it continued in the "religious renunciation" by the romantics of the ideals of the Enlightenment, in the struggle of the twentieth-century Christian renaissance with positivism and atheism. And Russian literature — through Gogol, Dostoyevsky, Tolstoy, Chekhov and Solzhenitsyn — has unfailingly borne witness to the profound malady of our secular culture, to the tragic absurdity of an existence without God, to man's indestructible urge to find the true light. Without breaking through to absolute and unconditional values, culture inevitably ends by denying itself in what might be termed pseudo- or anticulture, in something which has the external appurtenances of culture but is essentially false, worthless, and inhuman. This process of psychologically casting off the dominating idols and temptations of modern civilization is bringing us back to that spiritual center in which culture first originated. On the basis of its genuine, though perhaps incomplete, religious experience, culture is posing many problems of Christianity anew, trying to find an answer to them in the Church and searching for support and a dialogue.

But it is precisely at this point that a certain fateful disjointedness of creative rhythms is revealed, for the Church is deaf to these queries and does not know how to answer them. Answers exist, they must exist, but how and in what language should one begin speaking? All the "modernism," all the "adaptation" introduced by the Church are in reality nothing other than manifestations of its *profound bondage to secular culture.* This capitulation is not always voluntary and more often than not is the result of a prolonged siege. And this siege can take different forms: in different historical periods, in different parts of the world and with varying degrees of activeness, the Church is opposed in one place by state atheism, in another by the ideology of science, and elsewhere by totalitarian regimes or the establishment of general material prosperity and comfort. Strategy and tactics change, but the result is usually the same: the consciousness of the Church turns out to be defenseless against hostile pressures. The Church closes up on itself, hoping to wait out the siege, then suddenly revolts and hurls anathemas, but ends up by trying to speak in that alien language imposed from outside. But how, in those circumstances, is it possible to speak about things that have been expressed only in the unchangeable language of Christian Hellenism or medieval scholasticism? By creating new concepts and a new liturgical language? By creating a new religious art? But then it is a long time since the Church seemed once and for all to renounce any desire to create cultural values or a new language for religious culture itself. It seemed to have overstrained itself in the period of its medieval supremacy. And now, in accordance with the universal principle of freedom of worship, we Christians are prepared to settle conclusively for our compulsory autonomy. In the huge and as yet unfinished building of culture, we have been magnanimously given the use of a corner with icons and lamps, and we seem to have reconciled ourselves to this fact. Certain modernists still think that all is not yet lost: icons can be replaced by a more modern "religious" art, and lamp oil by electricity. And indeed, the possibilities for renovation and adaptation are not yet exhausted. But would it not be self-deception to think that the light of the lamp, however much we cherish it, is that *Light for the World* that is destined to transform our whole life and with it the whole universe?

"The Spirit breathes where He will, and you hear His voice, ignorant of whence it comes and whither it goes. . . ."

But we seem not to concede this mysterious freedom of the divine call to the world. We want to think that God speaks only through our Church organization, only through our rite, only through our doctrine and tradition. In this approach the Church easily becomes an idol. We turn it from a living, eternally growing and eternally developing organism expressing the unity of man with God into a frozen mechanical form, capable of receiving into itself only things that can be cut off and adjusted to it. But the Church is life, not an external form. Its mission, which we too often forget, is to make everything that seeks the Light and aspires to the Truth a truly living and growing part of the Body of Christ.

Today it is particularly important to overcome our enthrallment by *pseudoecclesiasticism*. Regular attendance at church or familiarity with the order of the Mass does not at all mean that only we are necessarily doing good. Our sojourn in the Church is not in itself a prerogative or patent on salvation. The secret of individual salvation is known only to God. We are called by Him to embody Christ's work in this world and to work for the establishment of the Kingdom of God. That is why our life in the Church is above all a *task* (a commandment), the task of achieving greater perfection, of growing in the fullness of the grace granted to us, and not an advantage that justifies everything we do. We have, indeed, been given a great deal, but that only means that still more will be demanded of us. Now we can surmise how the Church and Russia may escape from that terrifying blind alley in which they find themselves. It is evident that a better future for Russia is inseparable from Christianity. And if Russia is to have a renaissance, it can only be accomplished on a religious foundation. But will the Church have enough strength to start this renaissance? At the moment it is experiencing a profound crisis and itself needs a renaissance first. Many people cling to the vain belief that this is only a crisis of Church government, a crisis of power in the Church. In fact we are experiencing something much bigger — a crisis in Church consciousness itself, in the traditional concept of the congregation. In various conditions and forms this crisis has now affected the Christianity of the whole world. But the Russian Orthodox Church is experiencing it in a specific form. External lack of liberty is paralyzing its life and being internalized, it is taking root in its consciousness and becoming equated with Church tradition. And to many people it now seems unarguable that no creativity is possible, that it is doomed and most probably unnecessary. All that remains is to await the resolution of our earthly destinies and curse the bishops.

The most tragic thing of all is that these views are being taken over from a gutless and confused older generation by the young people and intelligentsia who are coming into the Church. It is tragic that they are forgetting and betraying their experience of spiritual emancipation. Against the background of their conservatively stylized "old people's" Orthodoxy it is difficult to believe that they have really experienced the joy of liberty in Christ and have felt the influx of the power of grace. Looking at them makes one think that too often conversion to Christianity, to Orthodoxy, means no more than a change of ideologies. But ideology, however infallibly true it may seem, is incapable of liberating man.

Today, as never before, a Christian initiative is needed to counter the godless humanism which is destroying mankind, and to prevent humanism from deteriorating into a nonreligious humanism. We are too passive in our attitude to the world. We do not carry our own religious will within ourselves, or our care for the world; we seem to have forgotten that we have been entrusted with the great task of transforming the world. We must begin by prophesying inside the Church about the genuine foundations for hope offered by Christianity, and not by restoring or modernizing things that amount merely to historical or cultural incrustations. We need new creative efforts, we need a new language. We must speak of what is beyond modernism and conservatism alike, of what is eternally living and absolute in this world of the relative, of what is simultaneously both eternally old and eternally young. Our historicism must be metahistorical, it must mean not only a breakthrough into eternity but the presence of eternity in our own time, metahistory in history.

Christian activism must lead not to a reformation but to a

transformation of Christian consciousness and life, and through it to a transformation of the world. Only when we have entered upon this path shall we be able to answer the challenge of godlessness to build our world on autonomous principles. Only then shall we be able to answer the call of those who are close to the Light, but who are prevented from communing with it by our own negligence and inertia.

Personality and National Awareness

VADIM BORISOV

There is a widespread, if sometimes inexplicit, feeling about that Russia has passed her Golgotha and is approaching some new historic milestone.

But what is this milestone? Is it the beginning of a collapse, of which the growing stream of emigrants would seem to offer material proof? Or is it the expectation of resurrection?

Hope and faith are locked in a struggle with despair and blind ill will; in the present debate on Russia notes of truly apocalyptic alarm are increasingly in evidence.

Are we an accursed and corrupt race or a great people? Are we destined to have a future, or was Russia only created, in the words of Konstantin Leontyev's [1] crazed prophecy, to bring forth from its vitals the Antichrist? What lies ahead — a yawning abyss or a steep and laborious ascent?

It is a dire symptom in itself that these unmentionable, taboo, half-forgotten yet everlasting questions occupy the thoughts and minds of every living being in Russia. Only when decisive historic changes are in the wind do these

1. Konstantin Leontyev (1831–1891), a conservative thinker who opposed aristocratic and aesthetic values to the prevailing liberal and Nihilist theories of his time. He died a monk in the monastery of the Holy Trinity. — TRANS.

questions pose themselves with such merciless urgency: thus it was at the beginning of the seventeenth and eighteenth, the beginning and middle of the nineteenth, and at the beginning of the twentieth centuries.

The future, as is well known, casts its shadow before it, and we who live in this shadow, remembering our predecessors' bitter but profound experience, need to distinguish its contours. If we hope to maintain a meaningful historical existence, indeed, we must.

Not so long ago it seemed impossible that the debate about Russia, after everything she has suffered, should revive. But present developments offer a glimmer of hope that an end to peremptory Marxist decisions and predeterminations of Russia's fate may now be near and that henceforward her crippled soul and body may *themselves* begin to seek ways back to health.

The debate also offers us a warning. The ideological monolith that has weighed for long years on Russian life and thought has done its work: Russian consciousness is scrambling out from under it toward an unknown future which is fragmented as never before. All the old unresolved dilemmas of Russian thought are rearing their heads again, intensified, complicated and distorted by our unprecedented experiences of the last half century. It is not rhetoric, but cold fact, that our people's very *life* now depends on their solution.

Unless we can discover *in ourselves* the source of some power to lead our ravaged consciousness back to a single spiritual center, all the present enthusiasm for social experiment may turn out to be Russia's last agony.

ONE

Of all the questions facing us, perhaps the most painful and contentious is that of Russian national rebirth, its potential, its principles, its form and direction.

Why the contention?

During recent decades many people have come to understand a long known but eternally neglected truth: that a people can perish without being totally annihilated physically — it is necessary only to remove its memory, its thought and its word, and the *soul* of the people will die. History may observe the numbing spectacle of the dead and soulless body's continued growth for a long time afterward, but eventually it witnesses the predestined collapse.[2]

That, it is widely thought today, is the fate in store for the Russian people.

But no man's heart, if Russia means any more to him than a "prison of the peoples," can remain indifferent to such an outcome. And this emotion gives rise to attempts, tentative perhaps, misdirected perhaps as yet, but *living* attempts to grope for ways to effect the salvation and rebirth of the national soul.

Different groups among our present educated class have different ways of understanding and approaching this already clearly defined aspiration for national rebirth — from unquestioning support for *any* of its manifestations to total aversion to the idea itself.

The recent and continuing controversy over A. Solzhenitsyn's "Letter to the Soviet Leaders" has shown up this specter for all to see.

Exacerbated national feeling among the various peoples of the Soviet Union is now a fact not to be concealed by braggart phrases about a "historic new community." In fact this community reveals itself as a none too solid ideological crust which can barely restrain the underground tremors of forcibly suppressed national energies. But whereas liberal-democratic circles in our society unfailingly support national independence movements among, say, the Baltic peoples, their attitude to similar tendencies in Russia herself is one of keen suspicion, alienation, fear and unconcealed hostility.

2. A. S. Khomyakov in his polemic with the "progressists" clearly understood that a people "may perfect its knowledge, while its morals decline and the country perishes; the administration may behave according to the rule book and therefore appear to be in order, yet the people decline and the country perishes. A center may fortuitously consolidate itself while all the limbs are weak and diseased, and the country yet again perish."

Everyone knows the immediate historical causes of this apparently paradoxical situation.

The intelligentsia's unwavering aversion to the false official patriotism into which Stalin strove to direct the genuine national exaltation of the war years (succeeding generations will forever associate this "patriotism" with the purges of "cosmopolitans" and arrests of Jews), plus guilt for the Russification of the fringe republics and hostility to official anti-Semitism — all this directly motivates the humanist protest against "Great Russian chauvinism" or — to put it another way — "nationalism."

However, a number of publicistic articles in recent years (by G. Pomerants,[3] R. Medvedev and others) and recently, unfortunately, the attitude of A. Sakharov, together with personal contacts with today's intellectuals, lead me to conclude that the true extent and purpose of this protest goes much further and deeper. It has often seemed to me that, with rare exceptions, these circles regard not just *nationalism,* as a specifically defined ideology (of which more later), but *any* symptoms of a Russian national psychology and awareness with skeptical hostility or at best guarded suspicion.

This is a replay of the situation which S. Bulgakov[4] once defined as typical of Russian prerevolutionary society — "the moral boycott and auto-boycott of national consciousness." The forms are new, of course, but it remains essentially the same as before. The boycott is nominally intended to defend the dignity of the *human personality.*

Our progressive, humanistically inclined intelligentsia makes no clear distinction in its mind between "national" and "nationalist," because it tends to suspect that national feeling by its very nature is morally inferior and immature.

Despite the fatal blows the twentieth century has dealt to our faith in man *as such* and the progressive enlargement of his rights, this faith for inexplicable and irrational reasons still remains the basic postulate of the moral consciousness of

3. For a discussion of Pomerants's writings, see pages 244–246, 259–261, 264–265, 270.— TRANS.
4. See note on page 20.— TRANS.

the modern liberal-democratic intelligentsia (I use this conventional term for want of a better one).

Now, as in the past, this faith inspires noble self-sacrifices, examples of which we can all call to mind.

But that same faith, as we shall see, is what lies at the heart of the process of denationalization of faithless humanist philosophy, and this reveals its inherent ambiguity and tragic contradictoriness.

The freedom of individuals and their unification in mankind as a whole are the alpha and omega of the humanist philosophy, the formula for the progressive development of the human race in history and its most rational outcome. The humanist ideal regards the *nation* as one of human society's transitional forms, which at a certain point (it is deemed to have arrived already) hinders the achievement of a higher form of human community and which is in any case inferior to that shining goal.

Ignoring the nuances, this philosophy, which is usually couched in socialist terms, is closely related to V. I. Lenin's famous dictum: "Socialism's aim is not only to abolish the fragmentation of humanity into small states and to end all distinctions between nations, not only to bring the nations closer together, but to bring about their fusion." [5]

Liberation from the bonds of nationhood is part of humanism's plan for the emancipation of the *human personality*. For this reason any intensification of national feeling, when not connected with a struggle for freedom from foreign political oppression (homegrown oppression is *our own!*), is regarded as atavistic reaction fit to be condemned unconditionally.

From this utterly rationalist point of view, finding the answer to questions about the relationship between the individual human personality and the nation and between the

5. Fichte in his early years formulated this striving to throw off the bonds of nationhood more individualistically and romantically: "Let those born of the earth, whose acknowledged fatherland is the crust of the earth, the rivers and mountains, remain citizens of the defunct state. . . . But the spirit whose likeness is the sun is irresistibly drawn and moves toward light and justice. We may rest serene in that feeling of universal citizenship. . . ."

nation and mankind presents no difficulty. The human personality's susceptibility to national feelings, its conscious affirmation of nationality, is *demeaning* to its dignity, subjecting its freedom to the dictates of blind tribalism, and stifling its rational aspirations in the chaos of patrimonial life. Also, insofar as the historical limitations of the national unit have been rationally identified and scientifically accounted for, it follows that any excessive emphasis on it or foolish clinging to national distinctions at the present time will hinder the future union of mankind and serve the forces of division and *reaction*.

I think I am not alone in frequently hearing reproaches and even severe moral censure addressed to Russian writers (the nation's greatest geniuses included) who lack the moral fiber to overcome this base instinct.[6]

But is the answer to these painful questions as obvious as the proponents of rationalist humanism would have us believe? And why are they so discouragingly certain of their moral rectitude?

To get to the bottom of this we must take a closer look at the central concept beloved of all humanists today — the *human personality.*

And at once we enter an area of total confusion.

It will be easy enough to receive an exposition of the precise rights that are due to the individual personality, and we shall, of course, be reminded of its lofty dignity. But if we ask, what *is* the human personality, the definition will probably be "a sum of psychological qualities," or words to that effect.

But we are hardly likely to receive a satisfactory answer to

6. Let us here note a characteristic attitude to Russian culture often encountered among today's intelligentsia. They can combine love of this culture and its "highest achievements" with contempt for Russian history, fear of the "bestiality" of the Russian people, and a half-mocking, half-condescending view of its spiritual values. They regard these "highest achievements" not as an organic phenomenon but as an unaccountable anomaly of Russian life. Evidently they have genuinely lost all understanding and feeling for the indivisibility of the individual genius and the genius of the people. Therefore the apparent contradiction between Russia herself and her spiritual culture fails to strike them as unnatural.

the question of *why*, precisely, must the human personality have all these rights, why must we acknowledge that one "sum of psychological qualities" is equal to another? What is the basis of such an assumption? We shall of course be referred to "natural justice" and the "social contract" and "it stands to reason" and "our innate moral consciousness," and more of the same, but only by some strange mental aberration can this be taken seriously as a sound basis for a juridical concept in the 1970s.

We discover with astonishment that so-called rationalist humanism actually lacks an adequate *rational* basis for its defense of the dignity and inalienable rights of the human personality — for which it has often risked both life and limb.

The American Founding Fathers who many years ago first propounded the "eternal rights of man and the citizen" postulated that *every* human being bears the form and likeness of God; he *therefore* has an *absolute* value, and consequently also the *right* to be respected by his fellows.

Rationalism, positivism and materialism, developing in opposition to religion, successively destroyed the memory of this absolute source of human rights. The unconditional equality of persons before God was replaced by the *conditional* equality of human individuals before the law.

Deprived of divine authority, the concept of the *human personality* could now be defined *conditionally*, and therefore inevitably arbitrarily. The concrete person became a juridical metaphor, a contentless abstraction, the subject of legal freedoms and restrictions.

And it is here, in the admission of the *conditionality* of the human personality, that we find the root of its calamitous ordeals in our barbarous world. If the human personality is conditional, then so are its rights. Conditional too is the recognition of its dignity, which comes into painful conflict with surrounding reality.

But conditionality, by its very nature, is neither indestructible nor eternally binding. A given condition can survive only insofar as the *force* which supports it remains in existence. Once the force is spent, nothing can *logically* prevent us from breaking the condition.

If the human personality is not absolute but conditional, then the call to respect it is only a pious wish, which we may obey or disregard. Confronted with a force which demands *disrespect* for the personality, rationalist humanism has no *logical* arguments with which to refute it.

In breaking the link between the human personality and the absolute source of its rights, and yet affirming them as something to be taken for granted, rationalist humanism has from the very outset been inherently inconsistent, as its more logical successors very quickly understood. Darwin, Marx, Nietzsche and Freud (and many others) resolved the inconsistency each in his own way, leaving not one stone upon another in the edifice of blind faith in man's dignity. They knocked the *human personality* off its phantom humanist pedestal, tore off and ridiculed its mantle of sanctity and inviolacy, and showed it its true station in life — as the cobblestone paving the road for "superman," or the drop of water destined with millions of others to irrigate the historical soil for the happiness of future generations, or the lump of flesh dragging itself painfully and uncomprehendingly to union with its fellows.

These men represented the theoretical, logical culmination of mankind's humanist rebellion against God. They declared "our innate moral consciousness" to be self-deception, noxious illusion, fiction — as demanded by a rationally ordered consciousness.

This century's totalitarianism, trampling the human personality and all its rights, rhinocerouslike, underfoot, is only the application of this theory to life, or humanism put into *practice*.[7]

Yet oddly enough, despite the logic of humanism's historical development, this initial variant of it (defined above as

7. The evolution we have only sketched here has been studied in detail by Russian thinkers — F. Dostoyevsky, S. Bulgakov, S. Frank, N. Berdyayev, Fr. Pavel (Florensky) and many others. Their writings are strongly recommended to the interested reader.

"rationalist humanism") has not entirely followed this high road of reason, but has survived practically unchanged on the sidelines until our own time, representing in fact an archaic survival from the eighteenth century.

It has maintained its tradition of moral feeling unnaturally married to *atheism of the mind* (not of the heart!) while still *believing* in the inalienable rights of man *as such*. But this *utopian* humanism refuses to acknowledge its historical affinity with the "humanism" which has become a reality. Furthermore, it even joins battle with it for these very rights.

The clash is, by an irony of history, between two elements — the initial and the final — of *one and the same* process. It is an unequal struggle, with *utopian* humanism at a painful disadvantage. As we have already said, it cannot *logically* oppose its brutal and consistent younger relative. The source of its courageous protest is irrational, for it is that very moral light brought into the world by religion, but "rationalist humanism" cannot acknowledge this without ceasing to be itself.

Its fate is tragic: it testifies both to the indestructibility of man's moral nature and to the hopeless dilemmas in which he is enmeshed when he overlooks the religious roots of that nature. It is precisely because of its atheism that humanism so often either slips into despair or, denying itself, adopts a belief in solutions through violence, when the human personality invariably becomes a *tool*.

A humane attitude to life (a more precise term than the ambiguous "humanism"), if it ignores its origins, rests on flimsy, shifting foundations. As Dostoyevsky once observed, such unmindful "humaneness is only a habit, a product of civilization. It may completely disappear."

Do we need to quote the examples that have confirmed the terrible truth of those words a thousandfold?

The vagueness and abstract nature of the humanist concept of the *human personality* undermines confidence in its ability to solve the problem of the relationship between *human personality* and the *nation*. Humanism has forgotten what the human personality is. And perhaps it has also forgotten what a nation is. So should we not in fact discuss the relationships between the *human personality* and anything whatever in the context of the teaching that gave birth to the very concept of the human personality, namely, *Christianity?*

TWO

But here we come up against the inspired objection of the Apostle Paul: "There is neither Jew nor Greek . . ."

Many who quote this objection (including A. Krasnov-Levitin in No. 106 of the *"Vestnik RSKD"* [8] — though there are few enough who *don't* quote it) regard it as so authoritative, incontrovertible and altogether crushing as to eliminate the entire question of relations between the human personality and the nation from the *Christian* point of view, as if it were not a question at all, or at any rate one long ago answered. For Christianity the *human personality* exists, the *nation* does not.

We do not propose to quibble with St. Paul, still less to dispute his authority, for he did write those words. But they did have a continuation which for some reason is invariably overlooked by the proponents of Christian "universalism" (or, to run a little ahead, pseudouniversalism): ". . . neither male nor female . . ."

Are its proponents bold enough to maintain that Christianity, with its teachings on marriage, makes *no* distinction between the sexes?

Did not the apostle to the heathen rather mean that there is no difference between Greek and Jew, man and woman, slave and freeman in *one particular respect?* He said so quite explicitly elsewhere: "For the scripture saith, Whosoever believeth on him shall not be ashamed. For there is no difference between the Jew and the Greek: for the same Lord over all . . ." (Rom. 10:11–12).

To take the scriptural argument further, have our "univer-

8. See pages 95 to 96 and note on page 96.— TRANS.

salists" ever stopped to consider texts like *"All nations whom thou hast made . . ."* (Psalm 86:9)? Do they remember that Christ brought the good news, not to scattered individuals, but to the people of Israel *as a whole?* Or Christ's words: "Go ye therefore and teach *all nations . . ."*?

And does this not mean, despite all their disclaimers, that the "nation problem" does exist for Christianity, and that attempts to discard it (or even morally destroy it) on the basis of half a dozen imperfectly understood words are, to say the least, unjustified and premature?

In our atheist age, however, even Christians tend to shy away from scriptural arguments. This obliges us to transpose the question into a somewhat — if not altogether — different plane.

What is a *nation?* What is the essence of this mysterious human community at which "universalists" of various kinds have chanted spells ("abracadabra vanish!") for a century and more, but which has obstinately refused to vanish? Is it common territory? A common economy? Language? Kinship? Or all of them taken together? Or perhaps something else altogether?

Dostoyevsky's notebook contains the following words: "The *nation* is nothing more than the *national personality.*"

He returned to this idea many times, it was one of his most intimate and penetrating thoughts. He understood the *national personality* not metaphorically, not in the abstract, but precisely as a *living personal unity.* He saw it as the *spiritual reality* that binds all the concrete, historical and empirical manifestations of national life into a single whole.[9]

Well, they will say, Dostoyevsky was a "mystic" and is not much in demand these days. But:

"A nation is not a collection of different beings, it is an organized being and moreover a *moral personality.* A wonderful secret has been revealed — the great soul of France."

9. This inspired intuition was philosophically developed in Russian literature by L. Karsavin, N. Trubetskoy, N. Lossky and others.

The author of these words was no mystic. It was the famous historian of the French Revolution, Michelet. Rather than weary the reader with quotations, we ask him to take our word for it that the same idea, although not always equally well defined, appears in many spiritually sensitive people of all ages and all nations, however different their personal philosophies.

Just one more quotation, then, a very characteristic one from A. Herzen, the great writer and little understood idol of the Russian intelligentsia, to whom the mystery of the nation as a personality was a matter of deep concern:

"It seems to me," he wrote, "that there is something in Russian life higher than the community and stronger than the might of the state; it is hard to capture in words, harder still to point to with the finger. I mean that inner, not quite conscious power which wondrously preserved the Russian people under the yoke of the Mongol hordes and the German bureaucracy, under the Tartar knout from the *east* and the corporal's staves from the *west;* that inner power which preserved the attractive open character and lively wit of our peasants under the humiliating oppression of serfdom, and which when commanded by the tsar to educate itself, within one hundred years replied with the resounding phenomenon of Pushkin; I mean, finally, that power of self-confidence which lives on in *our* breasts. This constant power has preserved the Russian people and its unwavering faith in itself, preserved it outside all forms and against all forms."

This sense of the nation as a *personality,* which has been expressed by individuals, corresponds with and confirms the people's awareness of its identity as embodied in folklore. Its image covertly governs our speech, for when we speak of the "dignity" of the people, its "duty," its "sins" or its "responsibility," we are making concrete, that is to say, unmetaphorical, use of terms that are applicable only to the moral life of a *person.*

Finally, the unfathomable mystery of the nation's ultimate destiny (here again we shall have to resort to the Holy Scriptures), the mystery of its *indestructibility* and *autonomy* unbounded by space and time, in other words the secret of its *metaphysical essence,* is revealed in the Apocalypse:

"And the nations of them which are saved shall walk in the light of it [the City of God] and they shall bring the glory and honor of the nations into it" (Rev. 21:24 and 26). And, says St. John the Divine, the disciple whom Jesus loved, this shall come to pass *after* the first heaven and the first earth have passed away.

This concept of the nation as a *person* cannot be completely translated into the language of reason and therefore remains altogether foreign to rationalism and positivism, not to mention materialism. (That is, specifically, the *philosophies,* since there are of course exceptions among their adherents.)

However, even those endowed with neither a religious outlook on life nor any special spiritual sensitivity can to a certain extent verify the *reality* of the nation's personality, as distinct from the empirical manifestations of national life. All that is required is to examine with care and without prejudice (not necessarily to live through at first hand!) the experiences of the Russian emigration throughout the last century or so.

Many Russians have shaken the dust of the hated and despotic fatherland off their feet, cursing and denouncing its monstrous face, and fled to Europe, the "land of sacred miracles," to liberty, equality and fraternity. But very soon, quite against their expectations and desires, these same Russians were overcome by a spontaneous sense of some irreparable loss. The trouble, as many of them understood, was not simply the result of an unfamiliar environment or a foreign language (most of them, after all, knew European languages and European conditions just as well as their own) but something else. They gradually came to see the "land of sacred miracles" as an "abomination of desolation," and their own existence in it — though often quite comfortable — as illusory and insubstantial.

And unexpectedly the bond with the motherland, this

"darkness unmasked," to use Marina Tsvetayeva's [10] phrase, came to be the only thing that mattered, with a direct bearing on the very essence of their being.[11] They came to realize that behind the outward appearances of the life of their people they had failed to perceive what was most important, the *essence* of which Herzen wrote. They had not suspected it before and only now, in their isolation, could they begin to divine its real meaning and understand Russia as a personality, to whom their own personalities were by some mysterious process indissolubly bound. In their dark homeland these people suddenly perceived a fount of light, and were drawn to it irresistibly even when inevitable destruction stared them in the face.

This is the secret of the spiritual nature of that famous and mysterious Russian nostalgia, the unaccountable feeling of having lost some *whole* whose lack makes man's life seem incomplete.

Slavophiles and Westernizers alike were stricken with it, positivists and mystics, Russian Orthodox and Russian Catholics; it led them to mental instability and often to irretrievable breakdown. Russia continues to haunt her outcasts and fugitives all their lives: it is not the immensity of her plains, nor the beauty of her "little birch trees" which have now become something of a joke, nor even any peculiar trait of the Russian soul, but *she herself*, her mysterious *face* which evidently possesses such fascination.

And it is perhaps because rationalism and materialism held such comparatively short sway in Russia that this emotion is so extraordinarily acute among Russian émigrés, demonstrating that their spiritual capacity to be aware of their participation in the whole has not altogether atrophied, that they

10. Marina Tsvetayeva (1892–1941), one of the finest Russian poets of the twentieth century, emigrated in 1922, but returned to the Soviet Union in 1939 as a result of her husband's return. In 1941 she hanged herself. — TRANS.

11. "Having started with a cry of joy," writes Herzen of his spiritual experiences, "upon crossing the frontier, I ended with a spiritual return to my homeland. Faith in Russia saved me when I was on the verge of moral destruction. . . . I thank my homeland for my faith in her and for the healing it gave me."

are actively conscious of the inclusion of their individual personalities in a more complex unity — the collective or, to use the traditional term of Russian thought, *"corporate" national personality.*

That is what we call the *nation.*

We have already said that *personality* in its original sense is a specifically Christian concept.

It was unknown to the ancient world, whose consciousness was totally individualistic. The Greeks, for instance, despised all barbarians, and the citizens of Rome despised all non-Romans.

We have forgotten the Christian origins of our idea of the "personal" as of something that gives *every* individual his qualities of absoluteness, unrepeatability and irreducibility to other individuals — and this insensibility threatens ultimately to render meaningless the words we all so willingly use.

We often confuse the concepts of *personality* and *individual* in our speech and use them as if they were synonymous, but in Christian thought they are poles apart.

This requires some explanation.

In Christian thought the world is not simply the arithmetical sum of its visible parts, but a definite hierarchy, all of whose levels are personalized. This applies even to the structure of the life of the Deity, Whose mystery is embodied in the triune dogma of the Three Persons of the One God; and it applies equally to the structure of the life of mankind, inasmuch as "Christianity," in the words of St. Gregory of Nyssa, "is an imitation of the nature of God." Christian ideology distinguishes in God a single *nature* and its existence in *persons* (or *personalities*). The same distinction lies at the heart of all Christian anthropology and may in our view also be applicable to the question of the true role and significance of the "nation as personality" in mankind.

The source of the Christian interpretation of this question is in two great historical events — the Incarnation and the Pentecost.

In Christ's time there were many peoples already existing

on earth, occupying various territories, speaking various languages, and warring with one another. Was their appearance merely a historical accident? The words of the Bible about the "nations thou hast made" answer this question in the negative; the existence of peoples was part of the plan of creation, forming part of God's design for the world. In the course of their history, however, the peoples had lost their common measure, which Christ then restored to them.

Having assumed the *perfect* nature of man in the Incarnation, Christ *forever* confirmed the natural unity of mankind, once enshrined in the person of the first man, "Old Adam."

But Christ did not come to do away with the design of the Creator. He did not become the flesh of history so as to abolish it, but in order to become its spiritual center, its course of energy and its purpose.

Man's *nature* is *one* — says Christianity — but "all nature is contained in somebody's personality and can have no other existence." [12] In other words, Christianity introduced to the world the concept of the *plurality of personalities of a single mankind.* Personalities not just *individual,* but also *national.*

This concept in particular is symbolized in the events of the Pentecost, when the Holy Ghost descended on the apostles and they were endowed with the gift of speaking in *different tongues.* "And they were all amazed and marveled, saying to one another, behold, are not all these which speak Galileans? And how hear we every man in our own tongue, wherein we were born? Parthians, and Medes, and Elamites, and the dwellers in Mesopotamia, and in Judea, and Cappadocia, and Pontus, and Asia, Phrygia, and Pamphilia, in Egypt, and in the parts of Libya about Cyrene, and strangers of Rome, Jews and proselytes, Cretes and Arabians, we do hear them speak in our tongues the wonderful works of God."

The Christian Church was born not in a single world language but in the *different tongues* of the apostles, reaffirming the plurality of national paths to a single goal.

12. The words of the authoritative theologian of the Eastern Church, Leontius of Byzantium.

We can now easily understand the Christian view of the difference between the personality and the individual and the new principle contributed to the so-called national question by the concept of the nation as *personality.*

The individual embodies the opposite of the common measure in mankind, a fragment of the one human nature, self-sufficient and absolute, consisting of uniform particles formed from a *mingling* of nature and personality. Individual men and individual nations are *impenetrable* to one another.

The *personality,* as opposed to the individual, is not a part of some whole, it comprehends the whole within itself. The personality is not a fragment of one nature, but embraces the whole fullness of nature; therefore the idea of personality *presupposes* the existence of a common measure in mankind.

(To the contemporary mind these meditations may, indeed probably do, seem exceedingly abstract and divorced from the alarming reality of today. But we shall soon see the *practical* consequences that follow from forgetting and distorting these Christian ideas.)

If the *nation* is a corporate personality endowed with its being by God, then it cannot be defined as a "historical community of people" or a "force of nature and history" (Vladimir Solovyov). The nation is a level in the hierarchy of the Christian cosmos, a part of God's immutable purpose. Nations are not created by a people's history. Rather, the nation's personality realizes itself through that history or, to put it another way, the people in their history fulfill God's design for them.

In this sense the *nation* is distinct from the empirical *people.* The history of a people chronicles its discovery of its own personality. There is no concrete moment in the life of a people that fails to manifest its personality, and conversely, no historical situation is capable of plumbing the *full depths* of its personality.

Different stages of its self-discovery may come into sharp conflict with one another, as happens in the individual life of a man; this can lead to terrible declines, but so long as the people remains aware of its *personal* unity — and therefore of its *freedom* — it can reemerge from even the deepest gulfs.

The acknowledgment by all members of a national unit of their *personal* unity is what we call *national consciousness*. It brings together all aspects and empirical manifestations of a nation's historical being; its aim, in the words of Vladimir Solovyov, is to achieve in the destiny and spirit of the people "what God thinks of it in eternity." A necessary precondition of the people's existence and development is *historical memory*. If this is destroyed, the people's self-awareness suffers pathological distortion; it comes to identify its personality, to its own detriment, with the present moment of its existence; it forgets that all empirical personality is imperfect and that the fulfillment of personal life can only be achieved by a continuous and conscious process of development.

The destruction of historical memory kills a people's spiritual yearning for this fulfillment, cripples its moral personality, undermines its faith in the possibility of the creative conquest of evil and its hope of rebirth.

If peoples are recognized as *personalities*, this leads to recognition of their *equality*, giving them all an indisputable right to be respected and loved by all others, affirming the absolute value of their national identity.

But how can the freedom of the individual human personality be reconciled with its membership in a national whole?

No man is born into the world as a creature without personality, a clean slate. If he is to exercise free self-determination in his earthly life he must *already* be, at the moment of his birth, a *qualitatively*, and therefore also *nationally*, *defined person*. This definition is admittedly only an ideal and potential one, a metaphysical foundation for our spiritual nature; it does not violate or diminish the gift of human freedom. Every person is free to evade the fulfillment of his personal destiny, free to reject God's design for him, to forget the roots of his being; but destroy these roots completely he cannot.

And whatever new characteristics a man may acquire in the ups and downs of his life, his innermost being and subconscious self always preserve some vague idea of his origins, of his "prototype." In many people this tends to come to the surface as an oppressive, restless dissatisfaction with life, a sense of some unfulfilled vocation.

But another way is always open to every human personality — the way of self-knowledge, plumbing the depths of one's own self and the spiritual source of one's being. On this path toward God a sense of *national awareness* sooner or later comes into its own — an awareness of the individual's metaphysical relationship with the corporate self of the people, and *through it* with the corporate self of mankind.

But all these correlations can be considered to be no more than the theoretical base of Christian consciousness. Real life is still very far from realizing them. As in the time of the early Christians, they only show the way by which mankind *may* achieve the fulfillment of personal existence.

In Christian terms this higher level of personal being is called the *Church*. Mankind as the Church is the fulfillment of the future, toward which the constantly changing reality of the existing world must strive so as to become one with its Creator.

But every personality, individual or national, being unique, approaches this union in its own way, striving to achieve fulfillment *within itself;* only thus is the true whole fulfilled.

Christianity does not ask mankind to deny the variety of the personalities composing it, nor to become an amorphous mass. It urges mankind to transform itself entirely, "unto the measure of the stature of the fullness of Christ" (Eph. 4:13). Every people, every individual person must achieve his fulfillment in the Church. When this comes to pass, when *all* nations have achieved this goal, this will be the perfect fulfillment of the *corporate personality* of mankind — Christ's Church, in which the nations' spiritual experience, their "glory and honor," will be laid at Christ's feet.

"All nations whom Thou hast made shall come and worship before Thee, O Lord; and shall glorify Thy name."

This is mankind's *free* and common purpose.

THREE

The destruction of the Christian base of the nation could not but have disastrous consequences for its later history.

That is not to say, of course, that it was not sick even in its Christian context — sometimes with abstract pseudouniversalism, sometimes with religious nationalism. These distortions in practice often caused suffering to numerous human victims, and it would be intolerable hypocrisy for Christianity to try to duck its historical responsibility for it.

However, the degeneration of national awareness started in earnest with the spread of atheism, rationalism, positivism and materialism.

As the result of this degeneration there arose two atheist ideologies (in the broadest sense) — *universalism* and *nationalism.*

Both are worldwide in their scope, both have appeared in past Russian history and still exert a powerful influence on its course.

We touched briefly on the former while expounding the "rationalist humanist" view of the national question. Now we can take a different and wider view of this ideology so as to evaluate its real significance and the role which, whatever the subjective intentions of its proponents, it has played in Russian history and *may* play in the history of mankind.

The beginning of the collapse of Russia's integral, Christian national awareness was unusually stormy, thanks to the brutal reforms of Peter the Great, the first Russian Nihilist. For reasons of space we cannot here go into details of this process, which led to the agonizing bisection of the national personality; we only sketch in the rough outline.

How did it happen that the "educated class" and the "people" in Russia came to be opposed to one another? What were the origins of the notorious problems of the "intelligentsia and the people," regarded as one of the most characteristic traits of recent Russian history?

213

This problem is sometimes oversimplified as the unscrupulous "disengagement" of the intelligentsia from the people, as if it were a deliberate act. This oversimplification, however, ignores the entire tragedy of a dichotomy of which Russian writers from Dostoyevsky — nay, from Pushkin — to Blok [13] have always been keenly aware.

For many Russians this "disengagement" took place subconsciously and at first they were not subjectively aware of it at all. They lost their faith in God while at the same time retaining their love of the "people" and often an altruistic desire to "serve" it.

But in their minds, without realizing it, they substituted the *social image* of the people for the *face* of the people — *since the people as a whole cannot be comprehended rationalistically and materialistically.* Then they were faced with the fatal question (which could only be asked at all when the national personality was sick): *who in Russia is to be regarded as the people?* Naturally enough, in an agricultural country like Russia, it was mainly the peasantry who came to be called the "people."

And it was to the peasantry that the intelligentsia decided to communicate their idea of "progress," "enlightenment," and the "universal" social forms that had developed in Western Europe.[14]

But it was precisely the "people" that proved to be most unreceptive to this salutary universal ideal, and it was in contact with them that the intelligentsia felt most "foreign" in its own country. Suddenly the intelligentsia saw the Russian people as no more than a "reactionary mass," clinging stubbornly to their superstitions and loath to acquire the fruits of European enlightenment.

"Progressive" Russian society swung to the belief that the Russian "people," in Nietzsche's celebrated expression, was "something to be overcome" — for its own good, of course.

13. See note 7 on page 156.— TRANS.
14. "The task of the educated class in Russia is to be the bearer of civilization to the people." I. S. Turgenev's words were quoted approvingly as far back as 1910 by the Cadet leader P. N. Milyukov in his attack on the *Vekhi* version of the intelligentsia's history.

That was the beginning of a process that in a revised form is still going on — the "salvation" of Russia from herself, salvation through the renunciation of her national personality and the acquisition of "universal" features.[15]

With the increasing fragmentation of Russian society, the concept of the "people" in liberal and populist thought became attenuated,[16] until at length it degenerated into Marxism with its theory of class hatred.

Adopting a platform of hostility on principle to the concept of a national community, taking the sociological abstraction of "class" to be the only reality, inscribing its banners with the slogan "the proletariat has no fatherland," Marxism became the consistent and pure embodiment of *national nihilism.*

It was not its progenitor, however; it undertook merely to finish the job of depersonalizing the people started by Russian "progressive circles" long before.[17] Its inspiration, like theirs, was the idea of "building in the desert" (Pisarev's [18] expression) and it detested, as they did, the "idols" which had for centuries defined the moral nature of the Russian people, enabling it to distinguish between "good" and "evil" and preserving its self-awareness as a *personality.*

15. "The masses, like nature," wrote the Westernist historian T. Granovsky in the 1840s, "are either senselessly cruel or senselessly kind. They stagnate under the burden of historical and natural factors from which only the individual personality frees itself through thought. This breaking down of the masses by thought constitutes the process of history."
16. Typical was the Russian press debate over the events of 3 April 1878 in Moscow, when the butchers of Okhotny Ryad savagely beat up the participants in a student demonstration. Publicists argued loud and long about whether the butchers could be regarded as "the people."
17. Here is how M. V. Tugan-Baranovsky, the Russian socialist intelligentsia's theoretician, defined that intelligentsia at the beginning of this century. What mattered in an intellectual of this type was that "he was permeated with revolutionary spirit and had the greatest disgust for Russian historical traditions, regarding himself in this respect as an out and out renegade. . . . As for traditional Russian culture . . . hostility to it is the most typical mark of the intellectual. . . . The Russian intellectual is uprooted from his historical soil and consequently selects the social ideal which seems best from the rationalist point of view. This is the socialist ideal — cosmopolitan, supranational and suprahistorical."
18. See note 4 on page 156.— TRANS.

In order to destroy and supplant those "idols," Marxism in Russia undertook a campaign "to overcome" the people the like of which world history had never seen.

A "new historic community of people" was to rise from the "ethnic masses" of the former Russian Empire, but first they had to be "transformed." How this "transformation" was brought about, first and foremost with regard to the Russian people, is now well enough known.

Within a short time the Russian people had been brought to a state of almost total ignorance of their own history, deprived of their national culture, almost deprived of their reviled and persecuted Church, which survived by a *miracle*, and became, as the transformers had intended, a reliable buttress of the present and future international.

All Europe of the Left, where the processes of "denationalization" and "internationalization" were also taking their course, applauded and still applauds this outstanding success of the "Russian Marxists." Now *it too* is beginning to fear it is lagging behind the country of progressive socialism, and is urging and goading its own governments to catch up.

The "teachers" of the West and the "disciples" of the East have changed places.

"Western Europe" has lost its monopoly as a measure of the "universal," a role which is increasingly being taken over by socialist Eastern Europe. (In the real East, meanwhile, a new and awesome claimant for this role is emerging into the open — Communist China, which *already* overshadows earlier idols in the eyes of the European "New Left.")

The universal human ideal was conclusively and *scientifically* defined in the slogan of "socialist integration," which was held to apply in principle to the whole of mankind. It is true that Western adherents of this concept still tend to be shocked by what they call the "Asiatic" traits of socialism as at present practiced, but this merely shows that their minds are still "weighed down by the nightmare of the past" (Marx), in this case the traditions of the national democracies.

This exchange of roles between the "enlightened" West

and the East with its "centuries of stagnating in savagery" has led to some confusion and muddle in the camp of the defenders of socialist "denationalization." Western radicals were extremely upset, and then openly annoyed, by what they saw as the "retrograde" movement in the USSR for democratic rights, for "living standards approaching those of the West" (A. Sakharov), against which the main thrust of their own opposition is (openly or secretly) directed. Increasingly the leftist press counterattacks in an attempt to neutralize the unfortunate (for it) impact of demands for legality in the socialist countries. Accusations made against "dissenters" in the Soviet Union range from ones of "naïveté" to "reactionary" — and from their own point of view the Western radicals, striving for socialism, are of course right.

Their freedoms are stale and dilapidated, they do not know what to do with them; they are tired of seeing "no signs on earth or in heaven" (Jean-Paul Sartre), tired of their desperate isolation in the world. And to save them from all this they need an *ideological* faith: as a prop for their existence, as a nostrum for a better tomorrow, as a basis for struggle. In the name of this faith and for the sake of dissolving their own chaotic will in the purposeful will of the *masses*, they are prepared to give up this excessively heavy burden of contentless freedom and the limitless rights of the free personality.

Therefore when voices are heard in the countries where the idea has come to pass defending these same rights and threatening to undermine their ideological faith, they prefer *not to believe* them. This *disbelief* of like-minded circles in the West deepens the Russian liberal democrats' mood of suicidal pessimism, despair and confusion. These moods may eventually lead to a thorough reappraisal of our intelligentsia's philosophical first principles (for some it is already beginning). For the moment, however, they are still dominated by the urge to reorganize the life of mankind on rational principles with the aid of science and technology, and committed to the convergence of East and West in order to bring it about. And still, of course, they condemn the growth of national awareness as an obstacle of the *normal* advance of universal progress.

Great as are the differences between today's socialists, they share a faith in the progress of universal social forms, in the advance of human societies toward a mechanical fusion, toward a higher level of existence. All varieties of socialism claim to be *scientifically based,* whether on Marxism or on some more contemporary scientific-rationalist approach.

Nevertheless, despite its pretensions to science, socialism is no more than *faith* in the ultimate triumph of reason on earth. How else could "progressive philosophy" have survived in the face of the monstrous, catastrophic evils and suffering that mankind has endured during the twentieth century and that should have put an end forever to all "scientific" attempts at rebuilding the world? Since man appears to have reached the ultimate in bestiality this century, we must ask the question: *what* is it that is developing *progressively?* It should be formulated as a question about human nature, about the instinct of evil in man and the conditions in which it comes to the surface.

Some part of mankind has certainly been devoting much frantic and unhappy thought to this subject.

But nothing of the kind has happened among the supporters (at least the majority of them) of the theory of progress. Faith, as one would expect, has proved stronger than the facts. And mankind, flying into the inferno, is once again being soothed by the lullaby of progress.

Now, however, after all that mankind has experienced, the jarring notes in the lullaby can scarcely fail to be heard. We are told that nothing irreparable has happened; it is simply that "progress" has zigzagged and deviated from the straight and narrow way by the will of "evil leaders" and — need one say — "imperialists." But now that the "evil leaders" are dead and the imperialists in their last agony, everything will be all right. . . . In any case, why worry? *"Marxism, like any other science, had the right to make an experiment"* — so wrote the Russian "liberal" Marxist Roy Medvedev in 1974.

Some of the defenders of the theory of progress are, how-

ever, people of great moral sensibility who admit that an
uninterrupted march toward technological perfection may
have fatal consequences for mankind. Among them is the
world-famous, courageous defender of human rights, Academician A. Sakharov. How does he propose to avoid this menace? In his opinion, "conditions for the scientific and
democratic regulation of economic and social life on a worldwide scale" must be created. "Progress must be continually
and purposefully adapting its forms so as to supply human society's needs, and above all preserve nature and the earth for
our descendants." This assumes that in conditions of democracy "human society's needs" will automatically become rational, and that these conditions will probably be created
(since A. Sakharov is an implacable enemy of violence) by
the "goodwill" of governments, economic necessity, and a
recognition of impending dangers. Power will no doubt be
expected to pass from the professional politicians to the scientists and administrators, who will tailor progress into the
requisite form.

But what is the *goal* of mankind? What *requirements* must
progress meet? What guarantees are there that men will display reason and goodwill?

Since A. Sakharov answers none of these questions, his edifice takes on an abstract and formal character.[19]

The unsavory history of the twentieth century has convincingly demonstrated that even the most progressive of the
democracies are helpless to control human malice armed
with the products of progress (as the survivors of Hiroshima
will testify). At best democracy expresses the opinion of the
majority, but this by no means proves that the majority is
right.

What does this leave us with? *Science,* perhaps?

This century has reposed, and still reposes, great hopes in

19. "If progress is the goal," wrote Herzen, "for whom are we working?
Who is this Moloch who retreats backward as the laborers approach instead
of paying them their just due, and has no answer for the masses who are soon
to perish but the sarcastic promise that after their death all will be well on
earth? Surely you would not sentence the people of today to the pitiful fate
of caryatids?"

science. "Science has become a social institution" is the unanimous refrain of all kinds of theorists of modern industrial society. Science raises the material standard of living, science gives us mass production, science puts an end to voluntarism in society, science eliminates the erstwhile chaos of history and opens up a new era of "planned," "positive" history for mankind, and so forth and so on. The task of science is to create a strictly ordered and stable whole out of mankind of a universal "scientist" type. This society's culture, permeated with the "scientific spirit," should be radically different from what was previously understood by the word "culture."

Jean Fourastier, a prominent theorist of the "scientific society," gives a striking description of this new culture. According to Fourastier, this society will create a completely different concept of the personality, adapted to the spirit of modern times. It will be characterized by an antitraditionalist cast of mind, the absence of *historical memory* which would hinder a "sterile" perception of reality, antiemotionalism, sobriety, matter-of-factness. Mass consumption means a change in people's methods of communication. Henceforth man will impinge on his environment "apropos of things, and not apropos of questions such as "is the world organized justly?" Everything that cannot be measured, everything that cannot be computed, in a word, everything *qualitative* must be expunged from the new culture. A new moral climate will reign in the new consumer society, whose main distinguishing feature will be empiricism, corresponding to the empiricism of contemporary science. Morality will be loosened and freed from dogma; the atmosphere of modernity "carefully eliminates difficult and painful questions from moral consciousness." All this, according to Fourastier, helps "scientific" principles to penetrate the minds of the masses and betokens the intellectual "liberation" of the personality. But this "liberation" is not the expansion of freedom in the traditional sense, it is its precise opposite. The new "personality," freed of the weight of tradition and the "stereotypes" of former life-styles, must correspond as closely as possible to the regulatory function of science, that is, its behavior must be totally subordinated to the demands of rationality, optimalism and efficiency — in the noneconomic sphere as well as in the production process, since no sphere of the new society will remain indifferent to production. "The technological environment demands . . . that man should live ever closer to the optimum; all deviation from the optimum is now regarded as disorder, whereas traditional society was more tolerant." The socioregulatory functions of science are carried out by the technocracy. "Technocracy is power exercised on behalf of the demands of . . . growth and size, which regards society merely as an aggregate of the *social resources* designed to be utilized in order to achieve the goals of growth and reinforcement of the apparatus which controls it." (The utopian socialist Saint-Simon, Fourastier's compatriot, once wrote: "The supreme law of human reason subjects everything to itself, rules everything; in its view *people* are only *tools*.") This projected society would of course have to be worldwide and "universal." The development, concentration and rational distribution of science postulate the disintegration of traditional national structures and the liquidation of "historic" cultures incompatible with the "scientific" cast of mind. The greatest obstacle to the creation of the "society of the future" is, in Fourastier's view, the "magical, synthesizing and metaphorical way of thought" among the mass of the people. "The masses and progress," he says, "are a contradiction in terms." (Let us recall that the people is "something to be overcome.") [20]

It needs no great penetration to see the resemblance between this picture and the ideal toward which contemporary Marxism strives — "the socialist reconstruction of the world." The latter merely maintains that this ideal cannot be fulfilled under capitalism. From the Marxist viewpoint the blueprint of the new "personality" as envisaged by the theorists of the "scientific" society must also suffer from one

20. During the 1960s Fourastier concluded that the twentieth century's sociopolitical experimentation and scientific experimentation were manifestations of one and the same antitraditionalist spirit of the New Age.

other vital flaw, namely, the lack of an ideological component, which experience has shown to be of far from negligible utility in exercising the "regulatory" function and which,
happily, does not come into conflict with the "scientific
spirit," since, as is well known, Marxist ideology differs from
"traditional" ideologies precisely in that it is the "only scientific" one. Correspondingly, society requires the regulator of
a scientific ideology, which would in effect squeeze out the
politically naïve technocracy.

The thinly veiled "convergence" of socialism and "tech-
nologism," which is now becoming increasingly visible, is
not fortuitous and rests on their as yet not fully acknowledged
spiritual affinity. Scylla and Charybdis will always find a
common language for negotiations, because they both share a
common nature and — more important — a common enemy.

What is the name of this enemy?

The prophets of the new universal society never speak it
aloud, perhaps because many of them are still vague about it,
but perhaps also because pronouncing it openly would mean
that their cause was lost. All the same . . .

As we have seen, the "new society" envisages the disappearance of the *personality* in the traditional sense of that
word, as we explained above. Its place is to be taken by the
sterile "universal man," deprived of all *qualitative definition,* a rational atom with rationally planned social behavior.

We have seen that the "new society" strives to eliminate
all former "nonoptimal" types of human society — the *nation*
first and foremost — that hinder the worldwide regulation of
the life of "mankind." (The abolition of religion and "magical
thought," as the chief sources of irrational experience, is
taken for granted.)

And so that the radiant field of reason shall never be
darkened by distressing recollections of these dispensable
things, the "new society" intends to destroy historical memory and make *history* nonexistent.

We have here a well-thought-out plan for the *destruction
of the hierarchy of the Christian cosmos,* a plan to turn mankind into an amorphous mass.

But an *impersonal, unstructured, formless existence* is impossible. Deprived of these qualities it *destroys* itself and turns into *nonexistence.*

"The spirit of self-destruction and nonexistence" — that is the name of the real driving force and regulator of "universal progress" without God or man, that is what lies concealed beneath the handsome exterior of "universalism," jeering mercilessly at the "universal men" it has tricked. Throughout history it has masqueraded under a variety of names, always doing its work of destruction; often it has been recognized and forced to disguise itself again, for its mighty opponent is *life* itself. In Russia it was recognized and *named* by Dostoyevsky, but *progressive* society would not believe him, preferring to label his prescience "reaction," and this disbelief has cost Russia dear.

It has cost the rest of the world dear too, which has had its own prophets; but they, if they were not stoned, were considered at best eccentric lunatics and were not taken seriously.

Now all the prophecies have come true. The edifice that took centuries to build on "rational foundations" proved a useless and damnable dwelling. The "temple of society" (Milyukov's [21] expression), to the horror of its architects, became a place of mass human sacrifice, equipped with torture chambers to the greater glory of the Future. It emerged that this laborious process of construction had *its own aims,* quite different from the ostentatious plans of the constructors, who were no more than unconscious, passive tools for the fulfillment of an aim they knew nothing of — the aim of *destroying man and the foundations of his human existence.*

That is the *real* price mankind is obliged to pay — and which it has to some extent paid already — for its abstract, mechanical unity. This fact is being increasingly clearly realized by twentieth-century religious, artistic and philosophical thinkers. However, opportunities for the dissemination and assimilation of their arguments are limited

21. Pavel Milyukov (1859–1943), eminent historian and leader of the main democratic political party at the time of the revolution, the Constitutional Democrats. Emigrated in 1920.— TRANS.

both from without (by both overt and covert methods of suppression) and even more so from within, for reasons inherent in contemporary man *himself*. They bog down in the welter of preconceived stereotypes which in modern man pass for intelligence, stereotypes that are reinforced hourly by all the mass media.

The vast majority of people live in the grip of a tortured yet infantile optimism which quickly swings into paroxysms of fear, but snaps back to its former condition even more quickly. There is no more dangerous mistake than to confuse this will-less, thoughtless, irresponsible "optimism" with man's irrepressible thirst for *life*. An opposite law is at work here, as ancient as that of self-preservation. The *law of the self-destruction of life* works in disguise, cunningly, but no less destructively for that.

But it is not an impersonal force, not some mighty Fate that rules man *independently* or *against* his will. It can act only when the personality consents to subject itself to it, only by its *free* choice. Even if many people of our century insist on their right *not to be* personalities, to deny their freedom and their consequent responsibility for events, this does not alter the situation: it merely shows that they have *already* succumbed to that law, *already* consented to the final destruction of their being.

Universalism's rationalist utopia, based on irrational faith in progress, is not just a harmless aberration that can be overcome by reason. It is the product of the collapse of an integrated self-awareness of the personality, the result of its renunciation of the true roots of all existence, the symptom of a dangerous spiritual sickness which ultimately leads to its destruction. The fulfillment of this utopia does not *raise* the standard of existence, as its adherents believe, but *lowers* it, bringing *disintegration* and finally *destruction*.

FOUR

Attempts under the banner of internationalism to bring this

destructive abstraction to fruition in history have always led to the mutilation and dislocation of living reality and brought about equally fearsome reactions.

We refer to the phenomenon known as *nationalism*, whose origins have not as yet been fully explained.

It is of course wrong to maintain that nationalism is a reflex that arises *solely* when national life threatens to disintegrate, although this is what most of its adherents say. This would mean that it has no existence of its own, except as a reflection of some other phenomenon, and must disappear when the conditions that gave rise to it no longer exist.

But it is a well enough known historical fact that nationalism exists in countries which are under no external or internal threat; nobody will have any difficulty in calling examples to mind. Threats to national existence and national humiliation in any form exacerbate nationalist feelings, but at such times their *particular* nature is practically indistinguishable in the universal national exaltation.

Only when life returns to normal do its own features become more or less distinct.

Nationalism must not be identified with national feeling, as so often happens. The latter is its tool, no more. Nationalism is above all an *ideology*, which directs the existing elemental national instincts into a particular channel.

This ideology starts from the concept of the *exclusive* value of the tribal characteristics of a given race, and the doctrine of its superiority to all others.

The same concept, in the form of egotistical national instincts, also existed of course in the pre-Christian world; it contributed to the distortion of national awareness in the Christian era; but it became an ideology only when the principles of Christianity started to crumble and be forgotten.

We discussed in some detail above how Christianity regards mankind as single in nature, but plural in personality, with every personality having an absolute value.

Like universalism, nationalism distorts this relationship by denying the absoluteness of *every* national personality; but it has its own way of getting there.

Unlike rationalist or materialist universalism, nationalism does its utmost to maintain the concept of a national community that cannot be disrupted by sociological factors. But having lost the suprasociological Christian concept of this community as a *personality,* it is forced to seek it, not *above,* but *beneath* the sociological surface of national life. And nationalism finds this community in the nation's ties of blood and kinship, and places this racially naturalistic perception at the heart of its ideology.

All the traits of the national personality as manifested in the people's history, or rather the traits which for whatever reason appear most desirable to the proponents of the nationalist philosophy, are held to be derived from this racial factor *by its very nature.* It is scarcely necessary to enlarge on the idea that this set of "natural" traits is always historically limited and therefore arbitrary. One need only recall the fate of the theory, formerly widely held in Russia, that autocracy and Orthodoxy were the external *attributes* of Russian nationality and together with it formed an indissoluble triune principle. Or the once no less popular conviction that serfdom was an inalienable national characteristic of the Russian people (this belief of the old Russian nationalists is often met with even today, in an updated form, in the West and in Russia herself).

Nationalism confuses the concepts of personality and nature, ascribing to nature the attributes of personality. As a result, the absoluteness of national *personalities* is transmogrified into the absoluteness of national natures, that is, the single nature of mankind is made to disintegrate into a multiplicity of *private* natures, while the personality is forced into an alien role as the *means* of this disintegration.

Thus mankind becomes a *mechanical* aggregation of *national individuals* or *units* that are totally connected internally, sharing no common measure and maintaining purely external relations with one another.

Nationalism is therefore an individualistic, antipersonal mode of awareness. A man's or nation's awareness of his or its personality is always grounded in an awareness of the personality of all others, in an acknowledgment of the absolute value of any personality.

The nationalist acknowledges such value only in the nation in whose bosom he happened to be born; he regards other nations either as tools or as obstacles to his nation's fulfillment of its own ends. Introverted nationalism, therefore, knows of no moral principles that might limit its claims, but only of an external force that hinders their satisfaction.

Hence the *cult of force* of one's own state that is so remarkably typical for nationalist ideologies.

Another most important principle of this ideology is concern for the inner condition of the nation, interpreted in a very narrow sense. Insofar as nationalism, as has already been pointed out, believes a people to be endowed with its particular characteristics by its very nature, it insists on biological purity for the preservation of the national type. If a nation declines, nationalism tends to blame the decline on an adulteration of this "purity"; conversely, if a national renaissance is to be achieved, purity must be reestablished.

These two symbols — racial purity and state power — are for nationalists the essential and sufficient conditions of so-called national well-being. All other factors of national life — religion, culture, political system — are subordinate to these primary conditions, but they are not fundamental to the existence of the nation, which is declared to be an end in itself.

However dissimilar universalism and atheist nationalism may appear to be on the surface, however great their hatred of one another, they have a great deal in common that does not immediately meet the eye.

These philosophies are distinct from one another not *qualitatively,* but only *quantitatively.* Nationalism pursues the *same goals* as universalism, only within the framework of a national state. Universalism calls for love of men and mankind as such, nationalism calls for love of the men of a particular tribe and the tribe itself as such.

This similarity of two apparently contradictory phenomena was once penetratingly remarked on by the Russian thinker Konstantin Leontyev:

"To love a tribe as a tribe is to exaggerate and deceive.
. . . The purely tribal concept contains nothing germinal,
nothing creative; it is nothing but a *private perversion* of the
cosmopolitanist idea of universal equality and sterile universal happiness. . . . The national principle without religion
. . . is a principle of slow but sure destruction."

We would like to end this essay as we began it. Russia has
reached some unrecognized historic milestone. Today we all
have the responsibility of restoring her national awareness,
which is still fragmented and dispersed. The greatest responsibility rests with the Christians, who not only *can* but *must*
participate in this essential spiritual work. The humiliated
and deafened Russian people needs as never before to become aware of itself as a *personality*, freely choosing its historical path.

Christians today are called upon to assist it to *recall* its
spiritual roots in history, but before doing so they need to
recall it *themselves*.

This article is an attempt to remind them of it. As the Russian philosopher said: "We were destined to give the world
vivid examples of the lunacy to which the spirit of present-
day enlightenment can bring people — but we also have a
duty to discover the strongest possible antidote to this spirit."

The Smatterers

ALEXANDER SOLZHENITSYN

ONE

The fateful peculiarities of the educated stratum of Russians before the revolution were thoroughly analyzed in *Vekhi* (*Landmarks*) [1] — and indignantly repudiated by the entire intelligentsia and by all political parties from the Constitutional Democrats to the Bolsheviks. The prophetic depth of *Vekhi* failed (as its authors knew it would fail) to arouse the sympathies of the Russian reading public; it had no influence on the development of the situation in Russia and was unable to avert the disastrous events which followed. Before long the very title of the book, exploited by another group of writers with narrowly political interests and low standards (*Smena Vekh* — *New Bearings*), was to grow blurred and dim and to disappear entirely from the memory of new generations of educated Russians, as the book itself inevitably disappeared from official Soviet libraries. But even after sixty years its testimony has not lost its brightness: *Vekhi* today still seems to us to have been a vision of the future. And our only cause for rejoicing is that now, after sixty years, the stra-

1. See Introduction, pages v–vi.— TRANS.

tum of Russian society able to lend its support to the book appears to be deepening.

We read *Vekhi* today with a dual awareness, for the ulcers we are shown seem to belong not just to an era that is past history, but in many respects to our own times as well. That is why it is almost impossible to begin talking about today's intelligentsia (a problematical term which for the moment, in this first part, we shall take as referring to "that mass of people who call themselves by this name," and an intellectual — an *"intelligent"* — "any person who demands that he be regarded as such"), without drawing a comparison between its present attributes and the conclusions of *Vekhi*. Historical hindsight always offers a better understanding.

However, being in no way obliged to preserve the comprehensive structure of *Vekhi's* analysis, we shall for the limited purposes of the present survey take the liberty of summarizing and regrouping *Vekhi's* conclusions into the following four categories:

(1) *Faults of the old intelligentsia* which were important in the context of Russian history but which today have either faded away, or still exist in a much weaker form, or have become diametrically reversed:

Clannish, unnatural disengagement from the general life of the nation. (Today there is a considerable feeling of involvement by virtue of the intelligentsia's employed status.) Intense opposition to the state as a matter of principle. (Today it is only in its private thoughts and among small circles of friends that the intelligentsia draws a distinction between its own interests and those of the state, delights in any failure on the part of the state and passively sympathizes with any show of resistance; in all else it is the loyal servant of the state.) Individual moral cowardice in the face of "public opinion," mental mediocrity at the individual level. (Now far outstripped by total cowardice when confronted by the will of the state.) Love of egalitarian justice, the social good and the material well-being of the people, which paralyzed its love of and interest in the truth; the "temptation of the Grand Inquisitor": let the truth perish if people will be the happier for it. (Nowadays it has no such broad concerns. Nowadays it is "let the truth perish if by paying that price I can preserve myself and my family.") Infatuation with the intelligentsia's general credo; ideological intolerance of any other; hatred as a passionate ethical impulse. (All this bursting passion has now disappeared.) Fanaticism that made the intelligentsia deaf to the voice of life. (Nowadays: accommodation and adaptation to practical considerations.) There was no word more unpopular with the intelligentsia than "humility." (Now they have humbled themselves to the point of servility.) Daydreaming, a naïve idealism, an inadequate sense of reality. (Today they have a sober, utilitarian understanding of it.) A nihilistic attitude to labor. (Extinct.) Unfitness for practical work. (Fitness.) A strenuous, unanimous atheism which uncritically accepted the competence of science to decide even matters of religion — once and for all and of course negatively; dogmatic idolatry of man and mankind; the replacement of religion by a faith in scientific progress. (The atheism has abated in intensity, but is still as widespread among the mass of the educated stratum; by now it has grown traditional and insipid, though unconditional obeisance is still made to scientific progress and the notion that "man is the measure of all things.") Mental inertia; the feebleness of autonomous intellectual activity and even hostility to autonomous spiritual claims. (Today, on the contrary, there are some educated people who make up for their withdrawal from public passion, faith and action by indulging at their leisure, in their closed shell and among their circle of friends, in quite intensive intellectual activity, although usually with no relevance to the outside world — sometimes by way of anonymous, secret appearances in *samizdat*.)

In the main *Vekhi* was critical of the intelligentsia and set down those of its vices and inadequacies that were a danger to progress in Russia. It contains no separate analysis of the virtues of the intelligentsia. Yet looking at *Vekhi* comparatively from an angle of vision that enables us to take account of the qualities of the educated stratum of the present time, we find that, among its faults, the authors of *Vekhi* also list

features which today cannot be viewed otherwise than as
(2) *Virtues of the prerevolutionary intelligentsia:*

A universal search for an integral world view, a thirst for
faith (albeit secular), and an urge to subordinate one's life to
this faith. (Nothing comparable exists today, only tired cynicism.) Social compunction, a sense of guilt with regard to the
people. (Nowadays the opposite is widely felt: that the people is guilty toward the intelligentsia and will not repent.)
Moral judgments and moral considerations occupy an exceptional position in the soul of the Russian intellectual: all
thought of himself is egoism; his personal interests and very
existence must be unconditionally subordinated to service to
society; puritanism, personal asceticism, total selflessness,
even abhorrence and fear of personal wealth as a burden and
a temptation. (None of this relates to us — we are quite the
reverse!) A fanatical willingness to sacrifice oneself — even an
active quest for such sacrifice; although this path is trodden
by only a handful of individuals, it is nevertheless the obligatory and only worthy ideal aspired to by all. (This is unrecognizable, this is not us! All that remains in common is the
word "intelligentsia," which has survived through force of
habit.)

The Russian intelligentsia cannot have been so base if
Vekhi could apply such lofty criteria in its criticism of it. This
will strike us even more forcibly when we look at the group
of characteristics depicted by *Vekhi* as

(3) *Faults at the time,* which in our topsy-turvy world of
today have the *appearance almost of virtues:*

The aim of universal equality, in whose interests the individual must be prepared to curtail his higher needs. The psychology of heroic ecstasy, reinforced by state persecution;
parties are popular in proportion to their degree of fearless-
ness. (Today the persecution is crueler and more systematic,
and induces depression instead of ecstasy.) A personal sense
of martyrdom and a compulsion to confess; almost a death
wish. (The desire now is for self-preservation.) The heroic intellectual is not content with the modest role of worker and
dreams of being the savior of mankind or at least of the Rus-

sian people. Exaltation, an irrational mood of elation, intoxication with struggle. He is convinced that the only course open to him is social struggle and the destruction of society in its existing form. (Nothing of the kind! The only possible course is subservience, sufferance, and the hope of mercy.)

But we have not lost all of our spiritual heritage. We too are recognizably there.

(4) *Faults inherited in the present day:*

Lack of sympathetic interest in the history of our homeland, no feeling of blood relationship with its history. Insufficient sense of historical reality. This is why the intelligentsia lives *in expectation of a social miracle* (in those days they did a great deal to bring it about; now they make it less and less possible for the miracle to happen — but hope for it all the same!). All that is bad is the result of outward disorganization and consequently all that is needed are external reforms. Autocracy is responsible for everything that is happening, therefore the intellectual is relieved of all personal responsibility and personal guilt. An exaggerated awareness of their rights. Pretentiousness, posturing, the hypocrisy of constant recourse to "principles" — to rigid abstract arguments. An overweening insistence on the opposition between themselves and the "philistines." Spiritual arrogance. The religion of self-deification — the intelligentsia sees its existence as providential for the country.

This all tallies so perfectly that it needs no comment.

Let us add a dash of Dostoyevsky (from *The Diary of a Writer*):

Faintheartedness. A tendency to jump to pessimistic conclusions.

And many more qualities of the old intelligentsia would have survived in the present one if the *intelligentsia itself* had remained in existence.

TWO

The Intelligentsia! How far does it reach, where do its

boundaries lie? The term is the one that Russians most love to argue over, yet it is used in widely differing ways and its very vagueness tends to diminish the value of any conclusions reached. The writers of *Vekhi* defined the intelligentsia not in terms of the level or nature of its members' education but according to their ideology, as if it were a sort of new, religionless, humanist order. Clearly they did not regard engineers or scholars in the mathematical and technical fields as part of the intelligentsia. Nor the military intelligentsia. Nor the clergy. However, neither did the intelligentsia itself at that time, the *intelligentsia proper* (humanistic, political and revolutionary) regard all these people as a part of itself. Indeed, *Vekhi* implies, and in the writings of *Vekhi*'s disciples [2] the implication becomes a firmly rooted conviction, that the greatest Russian writers and philosophers — Dostoyevsky, Tolstoy, Vladimir Solovyov — did not belong to the intelligentsia either! To the modern reader this sounds preposterous, and yet it was so in its day and the gulf was quite a deep one. What people prized in Gogol was his denunciation of the state system and the ruling classes. But the moment he embarked upon the spiritual quest that was dearest of all to him he was flayed by the journalistic press and excommunicated from progressive society. Tolstoy was prized for the same sort of denunciations and also for his animosity toward the Church and toward higher philosophy and creation. But his insistent moralizing, his summonses to the simple life, to nonresistance to evil and to universal goodness met with a condescending reception. The "reactionary" Dostoyevsky was altogether detested by the intelligentsia. He would have been trampled underfoot and forgotten in Russia — and would not be quoted at every turn today — had he not suddenly surfaced in the twentieth century to thunderous worldwide fame in the respected West.

Meanwhile, what about all those people who fell outside the intelligentsia proper — where were they to be fitted in? After all, they had their own characteristic features which

2. For example: *The Russian Religious Renaissance in the Twentieth Century* by N. Zernov.

were sometimes quite different from *Vekhi*'s specifications. The technical intelligentsia, for example, possessed only a small proportion of the characteristics outlined in *Vekhi*. It was not at all disengaged from the life of the nation, nor opposed to the state, nor fanatical, nor revolutionary, nor guided by hatred, nor possessed of a poor grasp of reality, and so forth and so on.

If we take the etymological definition of the word *intelligentsia* from its root, *intellegere* — that is, "to understand, to know, to think, to have an idea about something" — then, clearly, it would embrace a class of people differing in many respects from those who, in Russia at the turn of the century, styled themselves thus and were viewed as such in *Vekhi*.

G. Fedotov [3] wittily suggested that the intelligentsia should be defined as a specific group of people "united by the idealism of their aims and the unsoundness of their ideals."

V. Dal [4] defined the intelligentsia as "the educated, intellectually developed part of the population," but remarked thoughtfully that "we have no word for *moral education*," for that process of enlightenment which "educates both the mind and the *heart*."

There have been attempts to construct a definition of the intelligentsia on the basis of its spontaneous creative energy, regardless of external circumstances; on the basis of its non-imitative mode of thought; and on the basis of its independent spiritual vitality. The chief difficulty dogging all these searches has lain not in an inability to formulate a definition, or to characterize an actually existing social group, but in a disparity of *desires:* who *would we like* to see included in the name *intelligentsia?*

Berdyayev [5] was later to suggest an alternative definition to

3. G. Fedotov, originally a historian and member of the Russian Social Democratic party, turned to religion after the revolution and in 1925 was allowed to go abroad. He subsequently became a professor of theology.— TRANS.
4. The great Russian lexicographer (1801–1872) who composed the first comprehensive dictionary of the Russian language.— TRANS.
5. See note on page 55.— TRANS.

that discussed in *Vekhi:* he saw the intelligentsia as the aggregate of Russia's spiritually elect. That is, as a spiritual elite, and not a social stratum.

After the 1905–1907 revolution a gradual polarization of the intelligentsia began to take place: the interests of the younger, student generation took a new turn, and slowly an initially very narrow stratum emerged, attaching a heightened importance to the inner, moral life of man instead of to outward social transformations. So the authors of *Vekhi* were not entirely alone in the Russia of their day. But this fragile, silent process of the emergence of a new type of intelligentsia (in the wake of which the term itself would have splintered and acquired a more exact meaning) was fated not to reach completion in Russia: it was caught up and crushed in the toils of the First World War and then by the dizzy onrush of revolution. The word "intelligentsia" was more often on the lips of the Russian educated class than many others, but in the course of events it never did acquire a definitive meaning.

Since then there has been even less opportunity and time. The year 1917 marked the ideological collapse of the "revolutionary-humanist" intelligentsia, as it used to describe itself. For the first time it had to shift from isolated acts of terror, from its conceited cliquishness, from its received party dogmatism and from its unbridled public criticism of the government to taking real political action. And fully in accordance with the melancholy forecasts of the *Vekhi* writers (and, independently, of S. Bulgakov: [6] "the intelligentsia, in league with our 'Mongols' . . . will be the ruin of Russia"), the intelligentsia proved incapable of taking that action, quailed, and was lost in confusion; its party leaders readily abdicated the power and leadership which had seemed so desirable from a distance; and power, like a ball of fire, was tossed from hand to hand until it came into hands which caught it and were sufficiently hardened to withstand its white heat (they also, incidentally, belonged to the intelligentsia, but to a special part of it). The intelligentsia had

6. See note on page 20.— TRANS.

236

succeeded in rocking Russia with a cosmic explosion, but was unable to handle the debris. (Later, surveying the situation from abroad, the intelligentsia formulated excuses for itself: "the people," it turned out, "was not up to scratch," "the people had disappointed the expectations of the intelligentsia." But this was precisely what *Vekhi* had diagnosed: that the intelligentsia was deifying a people whom it did not know and from whom it was hopelessly estranged! Ignorance, however, is no excuse. Ignorant of the people and its own political capacities, the intelligentsia should have been ten times more careful of taking the people's and its own name in vain.

And just as the poker in the fable, carelessly stepped on in the dark hut, struck the simpleton on the forehead with sevenfold force, so the revolution treated the intelligentsia which had awakened it. After the tsarist bureaucracy, police, nobility and clergy had been dealt with, the next murderous blow caught the intelligentsia as early as 1918–1920, while the revolution was still young, and brought with it not only firing squads and jails, but also cold, hunger, hard labor and mocking contempt. The intelligentsia, in its heroic ecstasy, was unprepared for all this and (which it would never have expected of itself) drifted into the civil war in part under the protection of the former tsarist generals, and then into exile — not for the first time in some cases, though now the intellectuals were all mixed up with those same bureaucrats whom they had until recently been blowing up with bombs.

Life abroad, although much harder in its everyday aspects than it had been in the old Russia they so detested, did at least grant the remnants of the Russian intelligentsia a few more decades for excuses, explanations and reflection. The larger section of the intelligentsia — the part that remained in the Soviet Union — was not destined to enjoy such freedom. Those who survived the civil war no longer had the latitude of thought and expression with which they had previously been pampered. Threatened by the GPU [7] and

7. GPU: acronym for "State Political Administration" (a euphemism for the secret police), introduced in 1922 to replace the older name of Cheka (an ab-

unemployment, they were obliged by the end of the 1920s either to adopt the official ideology and pretend it was sincerely held and cherished, or else face ruin and dispersal. Those were harsh years when the steadfastness of spirit of both individuals and the masses was put to the test, a test that was applied not only to the intelligentsia, but, for example, to the Russian Church as well. It could even be said that the Church, which was utterly decrepit and demoralized on the eve of the revolution and possibly one of the chief culprits of Russia's decline, passed the test of the twenties with far greater merit: it too had traitors and timeservers in its midst (the "reformists"),[8] but it also brought forth a mass of martyr-priests whose steadfastness was intensified by persecution and who were driven at bayonet point into the camps. Admittedly the Soviet regime was far more merciless toward the Church, while the intelligentsia was titillated with a stream of temptations: the temptation to *understand the great Natural Order,* to acknowledge the newly arrived iron Necessity as the long-awaited Freedom, to acknowledge it *for themselves* today — the thumps of their sincere hearts forestalling tomorrow's kicks from the escort guards or the death sentences handed out by the public prosecutors; the temptation not to turn sour as part of that "putrefying intelligentsia,"[9] but to submerge their "I" in the Natural Order, to gulp down that hot draft of proletarian air, and to totter off in pursuit of the Progressive Class as it marched away into the radiant future. And for those who caught up, there was a second temptation: to apply their intellect to the

breviation of the Russian for "Extraordinary Commission"). Later in 1922 the name was changed to OGPU ("United State Political Administration"), then in 1934 to NKVD ("People's Commissariat for Internal Affairs"), in 1943 to NKGB ("People's Commissariat for State Security"), in 1946 to MGB ("Ministry of State Security") and finally in 1953 to KGB ("Committee for State Security"), its present designation.— TRANS.
8. A reference to members of the so-called Living Church group, who advocated collaboration between the Orthodox Church and the Revolutionary Government in the early twenties. They were heavily infiltrated by the secret police.— TRANS.
9. A phrase of Lenin's.— TRANS.

Unprecedented Creation of a new society, the like of which world history had never seen. How could they fail to fall for it! This fervent self-persuasion was the physical salvation of many intellectuals and it even seemed to have saved them from spiritual collapse, for they gave themselves up to their new faith in all sincerity and entirely of their own free will. (And for long afterward they towered — in literature, art, and the humanities — like veritable tree trunks, and only time's weathering disclosed that they were merely hollow bark and had no pith.) There were some who went into this "chase" after the Progressive Class hypocritically and laughing at themselves, for they had already realized the significance of what was happening and simply wanted to save their skins. Paradoxically, though (and the process is repeating itself in the West today), the *majority* went into it in complete sincerity, in a hypnotic trance, having willingly let themselves be hypnotized. The intoxication of the rising generation of young members of the intelligentsia reinforced the process: the truths of triumphant Marxism appeared fiery-winged, and for two whole decades, right up to the Second World War, we were borne along on those wings. (As if it were an apocryphal story I still recall the autumn of 1941, when the fires of deathly war were ablaze and I was trying for the nth time — and as unsuccessfully as ever — to fathom the wisdom of *Das Kapital*.)

In the 1920s and 1930s the composition of the old in telligentsia, as it formerly understood and viewed itself, underwent intensive change and expansion.

The first natural extension was of the technical intelligentsia (the "specialists"). However, this technical intelligentsia, with its firm professional footing, its tangible links with national industry, its conscience clear of the sin of complicity in the atrocities of revolution, and therefore under no compulsion to weave a passionate justification of the New Order or to curry favor with it — this technical intelligentsia displayed far greater spiritual resilience in the twenties than did the nonscientific intelligentsia, was in less of a hurry to accept the new Ideology as the only possible world view, and, moreover, because of the independent nature of its work, was able to hold out physically as well.

But there were other ways in which the old intelligentsia expanded — and disintegrated — and these processes were confidently controlled by the state. One was the physical interruption of the intelligentsia's family traditions: the children of members of the intelligentsia had virtually no right of entry to establishments of higher education (only personal submission and regeneration through the Komsomol [10] opened the door). Another was the hasty creation of the "workers' faculty" intelligentsia, poorly trained and hence a "red-hot" proletarian-Communist infusion. A third way was the mass arrests of "wreckers." [11] This blow hit the technical intelligentsia hardest of all: it crushed a small minority and left the rest frightened to death. In what was by then a countrywide atmosphere of general intimidation, the Shakhty [12] and "Industrial party" [13] trials, and a few other smaller-scale trials, speedily achieved their aim. By the beginning of the thirties the technical intelligentsia too had been reduced to a state of total submission, and during the thirties it too was well schooled in treachery: it learned to vote obediently at meetings for whatever penalties were demanded; when one brother was annihilated, another brother would dutifully step into his shoes, even to take upon himself the leadership of the Academy of Sciences; and by this time there was no military order that the Russian intelligentsia would have dared regard as amoral or would not have rushed promptly and obsequiously to execute.[14] This blow struck not only at the

10. See note on page 123.— TRANS.
11. See note on page 117.— TRANS.
12. At the Shakhty trial, held in the summer of 1928, fifty-three engineers were accused of "wrecking," or industrial sabotage, in the Donbas coalfield.— TRANS.
13. The "Industrial party" trial was a sequel to the Shakhty trial and the climax of the campaign against the engineers. The eight defendants were said to have built up a secret organization covering the entire country. All eight were shot.— TRANS.
14. This feverish zeal for carrying out the orders of the state was portrayed with great frankness in a recent *samizdat* publication, *Tupolevskaya*

old intelligentsia, but soon affected part of the workers' faculty intelligentsia as well: it selected its victims on the principle of their refusal to obey, and in this way bent the remaining masses ever more into submission. A fourth process consisted of "normal" Soviet replenishments of the intelligentsia with people who had received their entire fourteen years of education under the Soviet regime and whose genetic links did not go beyond it.

In the thirties the intelligentsia underwent yet another expansion, this time on a vast scale: by state design and abetted by the passivity of the public consciousness, millions of state employees joined its ranks, or, to be more accurate, the entire intelligentsia was assigned to the class of *employees* — for that was the only way one described or styled oneself at the time, whether one was filling in forms or being issued with bread-ration cards. All this strict regimentation drove the intelligentsia into the class of functionaries and officialdom, and the very word "intelligentsia" was abandoned and used almost exclusively as a term of abuse. (Even members of the free professions, through their "creative unions," were reduced to the status of employees. Since then the intelligentsia has continued to exist in this sharply expanded form, in this distorted sense and with a reduced level of self-awareness. By the time the word "intelligentsia" was partly rehabilitated after the war it encompassed many extra millions of petit-bourgeois functionaries performing any kind of clerical or modest mental work.

In the prewar years the party and state leaders, the ruling class, had insisted on maintaining an entirely separate identity from both the "functionaries" (for *they* had remained "workers") and even more from the putrefied "intelligentsia," and as "blue-blooded" proletarians had carefully fenced themselves off. After the war, however, particularly in the 1950s and even more so in the 1960s, when "proletarian" terminology flagged in its turn and became increasingly "Soviet," and leading members of the intelligentsia on the other

Sharaga (*The Tupolev Special Laboratory*), which reveals that even the most prominent persons were not immune to it.

hand were increasingly allowed to occupy high-level posts as the technological requirements for all forms of management grew, the ruling class also allowed itself to be referred to as "the intelligentsia" (a development reflected in the modern definition of the intelligentsia in the Large Soviet Encyclopedia), and the "intelligentsia" obediently accepted this expansion too.

It was thought as monstrous before the revolution to call a priest an intellectual as it is natural now for the same word to be applied to the party agitator and political instructor.

So, having failed to reach a precise definition of the intelligentsia, it would appear that we no longer need one. What is understood by the word in Russia today is *the whole of the educated stratum,* every person who has been to school above the seventh grade.

In Dal's dictionary the word *obrazovat'* as opposed to the word *prosveshchat'* is defined as meaning: "to give merely an outward polish."

Although the polish we have acquired is rather third-rate, it will be entirely in the spirit of the Russian language and will probably convey the right sense if we refer to this "polished" or "schooled" stratum, all those who nowadays falsely or rashly style themselves "the intelligentsia," as the *obrazovanshchina* — the semieducated estate — the "smatterers."

THREE

And so it has come to pass, and there is no arguing with history: they have driven us among the smatterers and drowned us in them (but *we let ourselves* be driven and drowned). There is no arguing with history; but in our hearts we protest and disagree: things cannot possibly stay the same as they are! Be it because of our memories of the past or our hopes for the future — *we* are different!

One Altayev (a pseudonym for the author of an article entitled "The Dual Consciousness of the Intelligentsia and Pseudoculture" which appeared in No. 97 of the *Vestnik*

RSKD),[15] while acknowledging that the intelligentsia has increased in numbers and has dissolved in and become one with the bureaucracy, still seeks a touchstone for separating it from the dissolving mass. He finds it in a "generic feature" of the intelligentsia which, he claims, distinguished it before the revolution and stil does so today, so that it can be accepted as a "definition" of it: the intelligentsia is "a unique category of people" which has never been duplicated in any other country and which lives with a "sense of its collective alienation" from "its own land, its own people and its own state regime." But leaving aside the artificiality of this defini tion (and the not so very "uniqueness" of the situation) it could be argued that a sense of alienation from its own *people* was precisely what the prerevolutionary intelligentsia (as defined by *Vekhi*) did *not* feel — on the contrary, it was confident of its plenipotence to speak in the name of the people; and the modern intelligentsia is in no respect alienated from the modern *state:* those who feel that way, either in their private thoughts or among their immediate circle of friends, with a sense of constriction, depression, doom and resignation, are not only *maintaining* the state by their daily activities as members of the intelligentsia, but are accepting and fulfilling an even more terrible condition laid down by the state: participation *with their soul* in the common, compulsory lie. How much further could they go? One could perhaps surrender only one's body, one's brain, or one's expertise and still remain "alienated" — but not if one surrenders one's soul! The old intelligentsia really was opposed to the state, and its opposition went as far as an open split and even an explosion — for that is what it came to — whereas our present-day intelligentsia, as that same Altayev, contradicting himself, writes, "has not dared to speak out under Soviet power, not only because it has not been allowed to do so, but first and foremost because it *has had nothing* to say. Communism was its own offspring . . . including even the idea of terror. . . . It was conscious of no principles that were essentially different from the principles

15. See pages 95 and 96 and note on page 96.— TRANS.

implemented by the Communist regime." The intelligentsia is itself "an accessory to evil and to crime, and this, more than anything else, is what prevents it from raising its head." (And eased its entry into the system of lies.) Albeit in a somewhat unexpected form, the intelligentsia in fact got exactly what it had spent many decades trying to achieve — and submitted without a struggle. And the one solace it has been able to suck on surreptitiously since has been that "the ideas of revolution were good, but were perverted." And at each turn in history it has comforted itself with the hope that the regime was beginning to mend, that a change for the better was just around the corner and that then, at last, collaboration with the authorities would be fully vindicated (Altayev sums it up with his brilliantly polished *six temptations* of the Russian intelligentsia: revolutionary, new-directionary, socialistic, patriotic, "thawistic" and technocratic, all arising consecutively and then continuing to coexist at any given moment in the present).

We submitted all right, abasing ourselves utterly and annihilating ourselves spiritually, so what in all fairness can we call ourselves other than *smatterers?* A melancholy awareness of our alienation from the state (since the 1940s only), of our helpless captivity in the grip of alien paws — this is not a generic feature inherited from the past, but the genesis of a *new* protest, the genesis of repentance. And the vast majority of the intelligentsia is by now fully aware — some uneasily, some indifferently and some arrogantly — of their present alienation from the *people.*

The problem of how to avoid being engulfed by the smatterers, how to keep a distance from them and preserve the concept of an intelligentsia, has been much discussed by G. Pomerants (this is not a pseudonym; Pomerants is a real person, an orientalist who has published a whole volume of philosophical essays and polemical articles in *samizdat*): "the healthiest section of modern society . . . you will find no other stratum so progressive." [16] But he too is thrown into

16. Most of the quotations from Pomerants on this and following pages are taken from his articles "The Man from Nowhere" and "Quadrillion."

confusion by this ocean of smatterers: "The concept of an intelligentsia is one that is very hard to define. The intelligentsia has not yet settled into a stable entity." (Not settled into a stable entity, a hundred and thirty years after Belinsky and Granovsky? [17] No, after the shock of revolution.) He is obliged to single out "the best part of the intelligentsia," which is "not even a thin layer but a handful of people; . . . only a small core of the intelligentsia is an intelligentsia in the proper sense of the word, . . . a narrow circle of people capable of independently rediscovering cultural treasures and values." He even writes: "belonging to the intelligentsia is a process." He suggests that we cease trying to delineate the contours, boundaries and limits of the intelligentsia and instead imagine a kind of field of force, as in physics: there is a center of radiation (the tiny handful), then a "stratum of the animate intelligentsia," and finally, furthest from the center, the "inanimate intelligentsia" (?), a stratum which is, however, "more mature than the philistines." (In earlier variants of the same *samizdat* article Pomerants divided the intelligentsia into the "honorable" and the "dishonorable," which he defined rather strangely as follows: "the honorable ones play dirty tricks on their neighbors only when compelled to, and take no pleasure in it," while the dishonorable ones, so he says, enjoy doing it, and that's the difference between them!)

True, Pomerants rises to the defense of this multimillion-strong class on the borderline between "inanimateness" and "philistinism" and writes with great feeling about the hard life of schoolteachers, general practitioners and bookkeepers — "the white-collar laborers." But his vigorous defense turns out to be more of an *attack* on "the people," showing that the man whose job it is to scan the payroll for

17. Vissarion Belinsky (1811–1848) was Russia's first great literary critic, a supporter of Pushkin, Gogol and Lermontov (often for the wrong reasons) and the founder of a vigorous radical school of literary criticism. Timofei Granovsky (1813–1855) was a professor of history at Moscow University, a leading liberal and the spiritual father of the "Westernizers," a group of thinkers who advocated the introduction of West European political and social institutions into Russia.— TRANS.

mistakes has a harder time than the collective farm girl who works in a stinking hen house.

That labor has been distorted and people maimed is certainly true. I myself, having spent a fair amount of time working as a schoolteacher, can passionately endorse these words and add many more categories to the list: construction engineers, agricultural technicians, agronomists, and so on. Schoolteachers are so harassed, hard-pressed and degraded, and live in such penury, that they have no time, scope or freedom left to form their own opinions about anything or even to seek and imbibe any spiritual food that has not already been contaminated. And it is not because of their nature or the poorness of their education that these benighted provincial masses lag so far behind in "animateness" in comparison with the privileged university intellectuals of the capital, but precisely because of their penury and social deprivation.

But none of this alters the hopeless picture of a bloated army of smatterers to which the standard certificate of entry is the most average sort of schooling.

FOUR

It is all very well to charge the working class at the present time with being excessively law-abiding, uninterested in the spiritual life, immersed in philistinism and totally preoccupied with material concerns — getting an apartment, buying tasteless furniture (the only kind in the shops), playing cards and dominoes or watching television and getting drunk — but have the smatterers, even in the capital, risen all that much higher? Dearer furniture, higher-quality concerts, and cognac instead of vodka? But it watches the same hockey matches on television. On the fringes of smatterdom an obsession with wage-levels may be essential to survival, but at its resplendent center (in sixteen republican capitals and a handful of closed towns) it is disgusting to see all ideas and convictions subordinated to the mercenary pursuit of bigger and better salaries, titles, positions, apartments, villas, cars (Pomerants: "A dinner service is compensation for lost nerves"), and — even more — trips abroad! (Wouldn't this have amazed the prerevolutionary intelligentsia! It needs explaining: new impressions, a gay time, the good life, an expense account in foreign currency, the chance to buy gaudy rags. . . . For this reason I think even the sorriest member of the prerevolutionary intelligentsia would refuse to shake hands with the most illustrious of our metropolitan smatterers today.) But what distinguishes the mentality of the Moscow smatterers more than anything else is their greed for awards, prizes and titles far beyond the reach of the working class or the provincial smatterers — the prize money is higher, and what resounding titles they are: "People's Artist (Actor, etc.) . . . Meritorious Practitioner . . . Laureate . . ."! For all this people are not ashamed to toe the line punctiliously, break off all unapproved friendships, carry out all the wishes of their superiors and condemn any one of their colleagues either in writing or from a public platform, or simply by refusing to shake his hand, if the party committee orders them to.

If all these are the qualities of the *intelligentsia,* who are the *philistines?*

People whose names we used to read not so long ago on our cinema screens and who passed for members of the intelligentsia if anyone did, who recently left this country for good, saw no shame in taking eighteenth-century escritoires to pieces (the export of antiques is prohibited), nailing the pieces to some ordinary planks of wood to make grotesque "furniture," and exporting them in that form. Can one still bring oneself to utter the word "intelligentsia"? It is only a customs regulation that prevents icons older than the seventeenth century from leaving the country. Whole exhibitions of later icons are at this very moment being staged in Europe — and not only the state has been selling abroad. . . .

Everybody who lives in our country pays dues for the maintenance of the obligatory ideological lie. But for the working class, and all the more so for the peasantry, the dues are minimal, especially now that the financial loans which used to be extorted annually have been abolished (it was the fake voluntariness of these loans that was so perfidious and so distressing: the money could have been appropriated by some other means); all they now have to do is vote every so often at some general meeting where absenteeism is not checked with particular thoroughness. Our state bailiffs and ideological inculcators, on the other hand, sincerely believe in their Ideology, many of them having devoted themselves to it out of long years of inertia or ignorance, or because of man's psychological quirk of liking to have a philosophy of life that matches his basic work.

But what of our central smatterers? Perfectly well aware of the shabbiness and flabbiness of the party lie and ridiculing it among themselves, they yet cynically repeat the lie with their very next breath, issuing "wrathful" protests and newspaper articles in ringing, rhetorical tones, and expanding and reinforcing it by their eloquence and style! Where did Orwell light upon his *doublethink*, what was his model if not the Soviet intelligentsia of the 1930s and 1940s? And since that time this doublethink has been worked up to perfection and become a permanent part of our lives.

Oh, we crave *freedom*, we denounce (in a whisper) anyone who ventures to doubt the desirability and necessity of total freedom in our country. (Meaning, in all probability, not freedom for everyone but certainly for the central smatterers. Pomerants, in a letter to the twenty-third Party Congress, proposes setting up an association of the "nucleus of the intelligentsia," which would have a free press at its disposal and be a theoretical center giving advice to the administrative and party centers.) But we are waiting for this freedom to fall into our lap like some unexpected miracle, without any effort on our part, while we ourselves do nothing to win this freedom. Never mind the old traditions of supporting people in political trouble, feeding the fugitive, sheltering the passless or the homeless (we might lose our state-controlled jobs) — the central smatterers labor day after day, conscientiously and sometimes even with talent, to strengthen our common prison. And even for this they will not allow themselves to be blamed! A multitude of excuses has been primed, pondered and prepared. Tripping up a colleague or publishing lies in a newspaper statement is resourcefully justified by the perpetrator and unanimously accepted by his associates: If I (he) hadn't done it, they would have sacked me (him) from my (his) job and appointed somebody worse! So in order to maintain the principle of what is *good* and for the benefit of all, it is natural that every day you will find yourself obliged to harm the few ("honorable men play dirty tricks on their neighbors only when they have to"). But the few are *themselves* guilty: why did they flaunt themselves so indiscreetly in front of the bosses, without a thought for the *collective?* Or why did they hide their questionnaires from the personnel department and thus *lay the entire collective open to attack?* Chelnov (in the *Vestnik RSKD*, No. 97) wittily describes the intelligentsia's position as *standing crookedly* — "from which position the vertical seems a ridiculous posture."

But the chief justifying argument is: *children!* In the face of this argument everyone falls silent: for who has the right to sacrifice the material welfare of his children for the sake of an *abstract* principle of truth?! That the moral health of their children is more precious than their careers does not even enter the parents' heads, so impoverished have they themselves become. And it is reasonable that their children should grow up the same: pragmatists right from their school days, first-year students already resigned to the lie of the political education class, already shrewdly weighing their most profitable way into the competitive world of science. Theirs is a generation that has experienced no real persecution, but how cautious it is! And those few youths — the hope of Russia — who turn and look truth in the face are usually cursed and even persecuted by their infuriated, affluent parents.

And you cannot excuse the central smatterers, as you could the peasants in former times, by saying that they were scattered about the provinces, knew nothing of events in general and were suppressed on the local level. Throughout the years of Soviet power the intelligentsia has been well enough informed, has known what was going on in the world, and *could* have known what was going on in its own country, but it looked away and feebly surrendered in every organization and every office, indifferent to the *common* cause. For decade after decade, of course, it has been held in an unprecedented stranglehold (people in the West will never be able to imagine it until their turn comes). People of dynamic initiative, responsive to all forms of public and private assistance, have been stifled by oppression and fear, and public assistance itself has been soiled by a hypocritical state-run imitation. Finally, they have been placed in a situation where there appears to be no third choice: if a colleague is being hounded no one dares to remain neutral — at the slightest evasion he himself will be hounded too. But there is still a way out for people, even in this situation, and that is to let themselves be hounded! Let my children grow up on a crust of bread, so long as they are honest! If the intelligentsia were like *this*, it would be invincible.

There is also a special category of distinguished people whose names have become so firmly and inviolably established and who are so protectively cloaked in national and sometimes international fame that, in the post-Stalin period at least, they are well beyond the reach of the police, which is plain as plain could be from both near and far; nor do they fear need — they've put plenty aside. Could not *they* resurrect the honor and independence of the Russian intelligentsia? Could not *they* speak out in defense of the persecuted, in defense of freedom, against rank injustices and the squalid lies that are foisted upon us? Two hundred such men (and they number half a thousand altogether) by coming forward and taking a united stand would purify the public air in our country and all but transform our whole life! The prerevolutionary intelligentsia did this in their thousands, without waiting for the protection of fame. But can we find as many as ten among our smatterers? The rest feel no such *need!* (Even a person whose father was shot thinks nothing of it, swallows the fact.) And what shall we say about our prominent men at the top? Are they any better than the smatterers?

In Stalin's day, if you refused to sign some newspaper smear or denunciation, or to call for the death or imprisonment of your comrade, you really might have been threatened with death or imprisonment yourself. But today — what threat today induces our silver-haired and eminent elders to take up their pens, obsequiously asking "where?," and sign some vile nonsense concocted by a third person about Sakharov? Only their own worthlessness. What force impels a great twentieth-century composer to become the pitiful puppet of third-rate bureaucrats from the Ministry of Culture and at their bidding sign any contemptible piece of paper that is pushed at him, defending whoever they tell him to abroad and hounding whoever they want him to at home? (The composer's soul has come into direct and intimate contact — with no screen in between — with the dark, destructive soul of the twentieth century. He has gripped — no, it has gripped him with such piercing authenticity that when — if! — mankind enters upon a more enlightened age, our descendants will hear from Shostakovich's music how we were in the devil's clutches, utterly in its possession, and that we found beauty in those clutches and in that infernal breathing.)

Was the behavior of the great Russian scholars in the past ever so wretched? Or the great Russian artists? Their tradition has been broken: we are the smatterers.

What is triply shameful is that now it is not fear of persecution, but devious calculations of vanity, self-interest, personal welfare and tranquillity that make the "Moscow stars" among the smatterers and the middle stratum of "moderates" so pliant. Lydia Chukovskaya [18] is right: the time has come to count *some* people out of the intelligentsia. And if that doesn't mean all *these*, then the meaning of the word has been irretrievably lost.

18. Lydia Chukovskaya, the daughter of the well-known children's writer Kornei Chukovsky (1882–1969), is one of the Soviet Union's leading dissident writers and the author of two short novels, *The Deserted House* and *Going Under*. She was expelled from the Writers' Union in January 1974.— TRANS.

Oh, there have been fearless people! Fearless enough to speak up for an old building that was being demolished (as long as it wasn't a cathedral), and even the whole Lake Baikal area.[19] And we must be thankful for that, of course. One of the contributors to the present anthology was to have been an exceptionally distinguished person with a string of ranks and titles to his name. In private conversations his heart bleeds for the irrevocable ruin that has befallen the Russian people. He knows our history and our culture through and through. But — he declined: *What's the use? Nothing will come of it* . . . the usual good excuse of the smatterers.

We have got what we deserve. So low have we sunk.

When they jerked the string from on top and said we could be a little bolder (1956, 1962) we straightened our numbed spines just a trifle. When they jerked "quiet!" (1957, 1963) we subsided at once. There was also the spontaneous occurrence of 1967–1968, when *samizdat* came pouring out like a spring flood, more and more names appeared, new names signed protests and it seemed that only a little more was needed, only a tiny bit more, and we should begin to breathe. And did it take all that much to crush us? Fifty or so of the most audacious people were deprived of work in their professions. A few were expelled from the party, a few from the unions, and eighty or so protest signers were *summoned for discussions* with their party committee. And they came away from those "discussions" pale and crestfallen.

And the smatterers took flight, dropping in their haste their most important discovery, the very condition of continued existence, rebirth and thought — *samizdat*. Was it so long ago since the smatterers had been in hot pursuit of the latest items of *samizdat,* begging for extra copies to be typed, starting to collect *samizdat* libraries or sending *samizdat* to the provinces? Now they began to burn those libraries and cherish the virginity of their typewriters, only occasionally borrowing a forbidden leaflet in some dark passageway,

19. A reference to the extensive industrial pollution of Lake Baikal and its surroundings and to recent protests on environmental grounds.— TRANS.

snatching a quick look at it and returning it at once as if they had burned their fingers.

Yes, in the course of those persecutions a definite *core of the intelligentsia* did take shape and emerge into view, consisting of people who continued to risk their necks and make sacrifices — by openly or in wordless secrecy keeping dangerous materials, by fearlessly helping prisoners or by paying with their own freedom.

But there was another "core" that also came to light and discovered an ingenious alternative: to flee the country! Thereby preserving their own unique individuality ("*over there* I shall be able to develop Russian culture in peace and quiet"). Or saving those whom they had left behind ("from *over there* we shall be better able to defend your rights here"). Or, finally, saving their children, who were more precious than the children of the rest of their compatriots.

Such was the "core of the Russian intelligentsia" that came to light and that could exist even without Russia. But all this would be forgiven us, would arouse only sympathy — our downtrodden degradation and our subservience to the lie — if we meekly confessed to our infirmity, our attachment to material prosperity, our spiritual unpreparedness for trials too severe for us to bear: we are the victims of history that happened before our time, we were born into it, and have tasted our fair share of it, and here we are, floundering and not knowing how to escape from it.

But no! We contrive in this situation to find tortuous excuses of stunning sublimity as to why we should "become spiritually aware of ourselves without abandoning our scientific research institutes" (Pomerants) — as if "becoming spiritually aware" were a matter of cozy reflection, not of harsh ordeal and merciless trial. We have not renounced our arrogance in the least. We insist on the noble, inherited title of intelligentsia, on the right to be the supreme arbiters of every spiritual manifestation in our own country and of mankind: to make peremptory judgments about social theories, trends, movements, historical currents and the activities of prominent individuals from the safety of our burrows. Even as we put on our coats in the lobbies of our institutes we grow a head taller, and by the evening over the tea table we are already pronouncing the supreme judgment and deciding which actions and which of their perpetrators the "intelligentsia will forgive" or "not forgive."

Observing the pitiful way the central smatterers actually behave in the service of the Soviet state, it is impossible to believe the high historical pedestal they see themselves as occupying — each placing himself, his friends and his colleagues on that pedestal. The increasingly narrow specialization of professional disciplines, which enables semi-ignoramuses to become doctors of science, does not bother the smatterer in the slightest.

So powerful is the effect upon all educated people of the smatterers' high opinion of themselves that even Altayev, that stubborn exposer of the smatterers, bows to tradition in the interval between his exposures: "Today [our] intelligentsia manifestly holds the fate of Russia, and with it that of the whole world, in its hands"! Bitter laughter. . . . On the strength of Russian experience and in the face of the confusion in the West at the present time, it *could* — but its hands are feeble and its heart failing.

In 1969 this surge of self-satisfaction on the part of the scientific and technical smatterers spilled out into *samizdat* with an article by Semyon Telegin (pseudonymous, of course), entitled "What Is to Be Done?" The tone is that of a breezy, pushing know-it-all, quick at side associations and with a familiar, low wit (*Russisch kulturisch*), at one moment showing his contempt for the population with which he is obliged to share the same plot of dry land ("the human pigsty"), at another indulging in rhetorical flourishes: "But has my reader ever thought . . . ?" The author takes his "creative principle, source of ethics and humanism" from the apes, and believes that the best way out for the disillusioned is "the football stadium" and the worst "to join a sect."

What is important, though, is not so much the actual author as the circle of people who share his views and whom he plainly recommends as "progressive intellectuals" (party members, for they sit about at party meetings and are in charge of "individual work areas"): "We are the flower of thinking Russia," who "create a philosophical environment of our own in which we can live without becoming entangled in contradictions. . . . Imagine a class of highly educated people armed with the ideas of modern science, able, independent, fearless thinkers, altogether accustomed to think and fond of thinking, but *not* plowing the land."

Nor does Telegin hide these other peculiar features of his associates: "We are people accustomed to think one thing, say another and do a third. . . . The total moral demobilization has affected us too." What he has in mind is *triplicity*, a triple code of morals, "for oneself, for society, and for the state." But is this a sin? Telegin cheerfully maintains that "herein lies our *victory*"! What was that? Ah, the regime would like us to *think* as subserviently as we speak and work, but we *think* — fearlessly! "We have asserted our inner freedom"! (Astonishing: if secretly making a gesture of contempt in your pocket is inner freedom, what is inner slavery? We are inclined to define inner freedom as the ability both to think *and* act untrammeled by external fetters, and outward freedom as a situation when there are no fetters at all.)

It is precisely in Telegin's article that the "flower of thinking Russia" has comprehensively and very openly expressed itself. Let us familiarize ourselves with its contents — it will be an enriching experience.

"Under a regime of oppression," claims Telegin, a *new culture* has arisen, "a system of relationships and a system of thinking"; it is "a colossus on two legs — art and science." In the artistic sphere there are the guitarist-balladeers and independent *samizdat* literature. In the field of science there is "the powerful methodology of physics" and stemming from it "an entire philosophy of life," and beyond this "there are dozens of outgrowths and local subcultures sprouting in the drawing offices of planning departments, the corridors of research institutes and the foyers of institutes of the Academy of Sciences. . . . There is scope for creative people here, and there are plenty of them. . . . Science cannot be curbed by any authority" (oh, yeah). And — it will be possible to "apply the methodology of physics to the subtleties of ethics," and "This subterranean culture will act like yeast on the tribe of new, whole people, giants, who will spring up and to whom our fears will seem ridiculous."

There follows a daring plan explaining how this culture is to be used for our salvation. The crux of the matter is that "to speak out openly against the conditions of our existence . . . is not always the best way. . . . One evil will not cure another . . . secret conspiracies and new parties" will not help and are not wanted, nor must there be any calls for revolution.

With the last conclusion we heartily agree, although the author bases his argument on erroneous premises: he attributes the fall of autocracy solely to society's rejection of the idea of the bureaucratic state and not to any revolutionary activity. This is not true, and no parallel can be drawn here: there was very real revolutionary activity, autocracy was not defended one-tenth as fiercely as it should have been and the intelligentsia was determined to sacrifice itself. But we do agree with his practical conclusion: that we abandon the idea of revolution, and "not make plans for the creation of a new mass party of the Leninist type."

What, then, are his proposals? They are as follows: "initially no great sacrifices are envisaged" (which is very reassuring for the smatterers). Stage 1: "nonacceptance of the oppressors' culture" and "building a culture" of our own (to start with, by reading *samizdat* and displaying a high level of understanding in the smoking lounges of research institutes). Stage 2: making "efforts to disseminate this culture among the people," and even "actively bringing this culture to the people" (the methodology of physics? or the guitar songs?), "inculcating into the people an understanding of what we ourselves have come to understand," for which we need to seek "roundabout methods." This approach "will require first and foremost not courage [for the nth time this soul-soothing balm!] but the gift of persuasion, clarification, the ability to awaken the attention of the people and hold it over a long period of time without attracting the attention of the authorities. . . . Russia needs not only platforms and fanatics but also . . . vehement critics and skilled missionaries of the new culture. . . . After all, we find a common language with the people when we talk about football and fishing — we need to find concrete ways of going to the people. . . . And surely, with our philosophy [etc., etc.] . . . we shall be able to cope with a problem that even semi-illiterate preachers of religion have tackled successfully?"! (Alas, alas, this is where the smatterers betray their arrogance and shortsightedness, for it is not a question of literacy, but of *spiritual power*.)

We are quoting at such length because these are the views not of Telegin alone but of all the self-assured ideologists of our central smatterers. No matter which one we listen to, this is all we ever hear: a program of *cautious enlightenment!* An article by Chelnov (in the *Vestnik RSKD*, No. 97) is entitled, exactly like Telegin's, though not by any design, "What Is to Be Done?" His answer is: "create secret Christian fraternities," and he relies on a millennial improvement in morals. L. Ventsov's "Think!" (in *Vestnik*, No. 99), also by no design, offers the same remedy as Telegin! For a brief period a profusion of journals and more journals sprang up in *samizdat: Ray of Freedom, The Sower, Free Thought, Democrat*, all of them strictly clandestine, of course, and all of them offering identical advice: just don't reveal your face, just don't break the rule of secrecy, but slowly spread a correct understanding among the people. . . . What *is* this? The same thousand-year-old pastoral that has been outdistanced a hundredfold by the events of the space age. It seemed so easy: philosophize in one's burrow, hand the results over to *samizdat*, and the rest will happen *automatically!*

But it won't.

In the warm, well-lit, well-equipped rooms of their research institutes the "pure" scientists and technicians, while roundly condemning their brothers in the arts for "toadying to the regime," have become accustomed to overlooking their

own innocuous service to the state; but that service is no less
terrible, and history will make them answer no less harshly
for it. Suppose that tomorrow we were to lose one-half of all
our research institutes, the most important and secret ones,
would science be brought to a halt? No, but imperialism
would. "The creation of an antitotalitarian culture can also
lead to *material* freedom," affirms Telegin, but *how* are we to
understand this: Scientists (and now that science has become
an industry they are essentially qualified industrial workers)
spend their whole working day turning out *material* appurtenances — if not of "culture" then of civilization — that is,
materially reinforcing the lie, and everywhere voting, agree-
ing with and repeating whatever they are told — is *this* the
kind of *culture* that will save us all?

In the years since Telegin's article there have been many
public opportunities for the *tribe of giants* at least to shrug
their shoulders or to take just one breath, but no! They
signed what was required of them against Dubček, against
Sakharov, against whoever they were ordered to, and making
rude signs in their pockets they scuttled off to their smoking
lounges to develop a "professional subculture" and hammer
out a "powerful methodology."

Do psychiatrists at the Serbsky Institute [20] perhaps live by
the same "triple moral code" and pride themselves on their
"inner freedom"? And sundry procurators and judges in high
places? For there are people of refined intellect among them,
in no way inferior to Telegin's giants.

This smug declaration is as deceptive as it is confused in
that it comes very close to the truth — which warms the reader's heart — and then at the critical danger point veers
abruptly onto another tack. *"Ohne uns!"* exclaims Telegin.
Right. "Refuse to accept the oppressors' culture!" Also right.
But when, where, and in what respects? Not in the cloak-
room after a meeting, but *at* the meeting — by refusing to
repeat what we do not believe, by refusing to vote against
our will! And in *that* little office, by refusing to sign anything

20. One of the most notorious of the psychiatric hospitals where political
dissidents are detained.— TRANS.

258

that we did not compose in all good conscience ourselves. This has nothing to do with rejecting some sort of "culture." Nobody is foisting "culture" on us, it is *lies* they are foisting upon us and it is only *lies* that we must not accept, but *at once,* right *then* and right *there* where we are being asked to accept them, instead of venting our indignation later in the evening over the tea table at home. We must reject lies *on the spot,* without thinking about the consequences for our salaries, our families and our leisure for spreading the "new culture." We must reject lies without worrying whether others will follow in our footsteps and without looking around to see if the rest of the population is catching the habit.

And it is because the answer is so clear and reduces to such a simple, straightforward form that the anonymous ideologist of the arrogant, shallow and sterile tribe of giants evades it with all the oratorical brilliance he can muster.[21]

So for the time being let those who feel unable to take the risk spare us in our filth and baseness their witty arguments, exposures and explanations of the origins of our Russian vices.

FIVE

And how do the central smatterers see their place in the country in relation to their own people? Whoever supposes that they repent of their lackey's role is mistaken. Even Pomerants, who represents quite a different group of the Moscow smatterers — unestablished, nonmanagerial, non–party members, working in the humanities — takes care to extol "the Leninist cultural revolution" (which destroyed the old modes of production, a very valuable service!) and to defend the form of government which existed from 1917 to 1922 ("a temporary dictatorship within the framework of democracy").

21. *Samizdat* versions differ. And later Telegin altered the ending, adding: "The first steps are boycott, nonparticipation and indifference." Indifference is nothing new; but as for nonparticipation — in what?

And "the bourgeois, of course, fully deserved the despotic treatment he received at the hands of the victorious revolutionaries. His cowardice and his servility are the breeding ground of despots." *His* servility, not *ours!* But in what respect is the behavior of the central smatterers more commendable than that of the so-called bourgeois?

Neither those who sing the praises of the smatterers nor their detractors voice as much as a suggestion of any *guilt* toward the people for the past or present, the guilt which so tormented the prerevolutionary intelligentsia. In this respect they are unanimous, all of them, even Altayev: "It might not be such a bad thing if the people themselves were to become aware of their guilt toward the intelligentsia."

All the comparisons that the central smatterers draw between themselves and the people are in their own favor. Pomerants: "The intelligentsia is a measure of social forces — progressive and reactionary. When set against the intelligentsia *the entire people coalesces into a reactionary mass*" (emphasis added). "It is that section of the educated stratum of society in which spiritual development takes place, old values are destroyed and new ones arise, and in which one of the steps from animal to God is taken. . . . The intelligentsia is precisely that which it has sought in others, in the people, in the proletariat, and so on: the ferment that sets history in motion." Furthermore: "Love of one's people is far more dangerous [than love of animals]: there is no threshold here to prevent one from going down on all fours." And simply: *"The backbone of a new people is being formed here . . .* a new something will replace the people . . . the people involved in creative brainwork will become the chosen people of the twentieth century"!!!

Telegin says the same thing, and so does Gorsky (yet another pseudonym, writing in *Vestnik*, No. 97): "The road to supreme values lies elsewhere than in fusion with the people." At the opposite pole from the opinion of their foolish predecessors in the intelligentsia.

Or take religion. Pomerants: "The peasants' understanding of religion is imperfect," that is, philosophically crude: "You can call it God, the Absolute, the Void . . . I have no particular preference for any of these words." Simple, sincere devotion to the faith, to its precepts and even its rights — ugh, their understanding is imperfect, just as they don't understand agronomy. (With peasant agronomy there was grain enough and the soil wasn't exhausted, but now that things are scientifically done we shall soon be without soil altogether. But then Pomerants's entire argument is no doubt directed against the *pochvenniki,* or "men of the soil," [22] and his ideal is "people of the air, who have lost all their roots in everyday existence.") On the other hand "the intellectuals are today seeking God. Religion has ceased to be the mark of the people. It has become the mark of the elite." The same point is made by Gorsky: "To confuse a return to the Church with going to the people is a dangerous prejudice."

One of them is writing in Moscow *samizdat,* the others in a Paris journal. It is unlikely that they know each other, but what unity! One cannot pick a single hole in it. Which means that it is not just the invention of individuals, but a *trend.*

But what do we recommend for the people, then? Absolutely *nothing. There is no people,* this is something else about which they all agree: "Culture, like a snake, simply sheds its skin, and *the old skin, the people,* lies lifeless in the dust." "The patriarchal virtues are irretrievably lost to mankind," "the muzhik can be resurrected only in opera houses." "We are not surrounded by the people. The peasantry in the developed countries is becoming too small to surround us," "peasant nations are hungry nations, and nations whose peasantry has vanished are nations in which famine has disappeared." (This was before we ran into a technological dead end.)

But if this is the smatterers' interpretation of the general situation of peoples, how do they view the future of nations? This has been thought out too. Pomerants: "Nations are local cultures and will gradually disappear." And "the position of

22. The name of a group of writers and thinkers in the mid-nineteenth century who advocated a kind of Christian naturalism, which was to be achieved through a study of organic historical, social and spiritual forces inherent in the Russian people.— TRANS.

the intelligentsia is always to be halfway between. . . . Spiritually all intellectuals nowadays belong to a diaspora. Nowhere are we complete strangers. And nowhere do we feel quite at home."

It is on this spirit of internationalism and cosmopolitanism that our entire generation was reared. And (leaving aside — if we *can* leave it aside! — the nationalities policy *as it was in practice* in the 1920s) there is great spiritual nobility and beauty in it, and mankind is probably destined one day to rise to those noble heights. This view preponderates widely in European society too at the present time. In West Germany it is creating a mood in which people are not particularly concerned about the reunification of Germany, and see no mystical imperatives in German national unity. In Great Britain, which still clings to the illusion of a mythical British Commonwealth and where society is keenly indignant over the slighest racial discrimination, it has led to the country's being inundated with Asians and West Indians who are totally indifferent to the English land, its culture and traditions, and are simply seeking to latch onto a ready-made high standard of living. Is this such a good thing? It is not our business to judge from a distance. But despite the prognostications, imprecations and denunciations, this has turned out everywhere to be the century in which nation after nation has come to life, become aware of its existence and gathered itself up. And the miraculous birth and consolidation of Israel after two thousand years of dispersal is only the most striking of a multitude of examples.

One would think that our authors would be aware of this, yet they ignore it in their arguments about Russia. Gorsky is irritated by "unthinking patriotism," by "instinctive dependence on innate and atavistic elements," and would deny us the right *simply to love* the land of our birth irrationally and unpremeditatedly, demanding instead that each of us rise to "an act of spiritual self-determination" and only thus choose a homeland for ourselves. Among the unifying features of a nation *he makes no mention of a native language!* (which makes him a worse theoretician even than Stalin), nor of a *sense of the history* of the country. He acknowledges, as a merely subsidiary factor, "an ethical and territorial community," but sees religion as the basis of national unity (this is true, but the religion may extend beyond the nation) and again a loosely defined "culture" (perhaps the same culture that Pomerants says "slithers like a snake"?). He insists that the existence of nations is a contradiction of the Pentecost. (While we for our part thought that by descending upon the apostles with many tongues the Holy Ghost confirmed the diversity of the nations of mankind, as they have existed since that time.) Irascibly he thunders that for Russia the "central creative idea" must be *not* "national rebirth" (it is *he* who puts the expression in quotation marks and forbids us to entertain such a foolish concept) *but* "the struggle for Freedom and spiritual values." We, in our ignorance, fail to see any opposition here: how can spiritually lacerated Russia retrieve its spiritual values other than by national rebirth? To this day the entire history of mankind has run its course in the form of tribal and national histories, and all important historical movements have begun within the national framework, and none of them in Esperanto. A nation, like a family, is a natural, uncontrived association of people whose members are innately disposed toward one another, and there are grounds for inveighing against such associations or calling for their abolition today. What comes afterward will be clear in the distant future, when we are not here.

This, of course, is a point made by Pomerants too. He assures us that "from the standpoint of nationality all cats are gray. . . . Fighting the customs of one's native land when one's feet are firmly planted on one's native soil is about as simple as dragging oneself out of a bog." And once again we are too stupid to comprehend: from *what* soil should one fight the vices of one's *own country?* International soil? We have already experienced that fight (carried out with Latvian bayonets and Magyar pistols) with our ribs and the backs of our necks — no thank you! We must reform ourselves *by ourselves* and not invoke other wise men to be our reformers.

People will ask why I have fastened onto these two, Pomerants and Gorsky, or rather, these one and a half (a half for the pseudonym), two with Altayev, or two and a half with Telegin.

Because they represent *a trend*, because they are all theoreticians, and because this is evidently not the last we shall hear of them. So just to be on the safe side let us chalk up the following. In the summer of 1972, when the forests of northern Russia were ablaze as a result of Soviet mismanagement (the concerns of *our* leaders were in the Middle East and Latin America), Semyon Telegin, a live wire, a rollicker and an atheist, put out a *samizdat* leaflet in which he rose to his full gigantic height for the first time and announced: this is your divine retribution, Russia, for your evildoings! What a breakthrough.

To find out how the central smatterers view the national problem, go to the leading smatterer families, the ones that keep pedigreed dogs, and ask them what they call their dogs. You will hear (many times over): Foma, Kuzma, Potap, Makar, Timofei . . . and this grates upon nobody's ears, and nobody feels any shame. After all, peasants are only "something you see in operas," there is no *people* left, so why should they not call their dogs by peasant christian names?

Oh, how is one to traverse the brittle ridge without offending one's own people by wrongful accusation and without condoning one's own vices when they are more grievous than another's?

SIX

But the picture Pomerants paints of the people is, alas, to a large extent true. Just as we are probably mortally offending him now by alleging that there is no longer an intelligentsia in our country, and that it has all disintegrated into a collection of smatterers, so he too mortally wounds us by his assertion that neither is there a *people* any longer.

"The people no longer exists. There is the mass, with a dim recollection that it was once the people and the bearer of

God within itself, but now it is utterly empty. . . . The people in the sense of a Chosen People, a source of spiritual values, is nonexistent. There are the neurasthenic intellectuals — and the masses. . . . What do the collective farm workers sing? Some remnants of their peasant heritage" and whatever is drilled into them "at school, in the army and on the radio. . . . Where is it, this 'people'? The real native people, dancing its folk dances, narrating its folktales, weaving its folk-patterned lace? In our country all that remains are the vestiges of a people, like the vestiges of snow in spring. . . . The people as a great historical force, a backbone of culture, a source of inspiration for Pushkin and Goethe, no longer exists. . . . What is usually called the people in our country is not the people at all but a petit bourgeoisie."

Gloom and doom. And not far from the truth either.

Indeed, how *could* the people have survived? It has been subjected to two processes both tending toward the same end and each lending impetus to the other. One is the universal process (which, if it had been postponed any longer in Russia, we might have escaped altogether) of what is fashionably known as *massovization* (an abominable word, but then the process is no better), a product of the new Western technology, the sickening growth of cities, and the general standardization of methods of information and education. The second is our own special Soviet process, designed to rub off the age-old face of Russia and rub on another, synthetic one, and this has had a still more decisive and irreversible effect.

How could the people possibly have survived? Icons, obedience to elders, bread-baking and spinning wheels were all forcibly thrown out of the peasants' cottages. Then millions of cottages — as well-designed and comfortable as one could wish — were completely ravaged, pulled down or put into the wrong hands and five million hardworking, healthy families, together with infants still at the breast, were dispatched to their death on long winter journeys or on their arrival in the tundra. (And our *intelligentsia* did not waver or cry out, and its *progressive* part even assisted in driving them out. *That* was when the intelligentsia ceased to be, in 1930; and is that the moment for which the people must beg its forgiveness?) The destruction of the remaining cottages and homesteads was less trouble after that. They took away the land which had made the peasant a peasant, depersonalized it even more than serfdom had, deprived the peasant of all incentive to work and live, packed some off to the Magnitogorsks,[23] while the rest — a whole generation of doomed women — were forced to feed the colossus of the state before the war, for the entire duration of the war and after the war. All the outward, international successes of our country and the flourishing growth of the thousands of scientific research institutes that now exist have been achieved by devastating the Russian village and the traditional Russian way of life. In its place they have festooned the cottages and the ugly multistory boxes in the suburbs of our cities with loudspeakers, and even worse, have fixed them on all the telegraph poles in city centers (even today they will be blaring over the entire face of Russia from six in the morning until midnight, the supreme mark of culture, and if you go and shut them off it's an anti-Soviet act). And those loudspeakers have done their job well: they have driven everything individual and every bit of folklore out of people's heads and drilled in stock substitutes, they have trampled and defiled the Russian language and dinned vacuous, untalented songs (composed by the intelligentsia) into our ears. They have knocked down the last village churches, flattened and desecrated graveyards, flogged the horse to death with Komsomol zeal, and their tractors and five-ton lorries have polluted and churned up the centuries-old roads whose gentle tracery adorns our countryside. Where is there left, and who is there left to dance and weave lace? Furthermore, they have visited the village youth with specially juicy tidbits in the form of quantities of drab, idiotic films (the intellectual: "We have to release them — they are *mass-circulation* films") — and the same rubbish is crammed into school textbooks and slightly more

23. Magnitogorsk is a major city in the Urals that underwent most of its development in the twenties and thirties and became a showplace of Soviet industry.— TRANS.

adult books (and you know *who* writes them, don't you?), to prevent new growth from springing up where the old timber was felled. Like tanks they have ridden roughshod over the entire historical memory of the people (they gave us back Alexander Nevsky without his cross,[24] but anything more recent — no), so how *could* the people possibly have saved itself?

And so, sitting here in the ashes left behind by the conflagration, let us try to work it out.

The people does not exist? Then it's true that there can be no national revival? But what's that gap there? I thought I glimpsed something: as a result of the collapse of universal technological progress, in line with the transition that will be made to a stable economy, there will be a restoration everywhere of the primeval attachment of the majority of the people to the land, to the simplest materials and tools, and to physical labor (which many satiated town-dwellers are even now instinctively seeking for themselves). Thus in every country, even the highly developed ones, there will inevitably be a restoration of some sort of successor to the peasant multitudes, something to fill the vacuum left by the people, an agricultural and craftsman class (naturally with a new, but decentralized, technology). But what about us; can the "operatic" peasant return no more?

But then the intelligentsia doesn't exist either, does it? Are the smatterers dead wood for development?

Have *all* the classes been replaced by inferior substitutes? And if so how can we develop?

But surely *someone* exists? And how can one deny human beings a future? Can *human beings* be prevented from going on living? We hear their weary, kindly voices sometimes without even seeing their faces — as they pass by us somewhere in the twilight, we hear them talking of their everyday concerns, which they express in authentic — and sometimes still very spontaneous — Russian speech, we catch sight of their faces, alive and eager, and their smiles, we experience their good deeds for ourselves, sometimes when we least ex-

24. Presumably a reference to Eisenstein's film *Alexander Nevsky.*— TRANS.

pect them, we observe self-sacrificing families with children undergoing all kinds of hardships rather than destroy a soul — so how can one deny them all a future?

It is rashness to conclude that the people no longer exists. Yes, the village has been routed and its remnants choked, yes, the outlying suburbs are filled with the click of dominoes (one of the achievements of universal literacy) and broken bottles, there are no traditional costumes and no folk dances, the language has been corrupted and thoughts and ambitions even more deformed and misdirected; but why is it that not even these broken bottles, nor the litter blown back and forth by the wind in city courtyards, fills one with such despair as the careerist hypocrisy of the smatterers? It is because *the people* on the whole *takes no part in the official lie,* and this today is its most distinctive feature, allowing one to hope that it is not, as its accusers would have it, utterly devoid of God. Or at any rate, it has preserved a spot in its heart that has still not been scorched or trampled to death.

It is also rashness to conclude that there is no intelligentsia. Each one of us is personally acquainted with at least a handful of people who have resolutely risen above both the lie and the pointless bustle of the smatterers. And I am entirely in accord with those who want to see, who want to believe that they can already see the *nucleus of an intelligentsia,* which is our hope for spiritual renewal. Only I would recognize and distinguish this nucleus by other signs: not by the academic qualifications of its members, nor the number of books they have published, nor by the high educational level of those who "are accustomed to think and fond of thinking, but not of plowing the land," nor by the scientific cleverness of a methodology which so easily creates "professional subcultures," nor by a sense of alienation from state and people, nor by membership in a spiritual diaspora ("nowhere quite at home"). I would recognize this nucleus by the purity of its aspirations, by its spiritual selflessness in the name of truth, and above all for the sake of *this* country, in which it lives. This nucleus will have been brought up not so much in libraries as on spiritual sufferings. It is not the nucleus that wishes to be regarded as a nucleus without having to forego the comforts of life enjoyed by the Moscow smatterers. Dostoyevsky dreamed in 1877 of the appearance in Russia of a generation of "modest and valiant young people." But on *that* occasion it was the "demons" ("the possessed") who appeared — and we can see where that got us. I can testify, however, that during the last few years I have seen these modest and valiant young people with my own eyes, heard them with my own ears; it was they who, like an invisible film, kept me floating in air over a seeming void and prevented me from falling. Not all of them are still at liberty today, and not all of them will preserve their freedom tomorrow. And far from all of them are evident to our eyes and ears — like spring streams they trickle somewhere beneath the dense, gray, hard-packed snow.

It is the method that is at fault: to reason along the lines of "social strata" and accept no other basis. If you take social strata you will end in despair (as did Amalrik).[25] The intelligentsia as a vast *social stratum* has ended its days in a steaming swamp and can no longer become airborne again. But even in the intelligentsia's former and better times, it was incorrect to include people in the intelligentsia in terms of whole families, clans, groups and strata. There might well have been particular families, clans, groups and strata that were intelligentsia through and through, but even so it is as an individual that a man becomes a member of the intelligentsia in the true sense of the word. If the intelligentsia was a stratum at all, it was a psychological, not a social, one; consequently entrance and exit always depended upon individual conduct, not upon one's occupation or social standing.

A stratum, a people, the masses, the smatterers — they all consist of *human beings,* and there is no way in which the fu-

25. Andrei Amalrik (b. 1938), a nonconformist Soviet writer, imprisoned in 1965 and subsequently exiled to Siberia for having produced "anti-Soviet" and "pornographic" works. In 1966 Amalrik was permitted to return to Moscow; in May 1970 he was again arrested on trumped-up charges as a result of his writings, and in July 1973 was sentenced to three years forced labor. This sentence was commuted in November 1973 to three years exile in Siberia.
For a discussion of Amalrik's writings, see pages 280–281 and note on page 280.— TRANS.

ture can be closed to human beings: human beings determine their future themselves, and whatever point has been reached on the crooked, descending path, it is never too late to take a turn for the good and the better.

The future is indestructible, and it is in our hands. If we make the right choices.

Now it is Pomerants who, among the many contradictory utterances he makes in his writings, comes out here and there with some strikingly truthful ones, and if we put them together we shall see that even from differing positions one can arrive at similar conclusions. "The present population is an amorphous mass between two crystalline structures. . . . It can assume a structure if an axis or a branch appears, however fragile, around which crystals will start to form." With this I agree entirely. However, doggedly devoted as he is to his intelligentsia ideals, Pomerants assigns this role of axis or branch exclusively to the intelligentsia. Since *samizdat* is not easily accessible we shall have to quote him at length: "The mass can crystallize anew into something resembling a people only around a new intelligentsia. . . . I am counting on the intelligentsia not at all because it is good. . . . Intellectual development in itself only increases man's capacity for evil. . . . My chosen people are bad, this I know . . . but the rest are even worse." True, "before salting something you must first become the salt again," and the intelligentsia has ceased to be that salt. Ah, "if only we possessed sufficient strength of character to give up all our laurels, our degrees and our titles. . . . To put an end to this cowardice and whining. . . . To prefer a clean conscience to a clean doorstep and to school ourselves to make do with an honest slice of bread without the caviar." But: "I *do believe* that the intelligentsia can change and that it can attract others to follow in its footsteps. . . ."

What is clear to us here is that Pomerants distinguishes the intelligentsia and sets it apart in terms of its *intellectual development,* and only *hopes* that it will *also* possess moral qualities.

Was this not at the heart of our old error which proved the

undoing of us all — that the intelligentsia repudiated religious morality and chose for itself an atheistic humanism that supplied an easy justification both for the hastily constituted revolutionary tribunals and the rough justice meted out in the cellars of the Cheka?[26] And did not the rebirth of a "nucleus of the intelligentsia" after 1910 arise out of a desire to return to a religious morality — only to be cut short by the chatter of machine guns? And is not that nucleus whose beginnings we think we already discern today a repetition of the one that the revolution cut short, is it not in essence a "latter-day *Vekhi*"? For it regards the moral doctrine of the value of the individual as the key to the solution of social problems. It was for a nucleus of this kind that Berdyayev yearned: "An ecclesiastical intelligentsia which would combine genuine Christianity with an enlightened and clear understanding of the cultural and historical missions of the country." So did S. Bulgakov: "An educated class with a Russian soil, an enlightened mind and a strong will."

Not only is this nucleus not yet a compact mass, as a nucleus should be, but it is not even collected together, it is scattered, its components mutually unrecognizable: many of its particles have never seen one another, do not know of one another, and have no notion of one another's existence. And what links them is not membership in an intelligentsia, but a thirst for truth, a craving to cleanse their souls, and the desire of each one to preserve around him an area of purity and brightness. That is why even "illiterate sectarians" and some obscure milkmaid down on the collective farm are also members of this nucleus of goodness, united by a common *striving* for the pure life. And the covetousness and worldly wisdom of the cultured academician or artist steers him in exactly the opposite direction — backward into the familiar lurid darkness of this half century.

What does an "axis" or "branch" for the "crystallization" of an entire people mean? It means tens of thousands of human beings. Furthermore, it is a potential *stratum* — but it will not overflow into the future in some huge and unobstructed

26. See note 3 on page 11.— TRANS.

wave. Forming the "backbone of a new people" is not something that can be done as safely and lightheartedly as we are promised, at weekends and in our spare time, without giving up our scientific research institutes. No, it will have to be done on weekdays, as part of the mainstream of our life, in its most dangerous sector — and by each one of us in chilling isolation.

A society so vicious and polluted, implicated in so many of the crimes of these last fifty years — by its lies, by its servility either willing or enforced, by its eagerness to assist or its cowardly restraint — such a society can only be cured and purified by passing through a spiritual filter. And this filter is a terrible one, with holes as fine as the eye of a needle, each big enough for only one person. And people may pass into the spiritual future only one at a time, by squeezing through.

By deliberate, voluntary sacrifice.

Times change, and scales too. A hundred years ago the Russian intelligentsia thought of sacrifice in terms of the death penalty. Nowadays it is considered a sacrifice to risk administrative punishment. And in truth this is no easier for abject, browbeaten characters to stomach.

Even in the most favorable circumstances (if the sacrificial impulse is felt by large numbers of people simultaneously) it will not be, as Pomerants anticipates, the caviar (already a museum piece) that they will have to sacrifice, but the oranges and butter with which our scientific research centers are so generously supplied. Malicious critics gleefully alleged that in *The First Circle* I exposed "the low caliber of love among the people" by quoting the proverb "people marry for cabbage soup and take a husband for meat" — while *we*, of course, love and marry Romeo-style! But there are many Russian proverbs to cater for different nuances and situations. There is this one too: "Bread and water make fine food."

This is the kind of food on which we shall have to demonstrate the caliber of *our* love for this country and its silver birch trees. To love looking at them is not enough. The harsh Northeast will have to be tamed — and it will be our precious smatterers' children who will have to go there, without waiting for the philistines to pave the way. And the clever counsels of anonymous authors — conspiracy and more conspiracy ("single-handed sorties are no use"), a thousand-year process of enlightenment, the surreptitious development of culture — are all rubbish! There is no way left to us to pass from our present contemptible amorphousness into the future except through open, personal and predominantly public (to set an example) sacrifice. We shall have to "rediscover our cultural treasures and values" not by erudition, not by scientific accomplishment, but by our *form of spiritual conduct*, by laying aside our material well-being and, if the worst comes to the worst, our lives. And when it becomes apparent that educational qualifications and the number of scholarly works published are utterly irrelevant, we shall become wonderingly aware of the presence beside us of those "semiliterate preachers of religion" we so despise.

It would be better if we declared the word "intelligentsia" — so long misconstrued and deformed — dead for the time being. Of course, Russia will be unable to manage without a substitute for the intelligentsia, but the new word will be formed not from "understand" or "know," but from something *spiritual*. The first tiny minority who set out to force their way through the tight holes of the filter will of their own accord find some new definition of themselves, either while they are still in the filter, or when they have come out the other side and recognize themselves and each other. It is there that the word will be recognized, it will be born of the very process of passing through. Or else the remaining majority, without resorting to a new terminology, will simply call them the *righteous*. It would not be inaccurate to call them for the moment a *sacrificial elite*. The word "elite" here will arouse the envy of no one, election to it being an extremely unenviable honor that no one will complain of being passed over for: come and join us, we implore you!

It is of the lone individuals who pass through (or perish on the way) that this elite to crystallize the people will be composed.

The filter will grow wider and easier for each subsequent particle — and the number of particles passing through it will increase all the time, so that on the far side these worthy individuals might reconstitute and re-create a worthy *people* (I have already explained my interpretation of the word *people*). So that a society might be formed whose chief characteristic would be not its level of productivity, nor its degree of prosperity, but the purity of its social relations.

There is absolutely no other way I can envisage for Russia.

All that remains is to describe the structure and operation of the filter.

SEVEN

People will laugh at us from outside: what a timid and what a modest step we regard as *sacrifice*. All over the world students are occupying universities, going out into the streets and even toppling governments, while our students are the tamest in the world: tell them it's time for a political education lecture, refuse to let them take their coats out of the cloak room, and nobody will leave. In 1962 the whole of Novocherkassk was in tumult, but at the Polytechnic Institute they simply locked the door of the students' quarters and nobody jumped out the windows! Or take the starving Indians, who liberated themselves from British domination by nonviolent, passive resistance and civil disobedience: but we are incapable of even this desperate bravery, neither the working class nor the smatterers, for we have been terrorized for three generations ahead by dear old Uncle Joe: how can you *not carry out* an order of the authorities? That would be the ultimate in self-destruction.

And if we set out in capital letters the nature of the examination we are going to set our fellowmen : DO NOT LIE! DO NOT TAKE PART IN THE LIE! DO NOT SUPPORT THE LIE! — it is not only the Europeans who are going to laugh at us, but also the Arab students and the ricksha-drivers in Ceylon: is this all that is being asked of the Russians? And they call that a *sacrifice,* a bold step, and not simply the mark that distinguishes an honest man from a rogue?

But it is all very well for the apples in another barrel to laugh: those being crushed in ours know that it is indeed a bold step. Because in our country the daily lie is not the whim of corrupt natures but a mode of existence, a condition of the daily welfare of every man. In our country the lie has been incorporated into the state system as the vital link holding everything together, with billions of tiny fasteners, several dozen to each man.

This is precisely why we find life so oppressive. But it is also precisely why we should find it natural to straighten up. When oppression is not accompanied by the lie, liberation demands political measures. But when the lie has fastened its claws in us, it is no longer a matter of politics! It is an invasion of man's moral world, and our straightening up and *refusing to lie* is also not political, but simply the retrieval of our human dignity.

Which is the *sacrifice?* To go for years without truly breathing, gulping down stench? Or to begin to breathe, as is the prerogative of every man on this earth? What cynic would venture to object aloud to such a policy as *nonparticipation in the lie?*

Oh, people will object at once and with ingenuity: what *is* a lie? Who can determine precisely where the lie ends and truth begins? In every historically concrete dialectical situation, and so on — all the evasions that liars have been using for the past half century.

But the answer could not be simpler: decide *yourself,* as *your* conscience dictates. And for a long time this will suffice. Depending upon his horizons, his life experience and his education, each person will have his own perception of the line where the public and state lie begins: one will see it as being altogether remote from him, while another will experience it as a rope already cutting into his neck. And *there,* at the point where *you yourself* in all honesty see the borderline of the lie, is where you must refuse to submit to that lie. You must shun *that part* of the lie that is clear and obvi-

275

ous to you. And if you sincerely cannot see the lie anywhere at all, then go on quietly living as you did before.

What does it mean, *not to lie?* It doesn't mean going around preaching the truth at the top of your voice (perish the thought!). It doesn't even mean muttering what you think in an undertone. It simply means: *not saying what you don't think,* and that includes not whispering, not opening your mouth, not raising your hand, not casting your vote, not feigning a smile, not lending your presence, not standing up, and not cheering.

We all work in different fields and move in different walks of life. Those who work in the humanities and all who are studying find themselves much more profoundly and inextricably involved in lying and participating in the lie — they are fenced about by layer after layer of lies. In the technical sciences it can be more ingeniously avoided, but even so one cannot escape daily entering some door, attending some meeting, putting one's signature to something or undertaking some obligation which is a cowardly submission to the lie. The lie surrounds us at work, on our way to work, in our leisure pursuits — in everything we see, hear and read.

And just as varied as the forms of the lie are the forms of rejecting it. Whoever steels his heart and opens his eyes to the tentacles of the lie will in each situation, every day and every hour, realize what he must do.

Jan Palach burned himself to death. That was an extreme sacrifice. Had it not been an isolated case it would have roused Czechoslovakia to action. As an isolated case it will simply go down in history. But not so much is demanded of everyone — of you and me. Nor do we have to go out and face the flamethrowers breaking up demonstrations. All we have to do is *breathe.* All we have to do is not lie.

And nobody need be "first," because there are already many hundreds of "firsts," it is only because of their quietness that we do not notice them (especially those suffering for their religion, and it is fitting that they work as cleaners and caretakers). I can point to several dozen people from the very nucleus of the intelligentsia who have been living this way for a long time, for *years!* And they are still alive. And their families haven't died out. And they still have a roof over their heads. And food on the table.

Yes, it is a terrible thought! In the beginning the holes in the filter are so narrow, so very narrow: can a person with so many needs really squeeze through such a narrow opening? Let me reassure him: it is only that way at the entrance, at the very beginning. Very soon, not far along, the holes slacken and relax their grip, and eventually cease to grip you altogether. Yes, of course! It will cost you canceled dissertations, annuled degrees, demotions, dismissals, expulsions, sometimes even deportations. But you will not be cast into flames. Or crushed by a tank. And you will still have food and shelter.

This path is the safest and most accessible of all the paths open to us for the average man in the street. But it is also the most effective! Only we, knowing our system, can imagine what will happen when thousands and tens of thousands of people take this path — how our country will be purified and transformed without shots or bloodshed.

But this path is also the most moral: we shall be commencing this liberation and purification with *our own souls.* Before we purify the country we shall have purified ourselves. And this is the only correct historical order: for what is the good of purifying our country's air if we ourselves remain dirty?

People will say: how unfair on the young! After all, if you don't utter the obligatory lie at your social science exam, you'll be failed and expelled from your institute, and your education and life will be disrupted.

One of the articles in the present collection discusses the problem of whether we have correctly assessed the best directions to take in science and are doing what is necessary to follow them. Be that as it may, educational damage is not the greatest damage one can suffer in life. Damage to the soul and corruption of the soul, to which we carelessly assent from our earliest years, are far more irreparable.

Unfair on the young? But whose is the future if not theirs?

Who do we expect to form the sacrificial elite? For whose sake do we agonize over the future? We are already old. If they themselves do not build an honest society, they will never see it at all.

January 1974

Does Russia Have a Future?

IGOR SHAFAREVICH

ONE

Hardly has the blessing of free thought begun to return to us than we are faced with this terrible, yet inevitable, question: *What is Russia's future and what is our part in her destiny?* A question intimidating in its magnitude and insolubility, but inescapable, for without an answer to it there is no answer to the rest of life's questions.

But even to think about it is terrifying, because of a doubt that one hardly dare put into words: *Is Russia still alive?* For the life and death of nations are not as easily defined as those of living organisms. A nation may have fulfilled its historic mission, its creative spirit may have abandoned it, while its body — the state — lingers on for decades, still capable of putting heretics to death or subjugating its neighbors. *Living* for a great country means more than simply not falling apart and making economic ends meet. It must also know why it lives, be aware of its mission in the world. Does Russia have such a mission now? [1]

1. "Belief in one's desire and ability to give the world a message, and to renew it with the abundance of one's vitality; belief in the sanctity of one's ideals; belief in the strength of one's love and yearning to serve mankind — this belief is the pledge of a nation's highest existence, and by this means

A. Amalrik,[2] in one of the most vivid and brilliant works of postrevolutionary Russian thought, recently gave his answer to this question. He concluded on the basis of many subtle observations and historical analogies that Russia is nearing the culmination of her historical journey. In his opinion a certain softening of the system does not indicate the beginnings of a deliberate policy of liberalization: it is a symptom of the senility of the regime, which is incapable of changing to meet the demands of the time, or of dealing effectively with the resistance it is encountering. But there are no other forces that can claim a leading role. The intelligentsia — or, as Amalrik calls them, the middle class — have been brainwashed by the bureaucracy, they make a cult of submission, they are too feeble to be capable of developing their own point of view or organizing themselves. Christian morality has been beaten and chased from the minds of the people, who now respect only force, but not personality or liberty. The Russian people, in the view of the author, has no concept of the equality of all before the law, or of freedom and its concomitant responsibilities, but identifies freedom with disorder. In its place they have another concept — that of justice. Even this is destructive, however, for its essential principle is: nobody must be better off than myself. With frightening plausibility Amalrik sketches our future: a lingering, unsuccessful war with China, a growth in the centrifugal force of local nationalisms, growing economic difficulties, especially over the provision of food, destructive and vicious outbursts of popular discontent and finally the collapse of Russia and its disintegration into smaller parts. He even forecasts when our eleven hundred years of history will come to an end — sometime during the 1980s.

So that is Amalrik's answer to our question: Russia is dead

alone can they endow succeeding human generations with all their vitality and organic drive, as nature herself ordained in creating them. Only a nation strong in this belief has the right to a higher life." Dostoyevsky, *The Diary of a Writer*, January 1877, Chapter I.

2. A. Amalrik. *Will the Soviet Union Survive until 1984?* He paid for his thoughts with his freedom. [See Andrei Amalrik, *Will the Soviet Union Survive until 1984?* (New York: Harper & Row, 1970).— TRANS.]

and about to decompose. Well, great states have indeed perished before, and our feelings of desperation and inner protest at the verdict on Russia do not mean that it is unjust. But these feelings urge us to accept the verdict only after rejecting *all* the alternatives and examining *all* the possible ways forward. And this is what Amalrik's book does not seem to do. He can say in one sentence that the Russians' idea of justice has turned into hatred of anything that is in the least individual or excellent, and in the next that Russians are prepared to die at the stake for justice — two statements which obviously do not hang together. It strikes me that the idea of justice as a force capable of influencing history is alien to Amalrik, that it lies on a different plane from the one he is accustomed to think in.

The value of his book, as I see it, is that it has followed *one* possibility through to its logical end, that it has exhausted *one* train of thought. If you look at history as the product of the interaction of economic factors, or from the point of view of the interplay of the interests of different social groups and individuals, and the rights that guarantee these interests, then Russia indeed has no future — Amalrik's arguments are unanswerable.

But there are, after all, historical processes that depend on quite other principles. We, of all people, should not overlook the example of the October revolution. Nobody had a better nose than Lenin for the tiniest ripples of social and class forces, yet a few days before the February rising he saw no prospects of a socialist revolution, arguing persuasively in a letter to some Swiss workers that such a revolution could not succeed in Russia, the most bourgeois-minded country in Europe.

Four hundred years earlier, for that matter, when an unknown monk named Luther challenged the greatest force in the world at that time, he seemed to be going counter to all social and historical laws.

It is with this in mind that I should like to reexamine Russia's future. Medicine has much to teach us about disease and death, but religion knows resurrection also. For the mysterious words of I Corinthians 15:21 are nowhere more applicable than in the life of nations: *"For since by man came death, by man came also the resurrection of the dead."*

TWO

These words seem addressed directly to us, showing us the way. If neither class, nor party, nor a fortunate combination of forces on the world political stage can halt the shadow of death descending on Russia, then it can only be done *by man*, through the efforts of individual human beings.

But is it not hopeless for men to endeavor to arrest the inevitable action of historical laws? This is a most serious objection, which must be tackled first of all.

How many generations have now been brought up to believe from childhood that the individual is powerless to influence the course of history, that history is predetermined by the impersonal factors of economics and production? So thoroughly indoctrinated are we with this idea that it never occurs to us to subject it to intellectual scrutiny. One might think it was impossible to understand the nature of the laws of history without first knowing what those laws were, but in all sciences laws are tested by comparison and experiment.

Let us perform just one experiment. Let us choose as our subject a law which seemed so self-evident to those who formulated it that they dubbed it the "iron" law. This was the "iron law of wages," according to which under the capitalist method of production a worker's wage was always equivalent to the *minimum* necessary to sustain life. Its corollary was the inevitable total impoverishment of the proletariat. Any reference to this prophecy now, and to others like it, is embarrassing. Not only are the workers of Western Europe and America getting continuously richer, but thanks to strikes and trade-union policy they receive far more than their labor is strictly worth, which is causing serious problems. Similarly with all the other prophecies made by these oracles — of revolution beginning in the most highly industrialized countries, of the collapse of capitalism under the impact of repeated periodic crises, of the withering away of the state under socialism, of the replacement of armies by a militia, of the abolition of specialization that distorts the human personality, of the impossibility of war between socialist countries — wherever you look, it's the same picture. Only one conclusion is possible — that there is no truth in these theories. Their authors either completely failed to understand the laws of history, or else did not say what they really thought.

But now let us look at their actions. The October revolution was made by people who were fanatically convinced that history could be manipulated, that even a small group of people could change its course so long as they knew how to go about it. In this sense October crystallized the character of the twentieth century. The idea that power is there for the taking spread all over the world, and *this* concept was really borne out by experience — in Italy, Germany, Latin America, China and Africa. Yet the men who began this whole movement preached that the individual is powerless before the irresistible laws of history. What a strange contradiction!

Judged by their actions rather than their words, the men who made the revolution believed that human personality, together with such attributes as conscience, self respect, love for others and for one's country, was the greatest force in his tory. How much energy was expended in paralyzing this force, in propagating the idea that morality, ethics, kindness or patriotism were ridiculous, unscientific, outmoded concepts, that man's only motivation was self-interest and the interest of the group, class or party to which he belonged. This propaganda was no mere literary exercise: when the soldier, the defender of the fatherland, deserted the front and turned his bayonet against his neighbor (the landowner), it served the same end.

And how well those efforts paid off! Here is the clue to the mystery of the abject submission which would otherwise be inexplicable: in order to fight for your life, fear is not enough — you need to have preserved your moral strength as well. Those who attended political meetings during the day to vote for the execution of the accused at the Industrial party [3] trial would sit waiting for their own arrest at night. The results were in direct proportion to the victim's commitment to this philosophy: the peasants, though broken in spirit, endeavored to resist and revolt, while Old Bolsheviks went to the camps with revolutionary songs on their lips and received their bullets in the cellar with cries of "Long Live Stalin!"

Denying the existence of historical laws is tantamount to refusing to understand history itself. But is it credible that history should be governed by laws that work like clockwork? Even in quantum mechanics it is considered theoretically impossible to eliminate the influence of the observer on what is being observed. History's laws must, of course, take account of a fundamental element — the influence of human beings and their free will. Politicians and all great historians have always taken this for granted. And at every turn of history, wherever it has led mankind — whether to the victory of Christianity or the October revolution — the decision has always been in the hands of men and depended on their free will.

THREE

The fact that in principle men can influence the course of history does not of course mean that we in our country can do so now. Each one of us is not merely an individual, but also a small component in a vast machine, which is subject to its own laws and makes demands on its components that take no account of their free will or their immortal souls. Once upon a time J. V. Stalin whimsically referred to us all as "cogs" and even proposed a toast to the health of the "cogs." Have the

3. The name of a nonexistent underground party alleged to have been founded by industrial managers. It was the pretext for one of the first big show trials in 1930. See also note 13 on page 240.— TRANS.

cogs strength enough left in their souls to withstand the pressure of the machine?

I am certain the strength is there, that anyone who wishes can take the first steps toward his liberation now, and that the obstacles in the way are not outside us, but within — in our lifelong habits.

Let us try to understand the concrete ways in which our freedom is circumscribed. Few people nowadays, and then only rarely, have to take decisions for which they might have to pay with their lives or their liberty. But at every step life presents us with choices touching upon one particular question, and that is whether to give in to force a little, to bow to pressure, or to stand our ground and straighten our backs. We are constantly being urged to join the party — should we join? We are pressed to become party agitators — so we participate in the infantile charade of elections that give us no alternatives? A child is born — do we christen him in church? We have been given an interesting *samizdat* article to read — do we type a copy for ourselves, do we pass it on to others to read? We are invited to a meeting where neither speaker nor audience believes a word of what is being said — do we go? We are asked to support someone who is being unjustly persecuted — do we sign a letter in his defense? Even the boldest action in these cases no longer entails imprisonment or the permanent loss of one's job. The risk is merely one of official displeasure, the loss of regular promotion and pay raises, no new television set, no bigger apartment, no official trip abroad.

A process of barter takes place in which we pay with parts of our own soul that are essential to its health and survival. Our sense of self-respect and self-confidence is replaced by ruthless hostility toward others and the cunning mentality of the slave. Worst of all, life loses its aura of happiness and meaningful purpose. The price we pay is sterility in art and science, lives wasted on week-long vigils in endless queues for objects that nobody wants, and unprecedented alcoholism unheard of elsewhere on this planet and destroying not only this generation but the genes of descendants yet unborn. What does life offer us in exchange? As a rule the bare necessities that keep starvation at bay and enable us to feed the children. These are not in question. What is, then? I would say: values that do not lie in the material sphere. Sometimes this is quite obvious, sometimes less so. A medal, for example, neither feeds you nor keeps you warm. A large and expensive automobile soon falls apart on our roads, parking in the cities is more difficult, and with speed limited by law you get to your destination no quicker than in the cheapest vehicle. A trip abroad can be important for a budding engineer's or scientist's career, but its attraction is far greater than its usefulness. An expensive new suit keeps you no warmer than an old one patched at the elbows. And so on. None of these values has a consumer significance, their meaning is quite different: they show a man's place in the hierarchy of surrounding society. Like paper money, they have no value in themselves, but are symbols of something that men value highly.

Evidently any society, in order to exist, has to arrange its members in some sort of hierarchy. The hierarchy of human society reflects that society's outlook on life. The people most skilled in the activities that are highly regarded by society possess the greatest authority. Society endows such people with symbols that underline their authority — nose ring, gold-braided uniform or Chaika [4] automobile. These symbols acquire an exceptional attraction for the members of that society, persuading them to behave in the way society prefers.

It is this force that is the greatest limiting factor on our present freedom. It springs not from machine guns or barbed wire, but from our own opinions, from our inward, unquestioning acceptance of the hierarchy of surrounding society, from our assumption that a high position in it really matters. Like a hen fascinated by the chalk line the hypnotist draws before her, we are petrified because we believe our chains to

4. The larger and more expensive of the two types of automobile produced by the indigenous Soviet auto industry. It is commonly used to carry top-ranking party bureaucrats and government officials.— TRANS.

be real. The road to freedom begins within ourselves, when we stop clawing our way up the rungs of the career ladder or of quasi-affluence. And just as we sacrifice the best part of our souls in pursuit of these will-o'-the-wisps, so when we give them up shall we find the real meaning of life.

This is a feasible way out. Christianity, which originated just when the ancient world was reaching its apogee, accepted neither the ancient world's philosophy nor its acknowledged hierarchy, and this was one of the secrets of its invincibility. In our time too there exist small circles measuring their values by entirely different standards from those of the world outside. Once this movement is established and broadly based, we shall gain a freedom that we cannot even begin to contemplate at this moment.

One dangerous aspect of this approach is its negative character. If life asks a man to sacrifice everything he holds most dear in exchange for a sham, for pieces of paper with a price written on them but corresponding to no real value, then the practical conclusions he should draw from this realization are obvious: he should refuse this exchange, turn aside from this path. But since all life in our country and all its manifestations are in the hands of the state, would not a painter, for example, in accepting this view, have to give up painting, a scientist to give up his science? Would we not end by refusing to take an active part in life itself and in any cultural activities?

People everywhere in the world tend to speak of contemporary culture as becoming more and more antihuman, saying there is no room for man in it any more, and there is a growing retreat from culture as a reaction against this trend. That is why our question has particular significance and relevance, not only for the fate of the individual in modern industrial society, but also for the future of culture.

In answering it we must remember that here we are dealing only with a general principle. In practice everyone takes stock of his own strength and decides how far he can go along this path. All we have to determine is whether or not this general principle is contrary to culture, whether or not it leads us away from a field in which man has an obligation to labor.

Let us take examples from several fields of endeavor. It is natural to begin with literature, since it has always played a special part in Russian life. The concept of the writer as a teacher, able to perceive the truth that remains hidden from others, is purely Russian and peculiar to our people.

It is in literature that our question can be posed in its clearest form. To climb the hierarchical ladder the writer generally has to perform functions that are diametrically opposed to the goals of literature: to conceal and pervert the truth instead of seeking it. Hence the appearance of that antiliterature glorifying Stalin, Dzerzhinsky and Yezhov, the Cheka,[5] the White Sea–Baltic Canal,[6] collectivization, the persecution of "enemies of the people," and the denunciations of parents by their children. In these circumstances the question — can one be a writer outside this organization? — hardly arises, for literature can only survive by keeping its distance from all this. And indeed everything beautiful, truthful and profound that has been created in our time was created by people whom fate, however cruel the means, nonetheless protected from being drawn into this zone which meant death to literature.

In the human sciences — philosophy, history and sociology — the picture is similar. The only difference is that even fewer people have managed to fight their way out of antiscience than out of antiliterature. As for the natural sciences, it would seem that here we have no freedom of choice at all. In order to become a scientist one has to study at university, gain a higher degree, have access to laboratories, accelerators and computers. But here too it is far from being so simple. The sheer scale, the superorganized character of modern science has been its misfortune, even its curse. There are so many scientists and their output is so great that it is impossi-

5. The Cheka was the original name of the Soviet secret police (1917–1922), whose first chief was Felix E. Dzerzhinsky. Nikolai I. Yezhov was chief of the secret police (when it was known as the NKVD), 1936–1938.— TRANS.
6. The White Sea–Baltic Canal was built with slave labor from Stalin's labor camps.— TRANS.

ble to read all the publications even in one narrow specialty. The scientist's horizon dwindles to a pinpoint and he exhausts himself trying to keep abreast of his countless competitors. God's design, the divine beauty of truth as revealed in science, gives way to a bundle of petty technical problems. Science becomes a race, millions speed along without the least idea of where they are going. There is still satisfaction in this race for the few with vision, who can see a few steps ahead, but the vast majority see nothing but the heels of the one immediately in front, feel nothing but the panting breath of the one treading on their heels behind.

But even if it were possible to surmount the fact that science no longer brings the satisfaction it is capable of giving, that it deforms those who practice it, there are other reasons why it cannot go on the same way indefinitely. The output of science is now doubling every ten to fifteen years, the number of scientists is growing correspondingly, and spending on science is rising at almost the same rate. This process has been going on for two hundred to two hundred fifty years, but now it is clear that it cannot go on much longer — for by the end of this century spending on science would exceed the whole of society's gross product. In practice, of course, insuperable difficulties will arise long before then — probably in the 1980s (remember Amalrik!). In other words, development in this direction is doomed and the only question that remains is whether science can switch to another way, whereby the discovery of the truth demands neither millions of men nor billions of money, the way trodden by Archimedes and Galileo and Mendel. That is the fundamental problem now, science's life-and-death question. It will hardly be solved by those already trapped like squirrels in its treadmill. Our hopes must rest on those who have not yet been caught in its momentum.

Finally, it is impossible not to mention that sphere of cultural activity that is perhaps more important than any other for the healthy life of a nation — religion. For hundreds of thousands of years it was the noblest and most powerful motive force of mankind, yet in the space of a few decades we have broken with it, though not because we have found something to take its place or something nobler. One can judge from the results how the nation's soul becomes crippled, not only in our own country but also in others, from Germany to China, where the state has tried to wrench the people away from religion. The entire history of mankind consists of brutalities, but never before has violence paraded itself so brazenly, declaring itself to be the benevolent tool of history's laws, and never before, therefore, has such a pitch of technical perfection been reached in turning man into putty in the hands of his fellowmen as in these countries in recent times.

Nietzsche's literary phrase "God is dead!" has become a reality in our country and by now the third generation is living in a terrifying world without God.

Here, I would say, is the key to the whole question: it is the efforts applied in this sphere that will determine the life, death or resurrection of Russia. This most vital of all the fields of activity for our people will require hundreds of thousands of hands and heads (let us recall that there were three hundred thousand priests in Russia before the revolution). And it goes without saying that only people who renounce the system of values offered by our present life can work in this field.

Does it not follow then that this path, far from leading us away from culture, will actually help us to find those most essential and most hidden paths which would otherwise be invisible?

FOUR

And so it turns out that we are no longer hopelessly fettered and bound, that there is a road that leads to freedom. But in order to follow it we must understand that it will require the renunciation of things which actually have no worth.

Thus we may take the first and perhaps most precious steps

toward freedom — our own and Russia's. But we must not close our eyes to the fact that they are no more than the first steps. One may be imprisoned even for typing a copy of some *samizdat* work, let alone for circulating one's own work in it. But nothing matters more at the present time than joining forces to debate the vital issues of our country's future — for no ideas can develop in isolation, undebated. Similar penalties threaten expressions of religious belief, and especially religious movements unwilling to submit to a convoluted system of repressive regulations. Any act of persecution causes revulsion and arouses protest, which in turn leads to more persecution. But when it comes to what might seem to be perfectly natural actions — distributing pamphlets or demonstrating in support of an arrested person — risk is not the word, imprisonment is a certainty. And loss of employment, especially if one has a wife and children to support, exile to Siberia, a concentration-camp sentence, or finally the nightmare of indefinite confinement in an insane asylum — none of these can be called *sham* sacrifices.

So we conclude: Russia's fate is in our hands, it depends on the personal efforts of each and every one of us. But the essential contributions to the cause can be made only through *sacrifice*.

This might seem a misfortune, but in fact it is an irresistible weapon and a source of unlimited power. Few social forces act so powerfully on people as the drive for self-sacrifice in pursuit of higher ideals. It may not always be so, but at decisive periods in history sacrifice acquires a glamour that cannot be explained by any theory of sociology. Experienced politicians know this fact empirically and take advantage of it: calls for sacrifice generally meet with a ready response among the people. One reason why the revolution succeeded in our country was undoubtedly the fact that only in revolutionary activity could the intelligentsia find an outlet for their yearning for great deeds and sacrifice. What theoretician would have forecast the heroic deeds of the last war? For the outcome of the war was determined by peasants who had already borne the heaviest burdens. How else can

291

this miracle be explained except by the fact that the war enabled people to stand up straight and hold their heads high, that it opened the way to honest, voluntary self-sacrifice, which life had hitherto denied them.

We know how joyfully the early Christians sacrificed themselves. So strong was this urge that many fathers of the Church warned against the search for a martyr's crown and taught that martyrdom is sacred only when not actively pursued but waited for. This comparison, alas, has little relevance for us. Of all Russia's sorrows, perhaps the greatest is that she still lives (or dies) without faith. Even if a cure is possible, the task is infinitely difficult; it will take every ounce of our energy, and it will scarcely be accomplished quickly. But there is another spiritual state, akin to faith and much more accessible to us: readiness for sacrifice. The concept of sacrifice has always been mysteriously linked with religion. Sacrifice offers the same sense of uplift and joy and gives a meaning to life. If more than just a few individuals can rise to the pitch where they are ready to sacrifice themselves, souls will be cleansed and the soil prepared for religion to grow in.

Sacrifice can give us the strength to overcome the many obstacles in Russia's path — on one condition: that such a path still exists. Which brings us back to the question with which we began this article: what is the purpose of Russia's existence now, and has she still a historic mission?

It is hard to believe that any country has ever suffered such a multitude of catastrophes as has been unleashed on Russia during the last half century. Surely they cannot have been senseless and in vain? Involuntarily one looks for some purpose in them, thinking that they must have been preparing us for something. So often in the life of a man or a people, suffering is the path to higher things. Indeed, Russia's present position is unique: the misfortunes heaped upon us have blotted out all the simple, easily discernible paths, forcing us to search for the one essential and untrivial path that can lead to our (and perhaps not only Russia's) salvation. We have already seen a few examples. It is incomparably easier for a

budding scientist in the West to get onto the conveyor belt of
modern science: he has no need to pretend to be fulfilling
some social task, nor to speak against his conscience at ideological seminars, while scientific information is far more accessible to him and international contacts far easier. Here, by
contrast, everything conspires to divert him from this fatal
path.

Many profound thoughts have been expressed, beginning
with Plato, about the need for the best individuals, the elite
of the aristocracy, to rule the people. But these systems have
always led to the destruction of the profoundest and most
beautiful attributes of the soul, and, instead of elevating,
have degraded both the members of the elite and those they
ruled. Is this not because the wrong method of rule was indicated? For it should really be effected not through *power* but
through *sacrifice*. In other countries and at other times this
may not seem so obvious, but for us this method of serving
the people is the only one. Destiny has brought us to this and
enabled us to taste these truths with our bodies and our
blood, whereas it has not been revealed to other nations half
so clearly.[7]

It has often been said that Russia cannot save herself alone
and solve only her own private problems. The English, while
maintaining the slave trade and holding India in bondage,
were able to build what was then the freest society in the
world. We cannot do this, and have proved the converse at
least: however great the misfortunes that Russia has brought
on other peoples, she has always brought even greater ones
on her own.

The whole of mankind has now entered a blind alley. It
has become clear that a civilization founded on the ideology
of "progress" gives rise to contradictions that that civilization
cannot resolve. And it seems to me that the path to Russia's

7. Let us take a more particular example, such as the method of dissemi-
nating literature. For us, *samizdat* is the only possibility, but in principle it
is also the ideal way: the distribution of works is independent of both the
censor and the advertiser. With the aid of modern technology this method
can be made fully effective. But for the West it would be difficult to give up
existing methods, which in any case have worked pretty well so far.

rebirth is the same as the path that will enable man to find a way out of his blind alley, to find salvation from the senseless race of industrial society, the cult of power and the darkness of unbelief. We were the first to reach this vantage point, whence the uniqueness of this path became visible, and it is now up to us to set foot on it and point the way to others. This is my idea of Russia's possible mission, the purpose which can justify her future existence.

The past half century has enriched us with experience that no other country has yet acquired. One of religion's most ancient ideas is that in order to acquire supernatural power, one must visit another world, one must pass through death. That is how soothsayers and prophets are said to have arisen: "I lay as a corpse in the wilderness and the voice of God cried out to me . . ."

This is now Russia's position. She has passed through death and may hear the voice of God. But God makes history through men, and it is we, every one of us, who may hear His voice. Or, of course, we may not hear it. And remain as corpses in the wilderness that will cover the ruins of Russia.

Notes on Contributors

MIKHAIL AGURSKY (born 1933) is the son of an American Communist who went to the Soviet Union and was shot in Stalin's great purge of 1937. He is a cyberneticist by profession, but was deprived of all employment after applying to emigrate to Israel. He is the author of a number of *samizdat* essays and of open letters in defense of Solzhenitsyn and Sakharov.

EVGENY BARABANOV (born 1943) is an art historian who formerly worked for the publishing house Iskusstvo (Art) and its associated journal, *Dekorativnoye iskusstvo* (*Decorative Art*). He was deprived of his post in September 1973 when placed under investigation by the KGB for sending copies of the clandestine journal *Chronicle of Current Events,* and unpublished material on Russian religious and cultural life, to the West. He admitted the charges, saying that he considered it his duty to save the Russian cultural heritage from destruction and that there was nothing illegal in sending information out of the country. In 1974 he was refused permission to emigrate.

VADIM BORISOV (born 1945) is a historian who studied at

Moscow University and the Institute of History of the Soviet Academy of Sciences. He was recently prevented from presenting his doctoral thesis on Russian Church history of the fourteenth and fifteenth centuries and has been deprived of all employment.

F. KORSAKOV and A. B. are the pseudonyms of authors for whom it would be dangerous to reveal their identities at the present time.

IGOR SHAFAREVICH (born 1923), the author of three essays in the present collection and its coeditor, is a mathematician and algebraist of world repute who is a corresponding member of the Soviet Academy of Sciences and former laureate of the Lenin Prize. He is an active member of the unofficial Committee on Human Rights (founded by A. D. Sakharov and others) and is the author of a *samizdat* study of the Soviet law on religion.

ALEXANDER SOLZHENITSYN (born 1918) is a Nobel Laureate for literature. He fought in World War II, and was imprisoned in various labor camps becaue of his outspoken criticism of the Soviet regime. Now living in exile in Switzerland, Solzhenitsyn is world famous as both a literary and a political figure.

Index

INDEX

slavery (*cont.*)
and serfdom, 116, 226. *See also*
labor camps
"smatterers": intelligentsia and,
242–259, 267–269, 273; and
materialism, 246–247, 258
Smena Vekh (New Bearings) (publication), 229
Social Democratic party: West German, 74; Russian, vi, 235n.3
socialism: as basic force, 45, 218; vs.
capitalism, 6–8, 29, 67–87; and
death, 61–64; economic, 28–29; experience and, 66; in history, 31–45;
as ideology, 29–31, 46–47, 52,
65–66, 93, 97; and individuality,
58–61; and internationalism, 91,
283; Lenin on aim of, 198; and
"moral heroism," 14–15; and
nationalism, 90–91, 93, 97; opinions on origin of, 27–28; and
"piecework," 15; and "pseudo-
socialism," 15; and religion (*see*
religion); "scientific," vi, 65–66,
221–222; and socialist "ideal," 47,
52–56, 215n.17; and "socialist integration," 216; and "socialist
novel," 41–43; "theory" vs. "practice," 45–48; and violence, 81;
world trend toward, 27–28
Solovki (Solovetsky Islands), 11
Solovyov, Vladimir, 157n.10, 174,
234; quoted, 210, 211
Solzhenitsyn, Alexander, 189, 295,
296 (biography); authorizes publication of "The Quiet Don,"
126n.12; imprisoned, 11; Lenten
letter of, 175–176, 177; "Letter to
the Soviet Leaders," 196; Nobel
Prize, quoted on, viii; and tradition
in Russian thought, vii
South Korea, 127
Soviet Union. *See* Russia; USSR
"speaking in tongues," 209, 263
Stalin, J. V. ("Uncle Joe"), 274, 284,
288; *The Economic Problems of
Socialism*, 48; and patriotism, 197;
purges of, vii, 157n.12, 197, 295;
and religion, 49; and the terror, 115;
and treatment of his own party,
11–12

Stalinism, 5, 12, 18; as "deviation"
from Leninism, 10–12
standard of living, 71, 94, 217, 224.
See also economy
Stepun, Fyodor, 120
Storch, Niklas: quoted, 40–41
Struve, Nikita, vi
Struve, Peter, v, vi
Suvorov, Alexander, 120
"Sverdlovka," 51
Sweezy, Paul H., 70
Symbolist movement, 175n.4
Symeon, St.: quoted, 183

Taborites, 37, 40
Taiwan, 134
Talantov, Boris, 175
Tambov, 11
technology: automation and computerization in, 82, 84; "catching
up" by USSR, 7, 99, 140; of corporations vs. military, 70; "progress" in,
15–16, 84, 219; technocracy and,
221. *See also* industry
technostructures. *See* conglomerates
Telegin, Semyon (pseudonym), 260,
264; quoted, 254–259 (*passim*)
Theodosius I (the Great), Roman emperor, 178
Third International, 124
"Third Rome," 124
Third World (backward countries), 7,
74
Tiam, Dudu: quoted, 28
Tibetans, 88
time-lag. *See* "catching up"
Titian, 189
Toffler, Alvin: *Future Shock*, 68
Tolstoy, Leo, 157n.10, 158, 161, 162,
174, 189, 234; *Confession*, quoted,
159–160
totalitarian society: "advantages"
under, 77–79; and Church, 79,
177–179; defects of, 79; vs. democratic system, 80, 85 (*see also* democratic system); and human personality, 201; and responsibility,
113; West and, 73–75
Toynbee, Arnold: *An Historian's Approach to Religion*, 52

306